CASTLES OF ENGLAND, SCOTLAND AND WALES

CASTLES OF ENGLAND, SCOTLAND AND WALES

Paul Johnson

Weidenfeld and Nicolson
London

To Daniel and Sarah

Colour photographs by John Miller
© George Weidenfeld and Nicolson

First published in 1989 by George Weidenfeld and Nicolson Ltd
91 Clapham High Street, London SW4 7TA
Text originally published in 1978 by
George Weidenfeld and Nicolson Ltd
and the National Trust

Cataloguing in Publication Data

Johnson, Paul
    Castles of England, Scotland and Wales.
    1. Great Britain. Castles, history
    I. Title

    ISBN 0–297–79574–0

House designer Ruth Hope
Typeset by Deltatype Ltd, Ellesmere Port
Colour separations by Newsele Litho Ltd
Printed by Printers Srl, Trento
Bound by L.E.G.O., Vicenza

Half-title page   Scotney Castle
Title page left   Bamburgh Castle
Title page right   Kidwelly Castle
Right   Castle Campbell
Page 6   Beaumaris Castle

CONTENTS

'And they that shall be of thee shall build
the old waste places; thou shalt raise up the
foundations of many generations; and thou shalt
be called, The repairer of the breach,
The restorer of paths to dwell in'

ISAIAH

CHAPTER ONE

'THE NORMAN YOKE'

Opposite: Pevensey, covering eight acres, was built by the Romans to protect the Sussex coast. It has high walls and towers but its chief purpose was as a concentration point for troops and supplies.

What is a castle? If you adopt a wide definition, there are many thousands in Britain. There are, to begin with, about 1,420 Bronze and Iron Age hillforts built south of the line of Hadrian's Wall, and another 1,100 or so north of it. Created in the 1,000 years before the birth of Christ, usually on high ground with one or more surrounding ditches, these forts were sometimes, as at Maiden Castle in Dorset, of great size and complexity. But the Romans found them easy to take, and in their place set up far more formidable stone defences. We all know Hadrian's Wall, with its forts, of which Housesteads has been fully excavated. But the Romans also built elaborate city defences, as at Colchester, and strong legionary forts, of which Caerlon-on-Usk, near Newport, is the best surviving example. In the third century AD they added a new type of coastal fort to resist sea-invaders, and the remains of these structures at Burgh in Suffolk and Portchester in Hampshire testify to the grandeur of Roman military architecture.

The Saxons, in their turn, used fixed defences, though their resources and skill were greatly inferior. Sometimes, as at Tintagel in Cornwall, they refortified a Roman stronghold (though the present walls date mainly from the 12th century). From Alfred's time onward they built walls and gatehouses to protect market- and county towns, though here again their work was usually replaced by stronger medieval walls. From the mid-11th century onwards there are references to Continental-style forts being built in England, near the Welsh borders, but none has been certainly identified.

It is, therefore, essentially with the Normans and their successors that we associate the castle in Britain. And this popular notion has much historical justification. The Normans were organizers and militarists of genius. They did not invent armoured cavalry; nor did they invent fortified bases; and they certainly did not invent the basic concept of feudalism, which was the holding of land from a superior lord in exchange for knight-service. But they were the first to combine all three and regulate the resulting system in a thoroughly businesslike manner. On a regular battlefield and in open warfare, their

Previous page
left: Durham Castle.

right: Richmond Castle.

heavy cavalry gave them an immense advantage, even against ferocious and well-disciplined infantry like Harold Godwinson's *housecarls*. Armour and horsepower won Hastings. But what turned their victories into conquests was the speed and skill with which they erected castles, to consolidate their territorial gains, and to terrorize and demoralize the subject population. This was the essence of 'the Norman Yoke', which became part of English folklore for six centuries, and which was still spoken of as a living memory during the Civil War of the seventeenth century, when the last of the Norman-founded castles passed out of use as military establishments.

Even so, it is doubtful if such a vast and perilous enterprise as the Norman conquest of England could have been carried through to success without the inspiration and energy of William I, a general and military administrator of the first rank. William was noted for many things, but not least for his skill as a builder. His religious fervour, like that of his race – so prodigal in the building of churches, cathedrals and abbeys – undoubtedly assisted his success as a military architect; indeed, clerical designers and craftsmen assisted him and his sons at all stages of their castle programme.

Ordericus Vitalis, one of the best of the early chroniclers, insists that the Saxons were defeated and conquered because they had not adopted the castle. The castle, in so far as it existed at all in England, was an alien import remaining in largely alien hands. Had the English possessed a system of castles on the Norman model, or even modernized and maintained the works of Alfred and his progeny, William's campaign after Hastings might have degenerated into a lengthy affair of sieges, during which he might well have run out of time and cash, and seen his fine army disintegrate. As it was, most of the English burghs fell without a fight or after a perfunctory defence.

However, the failure of the English to maintain modern fixed defences was only one side of the story. Equally important was the speed with which William provided himself with them. He came fully prepared. The chronicler Wace, writing a hundred years later but doubtless using lost sources, says that William brought over the materials for a prefabricated fort: that is, wooden sections already cut and drilled, together with the fittings. This was not a new idea: the Jewish historian Josephus says that the Romans usually carried with them, on the march, the dismantled sections of their siege engines, using muletrains. And the probability that Wace's story is true is strengthened by the fact that prefabricated forts, on the lines of William's, were later used by Henry II in Ireland, and by his son Richard I in the Mediterranean. Wace says the fort was erected immediately after the landing at Pevensey, and was complete by the end of the day. Thus William moved to Hastings from a fortified base, very likely a ditch and palisade, with a powerful gateway. Ordericus Vitalis says it had 'a very strong rampart'. Nor was this all. Immediately after his victory at Hastings, William consolidated his position by building a castle. The Anglo-Saxon Chronicle says: 'As soon as his men were fit for service, they constructed a castle at the town of Hastings.' The work is portrayed on the Bayeux Tapestry. After this, his first move was to Dover. There he found a rudimentary castle, built perhaps in the Norman fashion. But he was not satisfied, and spent eight days rebuilding and strengthening it. Then he went to Canterbury, and 'built a tower' (presumably of wood, with a defensive ditch). Before arranging the surrender of London, he crossed the Thames at Wallingford, where he deposited experts to start work on another castle. So William, like the methodical Romans before him, moved forward at each stage only when he had a prepared defence to fall back on. Later, after the formal surrender of the English clergy and nobility, and his coronation at Westminster, William had the country surveyed; and, according to William of Jumièges, he immediately ordered a vast programme of castle-building. What exactly were these castles of King William? From a hint in Ordericus Vitalis, who says that few motte-and-bailey castles were built at first, it may be that some of William's early English castles were simply ditch-and-rampart palisades, with a central wooden tower built on a natural prominence or a low man-made mound. Then, when more time was available, the mottes became more

ambitious. Certainly, Norman mounds vary from ten to a hundred feet in height, and measure one hundred to three hundred feet in diameter at their base.

Essentially, the Norman castle was a fortified post from which a small body of armoured cavalry could range over an occupied area, and to which they retired if attacked by superior force. It contained a hall, usually on the first storey of a wooden building, for security purposes, with offices below; a well; a kitchen; sleeping-quarters for the men and horses; storerooms and workshops and, as a rule, a chapel. All of this area was surrounded by a ditch outside a bank. The entrance was by a bridge across the ditch, to a gap in the bank, further strengthened by a high timber fence. The whole defensive area formed the bailey. In time a wooden watchtower was added to overlook the bailey. Towards the end of the eleventh century these watchtowers became more elaborate, and were placed on mounds of increasing height. Then the motte-top developed its own fence and gate, and was reached by a flying bridge, or a gangway, itself protected by a timber palisade. So we soon have a castle (or keep, or donjon) within a castle.

Timber motte-and-bailey castles were cheap and quick to construct. But they were temporary. When timber is in contact with earth it soon rots. The next stage, therefore, was to follow the Roman custom of raising timber buildings on stone sleeper-walls. The third stage came when the keep was entirely rebuilt in stone. Stone castles were still rare in William I's day, but not as rare as was once thought. He set the fashion by building a great stone tower at his own family castle of Rouen. And he always built in stone where existing fortifications made it possible, or the material was at hand. The Tower of London and Colchester Castle were of stone from the first. So were Launceston and Trematon in Cornwall, and Totnes in Devon, in an area where timber was scarce and stone plentiful. One difficulty which faces the historian is that evidence of early stone-construction has often been removed by plunder; at Topcliffe, Yorkshire, and Barnstaple, Devon, virtually every single stone has gone. What is certain is that no Norman king or

lord built in timber if there was time, labour and material to build in stone; for the great destroyer of early castles was fire, and a stone keep could be made virtually fireproof.

That is why the keep was always the first part of the castle to be rebuilt in stone. The lord then had privacy and safety, and a secure place to keep his documents, money and prisoners. There were usually three or four rooms, stacked vertically, with smaller rooms built into the thickness of the walls. Since everything had to go in and out through the same entrance in the keep, a form of lobby or landing (called the forebuilding) was soon added, and the upper floor of this often formed the chapel. The roof was a weak point. It was built first of thatch, later of wooden shingles (usually of oak), clay tiles, stone slates, and lead. But thatch and shingles could be fired; and heavy missiles could crash through tiles and slates. So walls were carried up above the roofs, to protect them from siege-engines, and the resulting parapet provided with a wall-walk, so becoming a fighting platform and developing into battlements. But the arcs of fire from the battlements did not cover the base of the wall, and so wooden galleries, holding archers and missiles, were hung out of the walls on brackets.

Apart from depictions in the Bayeux Tapestry, there is no contemporary English account of the building of a motte-and-bailey castle. But Jean de Colmien's *Vie de Jean de Warneton*, which dates from *c.* 1130 and deals with the Pas de Calais area, says:

> It is the custom of the nobles of that neighbourhood to make a mound of earth as high as they can and then dig about it as wide and deep as possible. The space on top of the mound is enclosed by a palisade of very strong hewn logs, strengthened at intervals by as many towers as their means can provide. Inside the enclosure is a citadel or keep, which commands the whole circuit of defences. The entrance to the fortress is by means of a bridge which, arising from the outer side of the moat, and supported on posts as it ascends, reaches the top of the mound.

Excavations at Abinger, Surrey, have revealed a small castle of this type: a mound with a thirty-five-foot diameter and flat summit, twenty feet above the bottom of the surrounding moat. The holes which held the posts have been discovered, and a timber bridge which spanned the moat, ascending from the outer side of the moat on the top of the mound. The castles of Dol and Dinan, which we see on the Bayeux Tapestry, were of this type. They could be built quickly, but unless they were rebuilt in stone they disappeared just as easily, leaving few traces except to the expert archaeologist. Abinger, raised c. 1100 and remodelled in 1140, had a longer life than most, surviving until the treaty of 1153, which led to the abolition of many such strongpoints.

In the years immediately after Hastings, William's aim was to put up as many of these small castles as he could conveniently defend; and his tenants-in-chief and officials fanned out all over England and its borders in compliance with his instructions. During this first phase, castles (usually of wood) were set up overlooking towns, on the highest ground available, and often adjoining a river. Between 1066 and 1071, Norman castles were built at Chester, Lincoln, Stafford, Tutbury, Shrewsbury, Wisbech, Norwich (probably), Richard's Castle, Warwick – at a place called 'Alrehede', Wigmore, Worcester, Huntingdon, Clifford, Hereford, Cambridge, Ewyas Harold, Monmouth, Oxford, Chepstow, Berkeley, Wallingford, Exeter, Montacute, Winchester (probably), Pevensey, Hastings and Dover. London and York had two each. The Norman experts liked to select their sites according to their own well-tried rules, derived from long and bloody experience; but in their haste to shackle the English while they were still leaderless and demoralized, they often used existing Roman or Saxon sites, merely adding the improvements they felt indispensable.

The Domesday Book, 1086–7, mentions directly forty-nine castles as existing at this date. The figure is incomplete because the Domesday clerks did not list a castle, or anything else, which was not relevant to their strictly fiscal purposes. But it is noteworthy that, of the forty-nine, as many as thirty-three were

Colchester is the oldest defended town in Britain. There are Roman, Saxon, Norman and late-medieval elements in its castle and defences. In the 1640s it was the site of the most important siege of the Civil War.

on pre-1066 sites. Some twenty-eight possessed artificial mounds (as, for instance, at Arundel). A more comprehensive calculation suggests that William and his men had set up or substantially remodelled thirty-three castles by 1071, and eighty-six by the time of his death in 1087. At this point, there was a fairly even distribution of castles over England, south of a Chester–Lincoln line. The distribution was denser on the Welsh Border, and on the east and south-east coasts, where the Norse threat was still acute. A line of castles also stretched as far north as Newcastle, for operations against Scotland.

Careful research enables us to piece together some of the details of this huge building programme. The earliest castles were largely put up under William's personal supervision. When the king returned to Normandy in 1067, his viceroys, William FitzOsbern and Bishop Odo of Bayeux, carried on the programme. FitzOsbern died in 1071, but by then, to our certain knowledge, he had built Berkeley, Chepstow, Monmouth, Clifford, 'Guenta' (either Winchester or Norwich) and Wigmore, and rebuilt Ewyas Harold. The king returned late in 1067 and immediately started to build Exeter. The next year, to subdue the northern Saxon lords, he built castles at Warwick, Nottingham, York, Lincoln, Huntingdon and Cambridge. By 1069 there was a second castle at York, and others at Montacute, Shrewsbury, Chester, Stafford and Worcester. Those at Ely and Peterborough followed in 1070, with Oxford in 1071 and Wisbech in 1072.

Not all these earliest castles had mottes, which were only gradually, during William's time, coming to be accepted as an indispensable part of a standard castle. Obviously construction of mottes varied enormously according to local earth and rock conditions. A natural rock (which made mining virtually impossible) with water available was the ideal mound. Building an artificial motte was much more complicated than just throwing up earth, which could not provide a stable foundation for timber, let alone stone. It had to be levelled up with reinforcing layers of rock, or hard-beaten earth, or covered with an outer crust of clay. Heavy superstructures set up on a poorly made motte soon began to lean outwards, and were a death-trap under siege. The ditches had to be carefully worked too. The simplest were v-shape. But wet moats were obviously desirable for a variety of reasons – throughout the Middle Ages the strongest castles nearly always had water-defences – and this was a more serious problem of earth-moving engineering, entailing the controlled diversion of streams and rivers. Even with dry ditches, the banks might well have timber faces, to bind the earth together.

For the heavy earth-moving work forced labour was employ-ed on a massive scale. This was a perfectly legal development of the Anglo-Saxon system: *burh-bot* (the duty to labour on town fortifications) became 'castle work'. It was regarded as one of the most onerous duties of an unfree man, and was soon commuted by money-payments, known as 'heckage', though there were many variations. (At Bamburgh, certain inhabitants were obliged to bring a tree-trunk for the castle works once a year; the imposition was known as 'trunkage' and was finally commuted for £10 in 1280.) Work often continued throughout the winter and, as we know from Henry of Huntingdon and Florence of Worcester, by night, when the men worked by the light of rushes and candles. In existing towns, castle building was a ruthless business. At Lincoln, 166 houses were pulled down to clear the site; at York, one seventh of the city. Later, when the first panic was over, castle sites were bought under due process of law, and owners of land and property compensated. Woods were purchased, wholesale and in their entirety, to supply timber, which was used in prodigious quantities. But much Norman work in England is in stone from the great Caen quarries, which produced fine cream limestone, shipped to English sites comparatively cheaply wherever water transport was possible. Later, native centres were developed at Barnack (?), Quarre and Maidstone, all on river-sites. As near the castle site as could be, sand and lime for the mortar were dug and burnt, lead cast and iron worked. For these castles the Normans often re-used well-made Roman bricks (as at Colchester and London), and they may have made bricks of their own too. Where stone was used for the walls, solid rock, quarried flat, was preferred for the foundation; otherwise they dug deep trenches, wider than the proposed walls, and filled them with rammed stone rubble, or hardwood stakes driven into the subsoil. In the many cases where earlier foundations were used, the Norman engineers laid a platform of timber over them.

Once the Normans had time to set up their castles in stone, their tremendous sense of beauty and quality, so powerfully expressed in Durham Cathedral, asserted itself, and the outer faces, at least, were if possible of ashlar, that is wrought smooth

Opposite: The Tower of
London, basically
Norman, guarded the
capital city and port for a
thousand years. It has
been a palace, a prison, a
zoo, a barracks (until
recently) and is now a
museum. The ground
plan shows the later
additions around the
central Norman keep.

stone. Behind these ashlar blocks a core of rubble, bound with mortar, was rammed home, while wood ties framed and bound the wall until the mortar set. Sometimes, the entire wall was of mortared rubble, which set within wooden shutters. The Normans were already developing powerful engines for siege-warfare, and such towers could be adapted for castle building; though they also used high cranes (medieval crane-wheels can still be seen in the towers at Canterbury, and at Salisbury and Peterborough cathedrals). When the walls were finished they were, if possible, coated with plaster and white-washed – a practice still reflected in the names of the White Tower in London, and the White Castle on the Welsh borders. Some of the earliest stone castles in England had primitive lead plumbing; and even glass has been found at Ascot d'Oilly and Deddington, though these were twelfth-century castles.

William's castle-building programme was continued re-morselessly by his successors, Rufus and Henry I. Under their direction or patronage the first identifiable architects emerge. Thus William II's chief lay castle-builder was Robert, Lord of Bellême, a warrior who was also described as a 'skilfull artificer', and who was responsible for castles at Arundel, Gloucester, Bridgnorth, Shrewsbury and Tickhill, and perhaps others. Even more prominent was Archbishop Lanfranc's protégé and master-builder, Gundulf, promoted Bishop of Rochester. He was 'very competent and skillful at building in stone', and thus dominated the second stage of the Norman programme, when stone was replacing timber. Gundulf built the White Tower in London, the first rectangular stone keep in England, and very likely the great keep at Colchester. The Tower can probably be dated from 1079, and Colchester from 1083. Gundulf had visited the Holy Land, and he may have seen and been impressed by the citadel at Saone (Sayun) built by Byzantine architects; its dimensions are close to those of the Tower, and its huge buttresses resemble Colchester's. But other influences were doubtless at work: the Conquerer's own 'old tower' at Rouen, now vanished, and the new stone church towers of the Norman age, which were essentially similar in

construction to military keeps, and were sometimes used for fighting purposes. The stone keep was an innovation, in that it compressed into one simple and highly defensive building the scattered structures (hall, chapel, service rooms, defences) of the traditional Carolingian palace. But it was an obvious and natural innovation, given the technology, in a hostile country being held down by a small, fierce minority.

Thus the closing decades of the eleventh century and the long reign of Henry I were marked by continuous castle-building, increasingly in stone, under royal direction. The Exchequer probably existed under Rufus, and became a great department of state under Henry I; but none of its documents survive from Rufus's time, and only one isolated pipe-roll from the reign of Henry I, so we do not possess the detailed accounts which, from the time of Henry II onwards, cast such a welcome (if fitful) light on royal building activities. But we can, from a variety of sources, gather some information. In 1087–8 Gundulf agreed with Rufus to build a high stone bailey wall around the wooden tower at Rochester – here, as it were, king and bishop shared the expense of a costly new structure useful to both. Then followed castles at Corfe, Ludlow and Richmond (York-shire), also with curtain walls, which contained projecting towers – thus enabling archers to cover the wall base without using wooden extensions. The Normans pushed north: in 1092, a castle and colony was founded at Carlisle; Bamburgh and Tynemouth were captured and refortified in 1095, and Norman lords were setting up castles at Edinburgh (1093), Invergowrie (1107) and in Lothian (1106). In 1093–4 they pushed farther into Wales from their bases at Monmouth and Chepstow, building castles at Pembroke, Cardiff, Carmarthen and Cardigan; at Pembroke, and at Abergavenny and Rhuddlan, they built fortified towns also. They reached Anglesey in 1094, and, on the mainland side of the Menai Straits, they built castles at Caernarvon, Bangor and Aber Lleiniog. In Cumbria castles had been established at Bowes and Brough as early as 1070–4, and in 1092–1102, Roger of Poitou built a massive stone keep at Lancaster. Stone castles seem to have been built in the north, and in Scotland, almost as soon as in southern England.

The rectangular stone keep, which dominated major castle-building in this period, was not exactly new, as we have seen. But it became a peculiarly Norman-Angevin institution. Keeps were characterized by exceptionally thick walls and wide, low-projecting buttresses. Sometimes they were set on a particularly firm mound, as at Lydford; more often on the hard ground of the bailey. They were from two to four storeys, and divided internally by a partition wall. The entrance was on the second storey (the third at Newcastle) by external stairs, later covered and protected by the forebuilding. The principal hall was on the second or third storey, often with an internal mural gallery, and with mural chambers opening off it. There were fireplaces, one (sometimes two) chapels, very deep walls (sometimes with lead pipes carrying the water up two or three storeys), and straight or spiral staircases, often in the thickness of the wall. The White Tower, the first, is of ragstone rubble with ashlar dressings, walls between twelve and fifteen feet thick at the base, ninety feet high, not counting the later corner-turrets, and with projections formed by the end of the chapel and the staircase. Rufus added an inner bailey (later destroyed) between the Tower and the Thames. The castle was expanded by a Middle Bailey (1190) and a Bell Tower under the Angevins; Edward I, around 1300, finished the Outer Bailey, the Outer Moat, three outer gates and the Barbican. But the core of the castle has always been, and remains, its Norman rectangular keep.

Gundulf's White Tower was followed by his massive keep at Colchester and its imitation, though half the size, at Canterbury, also dating from Rufus's time. Then came Pevensey, a very strong keep, which the king himself was later to spend six weeks attacking with siege-engines – and it surrendered only when supplies ran out. These square keeps were sometimes, in effect, gatehouses, as at Exeter. More often, however, they were inside a stone bailey wall (or, as at Pevensey, within a Roman structure). Thus at Rochester, where Gundulf had already built the wall, Archbishop Corbeuil was not only entrusted by Henry I with the castle, in 1125, but given

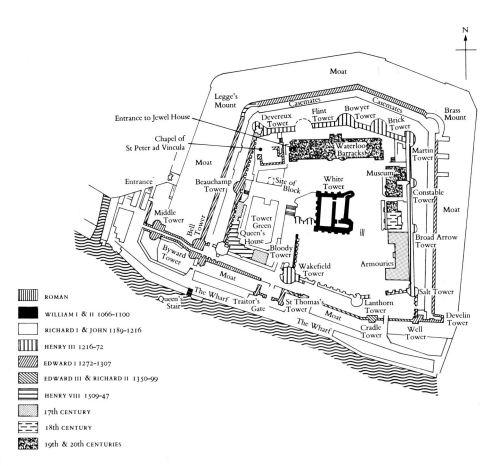

ROMAN

WILLIAM I & II 1066-1100

RICHARD I & JOHN 1189-1216

HENRY III 1216-72

EDWARD I 1272-1307

EDWARD III & RICHARD II 1350-99

HENRY VIII 1509-47

17th CENTURY

18th CENTURY

19th & 20th CENTURIES

permission to build an *egregiam turrim*. And the result was indeed an egregious, or outstanding, tower. It took thirteen years to build and rises 120 feet. Despite the ravages of the years, including a ferocious siege under King John, when the defenders continued fighting behind the partition walls even after the King's men had broken into the tower, Rochester is still perhaps the most menacing Norman keep in England.

Right: Hedingham, in Essex, is a superbly preserved Norman castle, with a keep modelled on the greatest of all, Rochester, but only three-quarters of the scale. It had the first genuine castle chimneys, concealed in a buttress.

Far right: The barbican of Lewes in Sussex, a Norman shell-keep castle with much of its 12th-century walls intact: seven feet thick, these rise nearly twenty feet from the courtyard to the wall-walk.

These great square stone towers continued to be built in England throughout the twelfth century. In the wake of Rochester came Hedingham, built on its model but only three-quarters the scale, Sherborne, Castle Rising, Kenilworth; then followed Norwich, Scarborough, Clun and Portchester; and finally, between 1150 and 1200, Bamburgh, Richmond, Newcastle and Dover. These buildings were among the strongest put up by mankind until the nineteenth century. Some are now ruinous, having been 'slighted' by the parliamentarians in the Civil War; others are virtually intact (Norwich, Dover), though with roof and walls missing or replaced. As the twelfth century progressed, refinements were added: portcullises, machicolations in the entrance passages, *meutrières* and arrow-loops. These defensive devices were built into the structure as the mechanics of siege-warfare improved. There was an unremitting technological battle between the two sides. Men were aware that the great stone keep, however strong, was not the perfect answer to enormous siege-engines and miners. The weakness lay in the corners, which could be prised open by men with crowbars working under cover. Some military engineers believed in the alternative to the shell-keep: that is, replacing the wooden palisades round the top of the motte by a strong stone wall, with the castle buildings ranged alongside it within. Then, in addition, the palisades of the bailey were converted into walls, with stone towers built at intervals to overlook the entire face of the curtain. These walls could be equipped with movable bridges, linking the various sections, but isolating them too if a particular section fell to assault. The general layout of such castles offered better protection against high-trajectory stone-throwing engines, like the pivotal-beam trebouchet, or the fixed-stop mangonel. They were also equipped with a massive gateway, usually the first part of the outer curtain wall to be converted to stone, with its own defensive barbican outside the castle perimeter. A shell-keep castle with a towered curtain placed less reliance on a single defensive feature than the tower-keep. It gave the defenders much more mobility within their perimeter, faced

the attackers with a greater variety of problems (and hazards) and meant the fight could go on even after they had won substantial successes.

Yet though one can produce a typology of castles, Roman-style uniformity was lacking. No two were alike. Topographical features, the taste or ingenuity of individual lords, availability of money, materials and labour combined to make each castle unique, once the primitive motte-and-bailey stage was over. Thus Windsor, though an outstanding example of the shell-keep castle, was in no sense an archetype. Its huge rock makes it a natural site for a Thameside fortress, and William I began to build there soon after the Conquest. It had a mound and a bailey, and may have been of stone from the start, for the mound is a natural hard chalk bed, capable of sustaining immense weights. Around 1075, the Normans scarped the mound all round, threw up a ditch, and built a double-shell stone keep. It soon became a royal resort, second only to the Tower and Winchester. Henry I held court there in 1114, and seven years later celebrated his marriage with Adela of Louvain within its walls. What walls? They no longer exist. The more important, and long-lived the castle, the less likely it is that the original masonry will survive, at any rate intact. Around 1175, Henry II added a curtain-wall, built halls and offices big enough to handle the court, and fortified the lower ward, so the castle could hold more troops. But he also, inevitably, remodelled the keep, building a new one inside the old shell, with wooden buildings inside this. Then, in about 1350, Edward III remodelled the interior buildings of the keep, providing it with a new entrance and approach. The keep was again altered in 1826 when it was refaced with stone, raised thirty feet to its present height of sixty-four feet – thus becoming the 'Round Tower' – and provided with new windows. So though it is correct to describe the Round Tower as a fine shell-keep, its interior woodwork, staircases and plaster ceilings are essentially four-teenth century, and its stonework is a bewildering mixture of the late eleventh, late twelfth, fourteenth and nineteenth centuries.

Warwick is another example of a fine natural site overlooking a river. Again it was fortified by the Conqueror, according to Ordericus Vitalis. It had a high mound with a shell-keep, fragments of which remain. On the south side its bailey was defended by the River Avon, and on all the other sides by a wide and deep moat. But alterations were incessant, for Warwick has always been held by kings or great subjects. It was refortified in the fourteenth century with a strong bailey wall, a gatehouse in the centre, and a powerful tower at either end on the east; and living quarters on a vast scale were built against the curtain overlooking the river. Then in the fifteenth century a large tower with corner turrets was added near the middle of the north curtain wall. In the sixteenth century it acquired a water-gate to the river; and, in the seventeenth, the old keep was transformed and prettified with turrets. Yet in basic plan Warwick is a Norman shell-keep castle.

Durham Castle, begun in 1072, has a keep in the shape of an irregular octagon with buttresses, on a mound of sandstone rock, its foundation going down to natural bedrock. It was set up as a strongly fortified residence for the bishops, who in Durham ruled a palatinate with its own system of laws and customs. The bishop was the king's viceroy, and his town, castle, palace and cathedral are correspondingly magnificent. Set on a high sandstone outcrop over the River Wear, and seen from the hill opposite on the west, the ensemble forms one of the finest architectural groupings in Europe, and is a unique triumph of Norman architectural, engineering and artistic skill, for the smallest details are as impressive as the whole. The concept is Norman; yet Durham is the creation of centuries. The castle is triangular: the buildings of the bailey ranged along the edge of the cliff over the river form the base, and the mound the apex. Some of the original late eleventh-century works remain – the chapel, part of the keep and the curtain walling, and a portion of the entrance gateway. But Hugh Pudsey, Bishop 1153–95, erected the palace buildings on the side of the bailey; and in the late thirteenth century the magnificent Bishop Anthony Bek built the great hall. The keep itself was gutted and

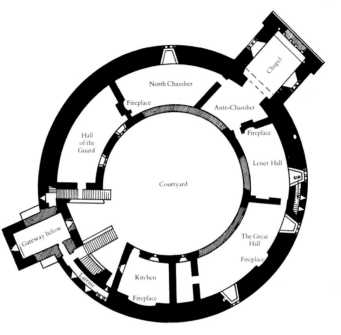

Far left: Durham, the old fortress of the Prince-Bishops who ruled the Palatine county of Durham, is part of the complex of castle, palace and cathedral which constitute the finest achievement of Norman architecture.

Left: The ground plan of Restormel, in Cornwall, a fine, virtually intact shell-keep, nearly 110 feet in diameter with walls 26 feet high and 8½ feet thick. Nothing remains, however, of the other defences.

transformed in the fourteenth century, and rebuilt again when the castle became Durham University in 1838–40.

Norman castles are so numerous and so varied that it is hard to select those with the greatest intrinsic interest. Thus, among outstanding shell-keep castles of the years 1100–50 are Lewes, Arundel, Cardiff, Restormel, Farnham and Berkeley, all with long and dramatic histories, and multiple layers of architectural growth. Lewes, built under William I, had two mounds, one at each end of a long, oval bailey. The original keep, of wood, was on the north mound. This was, perhaps, built in the first year or two after the Conquest. Then, in due course (*c.* 1080), the permanent stone shell-keep was set up on the south mound.

Opposite: Lincoln Castle, dominating the town and the Trent Valley, was first a Roman, then a Norman castle and saw its last siege in 1644. It was a prison as recently as 1878 and is still used as a shire-court.

Much of it is still there, an ovoid shell seven feet thick above a deeply battered plinth, nineteen feet high from the courtyard to the wall-walk, with its entrance gateway defended by a square tower. At Restormel, in Cornwall, the shell-keep is even finer and is virtually intact. It is nearly 110 feet in diameter, with walls twenty-six feet high and eight feet six inches thick. The bailey buildings and the other defences have gone. This was a Duchy of Cornwall property, and the Black Prince spent the Christmas of 1362 there, the castle being brought up to a fine state of repair in consequence. Thereafter it was allowed to decay, and we are lucky the keep survived; it is perhaps the best unaltered Norman shell-keep in England, rivalled only by the thirty-foot shell-keep at Rothesay, on the Isle of Bute.

Most Norman castles, however, are buried in later accretions, or ravaged hopelessly by time. Leicester, of great importance on its prominent site over the Soar throughout the Middle Ages, is such a confused casualty. It was an eleventh-century foundation, and suffered its first damage in the rebellion of 1101. The big mound of the original keep, once much higher, remains, and the lines of the original bailey, long since built up, are preserved as the parish boundary. The inner bailey is now termed Castle Yard, and the castle is a medley of buildings dating from the fourteenth, fifteenth, sixteenth and seventeenth centuries, including a 1695 court-house which incorporates a fragment of the original Norman great hall. This was built after 1150, and is probably the oldest surviving aisled and bay-divided hall in Europe. The timber roof is uniquely early, and many of the old oak pillars and struts which divided it into nave and two aisles are in their original positions. There is, too, a castle church, St Mary-in-Castro, originally founded as a collegiate college by Robert de Beaumont, 1st Earl of Leicester, in 1107, and now a bewildering medley of architectural styles, like the remains of the castle which encompass it. There are elements at Leicester which are of interest to the specialist; but for the amateur it is hard to make sense of what remains, or to visualize the castle in the twelfth- and thirteenth-century apogee of the Leicester earls.

One might say the same of Colchester Castle, or Lincoln, refortified about the same time (1068). Both were the sites of Roman fortresses, which had been repaired by the Saxons. Both are still in use, though not for military purposes. The span of time is enormous, nearly two millenia. Colchester was built on and around the Roman Temple of Claudius, which is the conjectural site of 'King Cole's Palace'. Earth was thrown up over the crumbling Roman walls to form a mound, topped by a wooden palisade. Then the temple ruins were stripped to floor level, and used as the base of the vast and massive keep, which was up to ninety feet high; plentiful supplies of Roman bricks and dressed stone, plus the rubble of the site, formed the materials. All this may have been accomplished in a frantic burst of activity during the threatened invasion by the King of Denmark in 1085. At Lincoln, the Normans had a natural hillsite covering a vast stretch of the Trent Valley, and an existing Roman enclosure, within which they set up two mounds. Some of the Roman walls were still in serviceable condition and were used as an outer bailey, while a lower Roman enclosure farther down the hill became the medieval city. Lincoln quickly became, and remained, a castle-town of great importance. It was prominent in the power struggle which broke out on the death of Henry I between Stephen (the Conqueror's nephew) and Matilda (Henry I's daughter), Stephen being taken prisoner in the process of trying to hold Lincoln. Later he got the castle back, and had his 'crown-wearing' there at Christmas 1146. In 1217 the royal forces of the infant Henry III raised the baronial-French siege, at the battle known as the 'Fair of Lincoln'; and in the Civil War it changed hands several times, being stormed by the Earl of Manchester's parliamentarians on 6 May 1644. It remains a shire-court and was in use as a prison until 1878 – in all, a fairly typical history for an important Norman castle.

Norman castles came in all sizes. Chepstow, set up by the Conqueror's regent, FitzOsbern, to open up the land route to south Wales, was placed on a natural leg-of-mutton shaped spur of sandstone overlooking a crossing point of the River

Opposite: Richmond dominates the entrance to Swaledale and was one of the strongest of the Norman rectangular keeps. On its spectacular site overlooking the river, the castle still looks formidable.

Wye. It also had a harbour, open to supplies from Bristol; and from it troops and materials could be pushed up-river, or along the coast. Most of FitzOsbern's hall and basic defences on the rock survive; but they are merely the nucleus for massive thirteenth-century additions by William the Marshall and, later, the Bigod earls of Norfolk, for vast sixteenth-century alterations and embellishments, and for changes which went on throughout the seventeenth century and even in the nineteenth, when it lost its roof and finally ceased to be inhabited. On the other hand, a great castle might be by-passed by history. Richmond, in Yorkshire, was begun by Alan the Red, son of a powerful Breton noble, the Count of Penthièvre, in 1071, to dominate the entrance to Swaledale. It was one of the strongest of the Norman rectangular keeps. Apart from the Tower and Colchester no other castle in England has so much masonry belonging to the first twenty years after the Conquest – though the great tower, still largely intact externally, was a mid-twelfth-century work, completed by Henry II. Its great hall is the oldest building of its kind, except for Chepstow. The castle, on its spectacular site overlooking the rocky river, still looks formidable. Perhaps it was too strong. There are high moors on three sides, and access for a large army with siege equipment must have been excessively difficult. In fact, Richmond was placed where it is precisely because the site is so strong; but if it dominates the entrance to the dale, it dominates little else. It was used as a prison for King William the Lion of Scotland, in 1174, but we have no record of any siege or fighting there. History passed it by. Was this because it was in the wrong place? No doubt the military engineer who sited and designed it for Alan the Red would argue that a castle which no one did, or dare, besiege had fulfilled its purpose, as a deterrent. But then, why was it allowed to decay? Castles were expected to pay their way, as a centre for the administration of estates, and the profitable dispensing of justice. A castle which did not return a profit tended to get neglected. In 1341 Richmond was reported to be in need of extensive repairs, and to be 'worth nothing' in yearly return. John Leland, seeing it

around 1540, called it a 'mere ruine'; it is a testimony to the massive scale and solid workmanship of its original construction that so much remains today.

There are many other castles without a military history, or at any rate a recorded one. Castle Acre, in Norfolk, may have fulfilled its deterrent purpose by being too strong to attack; though in its case the strength arose not from the nature of the site but from the scale of the stone walls and the depth and extent of its massive earthworks. It must have been one of the grandest motte-and-bailey castles in England, built by one of the richest and most powerful of the Norman superbarons, William de Warenne, first Earl of Surrey. There is a vast mound, and the foundations of a rectangular keep have been excavated on it; outside this was a powerful circular shell-keep 160 feet in diameter – a monster! Only the castle gate, with twin round towers, survives in full; but this is thirteenth century, and merely marks the perimeter of a huge fortified enclosure, covering a total area of fifteen acres, marked by walls which in places are thirteen feet thick. The ditches are exceptionally deep; the ramparts tower above. No other Norman castle has such impressive earthworks; and an unrecorded military history does not entirely surprise anyone who inspects the site today, even though the walls and towers have gone.

Castle Acre guards a priory of exceptional beauty and interest, founded by the heir of the lord who started the castle. The architecture of church and state were inextricably mingled in Norman times. Clerics designed and decorated castles as well as ecclesiastical buildings. At Castle Acre the great fortress and the magnificent priory rose together, built by the same workmen. We should not suppose that a castle was necessarily any less decorative than a contemporary church, at any rate internally. Sometimes even the external walls of a castle became a masterpiece of decorative masonry, as at Norwich, where the blind arcades of the keep rival anything in twelfth-century ecclesiastical embellishment. But of course, over the whole span of history, the survival chances of military architecture, and especially the elegant details, are much lower. At Kilpeck,

in Herefordshire, there is the usual conjunction of church and castle. The Romanesque church is one of the finest in Europe, covered within and without in grotesque carvings and mouldings characteristic of a school of Anglo-Norman sculptors who worked in these parts. Behind it is the remains of a motte- and-bailey castle of similar date, with a very strong counterscarp bank; once a formidable defence-work, though its military history is unknown. Was the castle once decorated like the church, at least on the inside? We cannot know, for virtually nothing of the stonework remains. The church, by contrast, is intact.

The need for decoration within a castle must have been all the stronger when we consider that it was the home of a rich man, the only one he had, unlike the church which he merely visited. There was a compulsion to make it more comfortable and beautiful, not least to express the ego of an ambitious man (and his wife) who had carved out an estate for himself in a hostile country. Even as the great stone keeps were rising, a conflict began to develop between comfort and security. The elegant walls of Norwich keep, with their swarming decorations, epitomize the way in which military considerations might be brushed aside. It may have been begun as early as 1094, along with the cathedral and bishop's palace. But even then it was archaic, outside the mainstream of the development of fortifications. Its openings were cut for lighting, rather than for their field of fire. At Castle Rising, also provided with elaborate external ornament, a comfortable gallery was simply hacked through the walls. These two keeps, finished in mid-twelfth century, were from a military viewpoint less efficient than the Tower and Colchester, built half a century earlier. But then the keep itself, the great military innovation of the eleventh century, was a dangerously inflexible concept. The idea of combining all the main accommodation and services in one building necessarily produced uncomfortable living conditions. The demands of social architecture and military engineering were often incompatible, or mutually antagonistic, and so produced compromises in which both suffered. Square

or rectangular shapes produce blind ground at the points of greatest vulnerability. So a polygonal or round shape was safer. But the need to stack rooms produced difficulties in either case. Unless expensively built of vaulted stone, floors involved timber which exposed the building to fire and collapse. Staircases built into the wall necessarily weakened it. Recesses for chimneys, fireplaces, sanitation and storage had to be hollowed out at the expense of the strength and stability of the main wall; window-openings, to admit light and air, were absolute weaknesses. They performed no military function. The designers replaced windows with small slits at the bottom of the main walls. But neither these, nor the windows, were of any use to defending archers. And all these openings and recesses were the first targets for the siege engineers, seeking to begin the process of reducing the keep to rubble.

Then again the entrance caused endless and often insoluble troubles. The entrance was the weakest point of all. So the strongest castle had only one, and only one door in the keep. And since even the single entrance was at risk, it had to have extra defences. These, by their very nature, increased the bottleneck. A strong keep always had a good, deep well; at Windsor it was 6 ft 4 ins in diameter, 165 feet deep and lined with dressed stonework to a depth of over sixty feet below the ground! But apart from water, everything else, and everybody, had to come and go through one door (like 10 Downing Street today). Even with a forebuilding to provide a landing, life could become intolerable. Most, perhaps all, of a castle's existence was spent in peacetime conditions, and the temptation to make life more comfortable at the expense of structural security often proved irresistible. Even under siege conditions, the keep-castle was not as formidable as it looked. The small force it could accommodate was no threat to an army – merely to the surrounding peasants. It might be impregnable, but it was also a trap. However massive, it could only hold a limited number of people for a limited time; and a relatively small detachment from an enemy army could lock them inside, until disease, starvation and plummeting morale compelled surrender. The

Rochester Castle is perhaps the most menacing Norman keep in England. It rises 120 feet and took thirteen years to build. It survived a ferocious siege under King John and still looks solid nearly eight hundred years later.

future lay with a rather different type of castle, as we shall see in the next chapter.

The Norman castle also posed a social and political problem. As we have seen, William I could not have conquered and held England without building castles in large numbers, and entrusting his tenants-in-chief with their custody. Many more came into existence as his successors pushed into Wales and to the north. At one time there may have been as many as a thousand motte-and-bailey castles, most of which have been plotted in a map in Dr Renn's *Norman Castles*. They were especially numerous in Wales and its borders. But this dispersal of power to feudatories necessarily posed a threat to the monarchy. The Conqueror was well aware of this. He increased his own power correspondingly, both in England and Normandy; in fact in the duchy his conquest of England gave him sufficient authority and means to enforce the rule, towards the end of his reign, that no castle might be built without his consent. This power of the duke over private castles is the earliest case we have of

Opposite: Farnham Castle in Surrey, a shell-keep castle which belonged to the Bishops of Winchester, was one of the first to be provided with comfortable living-quarters. Continuously occupied, it is now a conference centre.

interference in the customary rights of a Norman vassal. William seems to have established the right, formalized in the duchy customs of 1091 shortly after his death, to occupy any castle at will; and he undoubtedly exercised it in his last years, when many baronial castles were garrisoned by his troops. In a number of instances in Normandy important castles were not updated after about the end of the eleventh century, indicating a ducal ban on their modernization.

In England William introduced structural modifications in the feudal system to check baronial autonomy. He combined several thousand small estates into less than two hundred major lordships, held by tenants-in-chief. The lands forming a lord's endowment were known collectively as his 'honour' (i.e. 'that which gives a man distinction'). The lord's chief residence, his castle, was the head of the honour and its administrative and business centre. Thus, for instance, the lands of Roger de Busli, Ilbert de Laci and Henry de Ferrars emerge in the records as the honours of Tickhill, Pontefract and Tutbury, each with important castles called after them. The contemporary term for a district with which the distribution of land had been planned for the maintenance of a particular fortress was *castellaria*. The honour of William FitzAnsculf, for example, had its core in a large block of villages around his castle of Dudley. Other *castellariae* in the Domesday Book are Richmond, Caerlon-on-Usk, Richard's Castle, Ewyas Harold, Clifford and Montgomery. Such a consolidation of estates around castles enabled a small occupying force of Normans to hold down a nation. And from William's point of view a few large barons were easier to control than a multitude of small ones. Moreover, he established the point, maintained in theory at least until the days of Charles I, that the monarch might occupy at will any castle or house of a tenant-in-chief. He had a further institutional device to hold his great men in check. The knight's fee, the basic unit of military tenure in post-Conquest England, was a Norman institution. In England William was able to implant it from scratch, and completely subject it to his authority and purpose. The knight-service he accordingly imposed on his English

tenants-in-chief was so heavy that few of them could afford to enfief knights much in excess of what they owed the duke. Whereas in Normandy the size of a lord's military retinue bore no relation to the knight-service he had to provide, in England virtually all the baronial knights could be 'called up' by the king at the least threat of trouble.

The system worked, albeit with some outbreaks of trouble, well enough under the Conqueror and his two strong-minded sons. But any medieval monarchy, however strong, was vulnerable to a failure of male heirs. The Conqueror, Rufus and Henry Beauclerk permitted the construction of private wooden castles in some quantity. Major works, especially of stone, were either royal, or held by tenants-in-chief under stringent safeguards. Then came the disaster of the White Ship in 1120, which drowned Beauclerk's only son; and it is significant that, after this mishap, which foreshadowed a disputed succession, we first hear of major castle works by individual subjects.

With Henry's death in 1135 and the subsequent struggle between Matilda and Stephen of Blois, the great age of the 'adulterine castle' opened. The Anglo-Saxon Chronicle recorded: 'And they filled the whole land with these castles. They sorely burdened the unhappy people of the country with forced labour on the castles. And when the castles were made they filled them with devils and wicked men.' Many of the adulterines had very short lives. Thus Selby was captured within a week of the commencement of building. Wycombe, Reading, Blewbury, Heptonstall and Ipswich lasted only a few months or years, and there were many similar cases from the Welsh marches. Some were very small indeed, and have vanished virtually without trace. At the time they constantly changed hands, so that the historian is often bewildered by the problem of who owned what. Castles were taken by storm, lent, borrowed by force, stolen, pledged or sold for cash; others, such as Lincoln, Devizes, Downton and Harptree changed hands through various forms of trickery. At times, and in various areas of intense struggle, church buildings, being of stone, were involved. When the Earl of Chester sacked Lincoln,

Stephen turned St Mary's Church into a siege-castle. At Bampton, Oxfordshire, Matilda built a castle in the church tower. In Hereford, in 1140, the cemetery by the cathedral was the site of a siege-works, and arrows and stones were fired from the cathedral tower. The nuns were ejected from Wilton, and the monks from Romsay, Coventry and Bridlington, and the buildings fortified. At Cirencester a wooden castle was set up by the abbey. There was a great crop of counter-castles or siege-castles, set up either to assault or cancel out existing structures – at, for example, Dunster, Ludlow, Corfe, Arundel and Wallingford.

Not all the castles built during the anarchy were small and ephemeral. In 1138 Stephen's brother Henry was building castles at Bishop's Waltham, Farnham, Merdon, Taunton and Wolvesey. Farnham, with its fine shell-keep, is still in use today, and Wolvesey was described in 1141 as 'a house built like a palace with a very strong keep'. Moreover, many important existing castles, including royal fortresses, fell into baronial hands. We have a charter, dating probably from 1146, in which Stephen bribed the Earl of Chester to support him by handing over to him Lincoln, Tickhill, the New Castle in Staffordshire (Newcastle-under-Lyme), Belvoir, Rowley, Torksey, Derby, Mansfield, Oswarbec, Blyth and Lancaster, some of them already powerful strategic strongholds. Five years earlier, Geoffrey de Mandeville, Earl of Essex and one of the worst of the baronial ruffians, was given the hereditary constableship of London itself, plus the right to build a castle anywhere in his lands. Two years later, the *Gesta Stephani* noted: 'He not only had the Tower of London in his hand, but also castles of impregnable strength built around the city; and all that part of the kingdom which recognized the king he had so securely subjected to his control that, throughout the kingdom, he acted in the king's place.'

Nevertheless, the memory of the first three Norman kings was so potent that even during the anarchy at least some great lords sought to introduce elements of legality into the ownership and use of castles. Major tenants-in-chief always, if

possible, tried to obtain a legal basis for their actions, and their tenure of castles. The earliest licence to crenellate a dwelling-house (as opposed to strengthening a castle) comes from Bishopton in 1143. And, from about 1150, there is evidence that the greater barons were tiring of the Hobbesian struggle of 'every man against every man'. By that date, it was guessed, there were some 1,115 unlicensed castles. Incessant castle warfare posed grave problems to big landowners. Contemporary siege techniques were not equal to the easy reduction even of small castles. If a surprise assault failed, the attacker settled down to starving out the garrison, meanwhile living off the neighbouring countryside. Forced to abandon the siege, they destroyed the remaining crops and food supplies, to deny them to the defenders. Even when there was no actual fighting, the depredations of the 'castlemen' were intolerable. The barons might not care much about the sufferings of their peasants, but they hated to see their own revenues fall. Moreover, the greater lords found that their own vassals, by building castles which could stand up to anything short of a regular siege, were becoming uncontrollable. Hence the big men began to make private peace treaties among themselves, regulating areas where the royal writ no longer ran. Thus the Earl of Gloucester made a pact with the Earl of Hereford; and Robert de Beaumont, Earl of Leicester, made separate peace treaties with the Earl of Northampton, the Earl of Hereford and the Earl of Chester. The last of these is a virtual disarmament treaty, the text of which happily survives as a sort of charter. The Earl of Chester granted Mountsorrel Castle to the Earl of Leicester, provided the latter's castles were not used as bases for attacks on Chester's lands. Leicester agreed to destroy Ravenstone Castle, unless Chester agreed to let it remain; if the castle was held against one earl, the other was to assist in its destruction. The castle of Whitwick could be fortified. But neither earl was to build castles between a line Leicester–Donnington–Coventry–Hinckley–Hartshill, nor at Gotham, Kinoulton, 'or nearer', nor between a line Kinoulton–Belvoir–Oakham–Rockingham, 'or nearer', except by mutual consent. And in this demilitarized zone around Leicester both earls were to combine to destroy castles built by others.

There is no mention of the king, royal rights or the state in this quintessentially feudal document. But clearly one of its chief aims was to prevent the building of private castles, and reduce the number of existing ones – an aim that was traditionally associated with royal policy. Within a year or two, in 1153, the growing desire for peace found expression in the Treaty of Winchester, which composed the differences between Stephen and Matilda's son, the future Henry II, and opened the way for the peaceful accession of the first Angevin. It contained special provisions for the castles of London, Windsor, Oxford, Lincoln and Winchester. Stephen's reign thus marked the apogee of the private castle in England; the coming of Henry II not only brought the problem under control for two hundred and fifty years, but also opened a new epoch in military architecture.

Opposite: Rockingham, in Northamptonshire, was begun by William the Conqueror and still has a medieval gatehouse. However, most of the accommodation dates from Tudor times and the house was 'Gothicized' in the 19th century by Anthony Salvin.

CHAPTER TWO

PLANTAGENET CASTLES

Opposite: Orford, in Essex, is a superbly preserved example of an early polygonal keep, which superseded Norman square keeps in the later 12th century. It was probably designed by Henry II's military expert, Maurice the Engineer.

Previous page

left: Berkeley, one of the first castles with a turreted curtain-wall, though very ancient, is still the home of the Berkeleys. The de-throned King Edward II was murdered here in 1327.

right: Dover Castle.

Henry II was the ideal sovereign to end a period of anarchy dominated by unlicensed private castles. He held strongly to the view that the powerful and properly controlled royal castle was the very foundation of civil law, and that private castles, except in the supervised possession of men absolutely loyal to the crown, were the enemies of order. He came from a long line of centralizing castle-builders. The house of Anjou, the Plantagenets, had built up their power and imposed organized government on the crude feudalism of Anjou and Touraine very largely by building 'great stone keeps', from which justice was dispensed and enforced. This was the age of Fulk Nerra and Geoffrey Martel, in the tenth and eleventh centuries. Their successors were committed to the same principles, and all were expert castle-builders. Most of the new ideas in fortification came from the eastern Mediterranean, and were brought back to western Europe by crusaders. It was customary for leading crusaders to be accompanied by their master-mason and their 'engineer' (usually a master-carpenter, occasionally a smith). Henry II's grandfather, Fulk V, Count of Anjou, was a leading crusader for many years, an architect of many crusader castles and town walls, and in 1131 became King of Jerusalem. Henry's father, Geoffrey Plantagenet, was not only a castle-builder but a mechanical expert in a wider sense. A contemporary chronicler describes him as 'highly skilled in engineering and carpentry'. He specialized in sieges, and designed his own siege-works and siege-engines, of a type which had never before been seen in the West. During his siege of Montreuil-Bellay in 1151, the chronicler says he 'studied the work of Vegetius Renatus', author of *De Re Militari*.

Henry II inherited his father's literacy, expertise and passion-ate regard for the rule of law. And he founded in England a great line of builder-kings: Richard, John, Henry III, Edward I and Edward III; only two of his progeny, Edward II and Richard II, failed to become outstanding builders of castles and, perhaps in consequence, both were murdered in castle dungeons. Henry II's first problem, however, when he assumed control in England, was not to build but to destroy. Estimates of the number of castles he smashed to bits vary from 375 to 1,115 (the latter is certainly too high, since it represents the total of unlicensed castles). He was not a great general, but his defensive campaigns and his anti-baronial police actions were dashing, original and almost entirely successful. His ability to take even the strongest castles was famous. As a rule he did it by a lightning raid without warning, a rapid investment, and then a massive and shattering assault. At Malmesbury in 1153, according to Henry of Huntingdon, 'he threw himself straight into the siege, for delay was not his way, and soon took it'. By such means he seized a number of castles, especially in France, hitherto regarded as impregnable. This had important social consequences. In the 1130s and 1140s the balance of advantage had swung towards the defence, and as a consequence of castle-building, legitimate authority had become divorced from actual power. A handful of men in a strong castle could defy an army: in 1138, according to Richard of Hexham, nine men held at bay the entire army of David, King of the Scots. Henry II reversed the trend not merely by his huge siege-train and engines, improving on his father's ideas, but by the specialized force of mercenaries he formed for internal policing. These *routiers*, mainly from Flanders, were long-service foot-soldiers, fed and clothed by Henry, who had them specially trained and equipped for ruthless siege operations.

Thus Henry was able not merely to knock down and burn the wooden adulterines but to take by force any powerful stone castle which defied him. Happily, in England his reputation preceded him. His first act was to command all baronial occupiers to relinquish royal castles in their custody. When the Earl of York hesitated to comply, Henry moved swiftly and seized York, and the supposedly impregnable Scarborough, without a fight. In one case the king had to resort to force, against Hugh Mortimer, owner of Cleobury, Wigmore and Bridgnorth (the last a royal castle), all of which were simultaneously invested and stormed. The castles of Stephen's brother Henry, Bishop of Winchester, were declared forfeit and destroyed. There was a second great wave of destruction following the rebellion of 1173–4, which Henry put down in a masterful and ferocious fashion. Castles at Allington, Northallerton, Benington, Saltwood, Thirsk, Weston Turville, Dunham Massey, Kirby Malzeard and Groby had their walls pulled down and their mottes quarried away or levelled. The king saw to it that the 'slighting' was properly carried out; in 1180, for instance, the officials responsible for demolishing Owston Ferry Castle were fined for scamping the job. When the dust of the 'great war' had settled, says Roger of Howden, Henry 'took every castle of England into his hands, and removing the castellans of the earls and barons, put in his own custodians; he did not even spare his intimate counsellor, Richard de Lucy, the Justiciar of England, but took from him his own castle of Ongar'.

What Henry was doing was to enforce to the letter the right the king had always claimed to occupy and control any fortification beyond a certain size. Life-tenures and hereditary tenures of castles, becoming common under Stephen, were abolished. So Henry was establishing not merely the fundamental rule that all castles were at his disposal, but that no royal custodian should be personally identified with the castle he administered. Having established this framework, Henry could afford to relax the regulations as and when desirable. At the beginning of his reign private castles outnumbered royal ones by five to one. Within ten years most non-royal castles had been confiscated and destroyed or placed in reliable hands. The king did not forbid private castle-building completely. Faithful supporters were allowed, very occasionally, to build new castles, or expand and improve old ones. Thus his friend Robert FitzHarding, the real founder of the House of Berkeley, was allowed to refashion Berkeley Castle, providing it with one of the first turreted curtain-walls in England. Moreover, Henry largely financed the works. On a number of occasions he paid for improvements in private castles held by men he could trust. In the late 1150s he financed a strong new castle, with a stone keep, at Norham, Northumberland, held by Hugh Pudsey,

35

Bishop of Durham. In the 1173–4 rebellion, however, Henry felt that Hugh had betrayed his trust, and deprived him not only of Norham but of Durham and Northallerton also. But these works were too important to national defence to be slighted; Henry's method, in such cases, was to hold the castle under the crown, then return it under probation, taking it away again at the first hint of disloyalty – as he did with Norham in 1185.

Other castles held privately (as a rule) but financed by the crown were Bowes (1171), Harbottle (1157) and Wark-on-Tweed (1158–61). But Henry also steadily carried through an immense programme of royal castle-building and the systematic modernization of existing fortresses. Robert of Torigni, the Abbot of Mont St Michel, wrote: 'He improved or renewed nearly all his castles . . . and not in Normandy alone but in England, Aquitaine, Anjou, Maine and Touraine he worked at his castles and houses, either building new ones or restoring the old.' In some cases, refortification of royal castles was accompanied by building of town walls, forming large defended areas in which the castle served as keep. Henry was an innovator in military architecture, and in Maurice the Engineer, his leading expert, he had one of the finest craftsmen in the West. At Orford, built in the 1160s (the huge sum of £663 was spent in the year 1166 alone), he moved away from the rectangular keep, with its blind and vulnerable corners, towards the circular or polygonal keep, whose inspiration came from abroad, though whether it was Denmark, Sweden or France is unclear. Orford was habitable by 1168; and two years later it had a new-style curtain-wall with rectangular towers, now alas vanished.

At the same time Henry did not discard the rectangular keep. At Dover, under Maurice's direction, a vast building programme was carried out throughout the 1180s, at a cost of over £6,000. This included a big cubical keep, a curtain-wall with fourteen square towers, and two gatehouses, both powerful. Dover keep has an ingenious plumbing system, and is intrinsically strong; but it shows little improvement in military design over the square keeps built in England fifty years before

at London and Colchester. The great rectangular keep at Newcastle was also built by Maurice, at Henry's orders. Here the plumbing is even more elaborate than at Dover, water being conveyed by lead pipes to drawing places all over the keep; and the well, ninety-nine feet deep, is lined with stone all the way down. The cost was over £900.

These great fortresses were slow and expensive to build. The architectural historian John Harvey has calculated that the speed at which a fine stone church tower could be built averaged ten to twelve feet per season, running from spring to end-autumn. Evidence from Scarborough, Orford, Newcastle, Chilham, Bowes, Dover and Odiham, where the royal accounts shed some light, suggests that ten to twelve feet per season also applied to stone keeps. A big stone castle was an immense investment in time, money and skilled manpower, and it was therefore important to get the design right. On the face of it, it seems to us today that Dover and Newcastle were already obsolete when they were built, since rectangular keeps were being superseded by the circular or polygonal type. Why, then, did Henry II build the polygonal Orford, 1166–72, before he built Newcastle and Dover? One answer may be that Dover incorporated a number of other innovations, such as immensely strong mural towers, powerful gateways and the emergence of the new principle of concentricity – which was to dominate castle-building throughout the thirteenth and fourteenth centuries. Mural towers, especially if they projected, prevented mining since they covered every foot of the wall. Once a strong *enceinte* was put up, the keep became less important. Square or rectangular keeps were easier to build; and, from a domestic viewpoint, more convenient. Henry II had been brought up in such a keep, and may have allowed sentiment and comfort to influence him.

On the other hand, his illegitimate half-brother, Hamelin, who married the Warenne heiress Isabel in 1164, and so held the Earldom and estates of Surrey until his death in 1202, seems to have believed strongly in the cylindrical keep. At Conisbrough, in Yorkshire, where the 1st Earl of Surrey, who had

Dover Castle, mainly the creation of Henry II in the 12th century, is one of the greatest of all English castles. It was kept in repair as a working fortress, and garrisoned, until the mid-20th century.

fought at Hastings, had built a wooden motte-and-bailey castle, Hamelin set up the latest kind of military structure, one of the wonders of the reign, and still impressive. The castle is on a spectacular site, commanding a confluence of valleys and hills. Essentially it consists of a single bailey on a high natural mound, which is scarped all round and surrounded by a ditch. There is a curtain-wall seven feet thick and thirty-five feet high, with wall-towers at all important angles, built solid up to the wall-walk. The design is essentially an improved version of Orford. The keep is attached to the curtain-wall at its strongest point, with one side exposed to the field; hence, *in extremis*, the garrison might escape. It is of four storeys, with six immense buttresses, a wall fifteen feet thick above a very high batter carried round all the buttresses. Entrance is on the second floor, and both the basement below and the ceiling above it, are stone vaults, so that the bottom of the tower is both very difficult and deadly to loosen or mine, and impervious to fire. But at this point, characteristically, comfort begins to take over; not only are the floors of the third and fourth storeys of wood, but each has a two-light window, fireplace, lavabo and latrine built into the walls; and the fourth storey in addition has a richly decorated chapel built into a buttress, with a small sacristy attached. At the battlements, it is true, there are two fighting lines, one above the other. But even here a dovecote (for communications) has been carved out of one buttress, an oven out of another; and two buttresses contain water-cisterns, to save people the trouble of trudging down the spiral wall-staircases to the basement, to draw water from the well. The keep is built of fine limestone ashlar, and looks formidable; but the layout of the upper storeys betrays its weaknesses, which must have been known to an enemy since the internal arrangements of castles were easily discoverable in a military society where everyone knew each other. Moreover, the escape route provided by pinning the keep to the curtain-wall was another, and obvious, weakness.

But then who could design the perfect castle? Many fine castles were built in Henry II's reign, some for the crown, others for the king's close friends, supporters and office-holders (sometimes with the help of royal cash). Whereas under Stephen there had been a proliferation of castles in the midlands, the home counties and the south-west, there was now a shift to the north and the Welsh borders. A chronicler writing about 1200 listed almost a hundred castles in the English counties. The largest single group were in Yorkshire (twelve), with Shropshire (nine) second. Of the Yorkshire castles no less than seven were in the North Riding (to which should be added Bowes, which the chronicler omitted), the quintessential castle-country of England. These included a group of medium-sized castles, Pickering, Helmsley, Tickhill and Middleham, associated with hunting and the royal forests, though some of them were in private hands. Pickering stands on a lime-stone bluff on the south edge of the North Yorkshire moors, overlooking the Vale of Pick. William the Conqueror probably built a primitive castle here while harrying the north in 1069–70; fifty years later Henry I issued a charter from Pickering, presumably from a substantial castle. Then, in the last years of Henry II, entries in the pipe-rolls indicate it was being rebuilt and updated.

Pickering was near a vast stretch of royal forest, and a castle was necessary in such a spot not merely to provide accommodation and security while the king was hunting, but at all times to ensure that the forest laws were observed and enforced; like all castles it was an administrative centre and court of justice. Between 1100–1400 nearly all the kings of England visited Pickering for short spells of hunting, chiefly wild boar and deer, and the castle was normally in the custody of the sheriff. He was expected to return a profit, and usually did so, to judge from surviving accounts. In 1314, for instance, its revenue was £385 19s 3½d. Some £367 1s 9d was spent, but this included over £340 on building a new hall for the castle. In most years a large surplus was handed over in cash, derived from rents for land, profits from farming over 1,600 sheep, pasturing in the forest, commuted labour-services, and the profits of the court. Wool was stored in a wool house in the inner ward, and sold in

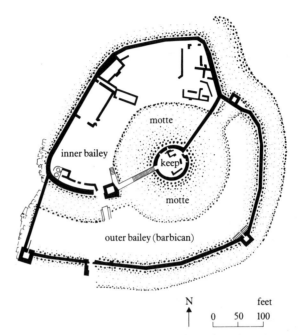

motte

inner bailey

keep

motte

outer bailey (barbican)

N   feet
0   50   100

Far left: Conisbrough was built by Henry II's half-brother, Hamelin, on a spectacular Yorkshire site overlooking valleys and hills. The keep is of four storeys, with six immense buttresses and a wall fifteen feet thick.

Left: The ground plan of Pickering in Yorkshire. Situated near a vast stretch of royal forest, it was built to provide accommodation and security while the king was hunting, and to enforce the forest laws.

large bales. Expenditure, apart from building, included the purchase of fetters for the prison, parchment for the accounts, and a chest and planks to construct a treasury in which to store the castle documents.

Tickhill, by contrast, was a private foundation, though it was clearly in royal hands during part of Henry II's reign, since Exchequer pipe-rolls show that £120 was spent on building a tower and bridge in 1178–80. With its moat, bridge, fine gatehouse and a good deal of surviving curtain-wall, this castle is a delightful sight today; but excavations show it once had an eleven-sided tower-keep, on a circular plinth and with pilaster buttresses – a formidable fortress. Henry II preferred to keep private castles of this kind in being, rather than slight them or allow them to decay. Architecturally, Tickhill was linked to Conisbrough; Middleham, another castle in this group, was linked to those with rectangular keeps from this period, such as Bamburgh, Carlisle, Appleby, Brougham and Norham, though

The ground plan of
Skenfrith, Gwent, an
early, red sandstone
Norman castle
commanding one of the
main routes from England
into Wales. A fine,
romantic ruin, it is well
situated on the west bank
of the River Minnow.

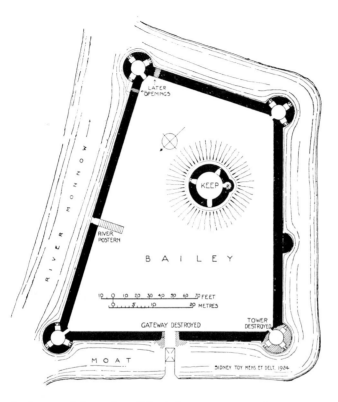

These medium-sized castles, whether in royal hands or owned by reliable friends, were seen by Henry II as part of an overall strategy for holding and administering an important area of the north of England, from which the crown derived substantial revenues. Henry did not, therefore, see each in isolation but as part of a group, capable if necessary of reinforcing and resupplying each other. They were operated in conjunction with the large royal castles of York, Scarborough, Richmond, Knaresborough and Pontefract, and together constituted a royal stranglehold on a huge chunk of wild countryside. Similar groupings can be observed in the Welsh borders, where the topography was somewhat similar, and the security problem also perennial. Thus Henry grouped Skenfrith Castle, an early foundation of William FitzOsbern's, a substantial and well-designed castle on the west bank of the River Monnow in Gwent, which still commands one of the main routes from England into Wales, with two other nearby castles, Grosmont and the White Castle. Each had its own tactical importance; but strategically they formed a unity. Four and five miles apart, the three made it a simple matter to control the area between Abergavenny and Monmouth, and between the Black Mountains the Wye, with the three main east-west routes that pass through it. The 'three castles' as they were known, were brought together by Henry as crown property; and they remained in common ownership and control, even when alienated by the crown, throughout the Middle Ages.

Both Henry II's regal sons, Richard and John, were tremendous castle-builders. Until well into the thirteenth century, the Holy Land continued to be the main testing-ground and inspiration for new ideas in fortifications and siege-techniques. Richard brought back from the Third Crusade not only new military concepts but a number of Frankish veterans from Syria. These included Pietro de Tanentonne and Martino de Nazareth, who built and operated *arbalistae*; and Mercadier the Brabançon and Master Ivo the Balistarius, also artillery engineers. With him, too, came a unit of Saracen warriors and the secret of Greek Fire, for centuries a Byzantine

the keeps of these five all had three storeys, and Middleham had two. At Middleham the keep stands in the centre, and largely fills a rectangular bailey, also cluttered with ranges of domestic quarters built during the fourteenth century. Within the keep are two wells, one at each end of its vaulted, fireproof basement. Middleham never seems to have been in royal hands until the fifteenth century, but this does not mean it was not under Henry II's supervision. As with Helmsley, with its square, turreted keep, half of it was blown down during the Civil War. This late twelfth-century castle, near Pickering on the road to the royal castle of Scarborough, was a quadrilateral enclosure with a double ditch, rectangular bailey and a square gatehouse: a substantial fortress of the second rank.

Pembroke, the great Anglo-Norman stronghold in south Wales, was provided by Richard the Lionheart with the first of the vast round towers which became the military fashion at the end of the 12th century.

monopoly, which was used at the siege of Dieppe in 1195. Richard had learnt a lot at the siege of Acre, and from his visit to the great Syrian fortress of Margat. He employed his knowledge in designing and constructing Château Gaillard, grandest of all the Angevin fortresses. By his day the accurate use of stone-throwing engines and mining techniques had been brought to the point where the existence beneath the walls of a single dead angle, or any place that could not be reached by missiles hurled by the defenders, imperilled the whole fortress. Gaillard was built so as to have no dead ground whatever. Like every other castle, however, it had a defect; in this case the stone bridge which connected the citadel or second court with the outer court – a defect seized on by Philip Augustus, King of France, when he took the castle from John. But Gaillard does not concern us, except as an influence. More important were the works Richard undertook in England. This included a radical refortification of the Tower of London, with an external wall and ditch costing £3,000. Richard also added the Bell Tower, an example of the new strong, rounded towers, which were now superseding the polygonal keep-towers of the Conisbrough and Orford type. His men added an even stronger and bigger tower of this sort – the first in Britain, in fact – to the great Anglo-Norman stronghold of Pembroke in south-west Wales. This was built of stone throughout, with vaulted roof and floors, and so completely fireproof. The inspiration seems to have come from Germany, where Richard, of course, was held in captivity in 1192–3.

John, too, spent large sums of money modernizing his castles, and building new ones, though little of his work has survived. The first recorded licence 'to fortify and crenellate with a wall of stone and lime' had been issued to owners of manor-houses in 1195. John issued nine in the years 1200–4. The usual type was a rectangular moated enclosure round the house, as at Kirkoswald, Ashley, Cottingham and Bridgwater. John did the same for his own hunting lodges, smaller houses and country villas. Though he lost Normandy, he campaigned vigorously and successfuly in Wales and Ireland; and in his last years, when the barons had joined hands with the French invaders, he showed himself a master of siege-technique.

John left his infant son Henry III about sixty castles, some of which were becoming obsolete, plus a large group of palaces and manor-houses. Henry's guardian, Hubert de Burgh, a leading expert on castles, took the work in hand, and throughout Henry's minority substantial sums were spent on repairs and improvements. Hubert did not confine his work to purely royal establishments. At Grosmont, in Gwent, one of the 'three castles' which came into his custody in 1201, he built a fine solar-hall around 1210, and then set in motion a scheme of building which, in the years 1220–40, replaced the old wooden Norman castle with a strong gatehouse, inner and outer bailey of stone (the outer bailey has now gone), and formidable towers. At Montgomery, some miles to the north, but still on the Welsh borders, he took the boy king on progress in 1223, and there showed him, according to Matthew Paris, 'a suitable spot for the erection of an impregnable castle'. The place is a natural site. The modern Shrewsbury–Montgomery road, following a Roman road, is the obvious invasion route from England into mid-Wales. There had been an Iron Age hillfort near here, an Anglo-Saxon base, and later a primitive Norman castle, abandoned around 1216. Here a spur of high ground terminates dramatically in the castle rock, with a spectacular view of the lower ground beneath; and Hubert built right on top of it, at a cost to the crown of over £2,000. Once finished, as a royal castle, it was granted to him for life in 1228, with £130 a year for its upkeep; in 1229 he got another 200 marks (£166 13s 4d) for 'enclosing' the castle, that is building the outer bailey wall; and in 1233 the tower was roofed in lead, perhaps marking its completion. Here, then, was another example of the crown financing a castle in the custody of a great private man, albeit a crown servant.

Such a course was, perhaps, inevitable, in some cases; but it was also risky, as Henry III's subsequent quarrel with Hubert indicates. But Henry continued the policy once he was of age to take decisions himself. He also began to build even more vigorously than his mentor, though his greatest work, West-minster Abbey, lies outside our scope. In the military sphere, his masterpiece is Kenilworth, in Warwickshire. This was a Norman foundation, given by Henry I to the Clintons, who built a massive square keep. Henry II took it back, compensating the Clintons in Buckinghamshire, and he, John and Henry III all spent large sums on modernizing it. But it was Henry III who turned it into the strongest fortress in the midlands, Nottingham perhaps excepted. He seems to have possessed quite a sense of military strategy, so that it is not entirely surprising that Edward I was his son. He recognized that unless a castle was built on a high, spectacular rock, like his Montgomery, the surest form of defence was water – not a narrow moat or even a river, but acres and acres of deep water. It was Henry and his experts who created the great lake at Kenilworth, by damming a series of streams which flow through the valley, and they erected two more lines of moats on the north side – the only one not protected by the lake-water. The water fortifications covered over a hundred acres, bigger by far than a similar scheme at Caerphilly, which we will come across in the next chapter. Water defences on this scale had to be kept in constant and expensive repair, but they had the inestimable advantage that the huge siege-engines, which dominated siege-warfare from the age of Henry II to the coming of large cannon, could not be easily, if at all, brought within range of the curtain-walls, let alone the keep. Henry, then, had the wit to build this powerful defensive system; but he lacked the political sense to hang on to it. He gave it to his sister Eleanor and her husband Simon de Montfort; and sixteen years later Simon based his revolt on Kenilworth, for a time even imprisoning Henry's son and heir the Lord Edward there.

The cost of most of Henry's building activities is recorded in some detail in the Exchequer and other accounts. The series of pipe-rolls begin with 1155, the first full year of Henry II and, apart from one missing year under John, are continuous; in the thirteenth century they are supplemented by a variety of other financial documents. Of course these royal accounts do not tell the whole story. On the pipe-rolls, the sheriff or constable usually gives only the total figure for 'the works of the castle'. But local taxes might be levied too, and unrecorded goods and customary services. We must assume that the sums given represent less than the true cost of the work. But in some cases, even as early as the reign of Henry II, it is possible to give detailed, season-by-season analyses, as at Orford, Chilham, Odiham, Scarborough, Newcastle and Horston.

Taking expenditure recorded in the pipe-rolls alone, the first three Angevin kings, 1155–1215, spent £46,000 on castle works – that is an average of £780 a year, at a time when the crown's basic revenues averaged under £10,000. During the thirty-three years of Henry II, some £21,000 was spent on ninety castles. Two-thirds of these cases consisted of minor work, repairs and maintenance. But expenditure exceeded £1,000 each on Dover, Newcastle, Nottingham, Orford, Windsor and Winchester. At Dover, the Exchequer payments came to nearly £6,500. By contrast, Richard spent little on castles in England, apart from the £3,000 he devoted to the Tower. But John spent over £1,000 a year on ninety-five castles, nine of them major works: Corfe, Hanley, Horston, Kenilworth, Lancaster, Knaresborough, Odiham, Scarborough and Norham. Henry III's expenditure on building was prodigious, altogether about £113,000 on royal castles and manor-houses in the years 1216–72, plus £40–50,000 on Westminster Abbey. This was about £3,000 a year, one-tenth of his average income of £30,000. Of this, about £1,500 went on castles, a total of £85,000 for the reign. He spent £7,500 on Dover, £15,000 on Windsor, and nearly £10,000 each on the Tower and Winchester.

This expenditure is not as profligate as it looks at first glance. Henry II was a shrewd financier who left a great deal of money. His aim in building and modernizing castles was to force lesser barons out of the business. By raising the level of military technology, he saw to it that only a few of the greatest private lords could afford to remain in the arms-race. Poorer barons had to be content with the new type of fortified manor-house – secure against a casual raid but useless against siege-engines.

Kenilworth, now a romantic ruin, was the 13th-century stronghold of Simon de Montfort. In the 16th century the Earl of Leicester, Elizabeth I's favourite, rebuilt it as a fortress-palace.

Hence Henry saved himself money, and he actually contrived to reduce the number of castles in royal hands, thereby saving more. This process continued. Throughout the thirteenth century, the number of castles, royal or private, which were kept not only in repair but up to date, fell steadily. Royal castles, as William of Newburgh put it, remained 'the bones of the kingdom', but the bones grew bigger and fewer. Under Henry III they were reduced from sixty to forty-seven. Moreover, the large sums Henry spent could be misleading. Even under John, much of the expenditure on castles was not military. Windsor, Winchester and Nottingham, for instance, were palaces, with all the comforts of Woodstock, plus more of the administrative resources of Westminster. John built his new castle at Odiham in Hampshire, for instance, 'to disport himself' in the New Forest. Under Henry III an even larger portion of the expenditure on royal castles went on domestic buildings and adornment. Of directly military expenditure, nearly all was repair and maintenance. Of course annual expenditure was directly linked to periods of political tension, rising and falling accordingly.

During periods of peace, the medieval mind having an incurable objection to looking far ahead, castles fell swiftly into decay. Maintenance was a constant struggle against storm damage, for a good castle was nearly always in an exposed spot, and the consequent dry rot; the results of poor workmanship were another constant problem, for most castles were built in haste, with forced labour. So towers and walls cracked and fell, and roofs were stripped even of lead by high winds. Money was always short, but if essential repairs were not done swiftly, the damage quickly became irreparable. The royal system of authorizing work was slow. Under Henry III, the sheriffs were given authority to spend up to £5 on repairs without a writ, but this tempted them simply to pocket the cash. Even after reducing the number of castles, the crown often found the burden of keeping them up unbearable. Lesser men might just give up. Benefield Castle in Northamptonshire was seized for debt in 1208; and many other private castles went out of use for

lack of cash. Garrisoning was costly. As early as 1130, a knight, ten sergeants, a watchman and a porter cost £21 a year to man Burton-in-Lonsdale Castle, and this was only a care-and-maintenance establishment. When, after the 1173–4 revolt, Henry II garrisoned Norwich on a wartime footing, it needed 300 men-at-arms, archers and engineers.

Of course, we cannot understand the medieval castle as an institution unless we appreciate its economic as well as its military functions. It did not stand in isolation but as part of a system, inseparable from its dependent area. A *castellaria* or *chatellenie* comprised castle, lands, feudal duties and fiscal arrangements – often very complicated ones if the castle was royal. Often, monopolies of mills, ovens and other basic services were created primarily to maintain castles; in fact the erection of a fortress made the creation of monopolies inevitable. This was one reason why castles were unpopular with the peasants. Townsmen might have a different attitude, especially in the 'new towns', created in increasing numbers from the time of Rufus onwards (Carlisle was the first), where merchants, shopkeepers and artisans were attracted by privileges and fiscal concessions. But they were milked, too, to keep the walls in repair. The possession of a stronghold without its 'natural' sources of revenue was abhorrent to the medieval mind; normally they expected it to make a profit. In January 1199 the peace terms drawn up between Richard I and Philip Augustus by the papal legate allowed Philip to keep those Norman castles he had already seized. Richard I was furious at this decision, but William Marshall, Earl of Pembroke, who had a much shrewder sense of military economics than his open-handed master, observed; 'You have gained all. The King of France wants peace. Leave him his castles until the next passage to the Holy Land, but keep the land which belongs to us. When he can get nothing from the land and has to keep up the castles at his own cost he will find that he is carrying a heavier burden than a war.'

Of course the flaw in the argument was that, in the long run, he who held the castles exploited their neighbourhood. A castle

Helmsley, in North Yorkshire, was a strong fortress of the second rank. Most of its outer defences are now gone, except an impressive square-turreted keep, half blown down.

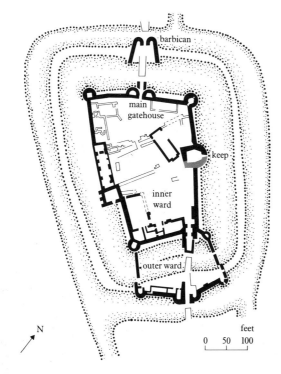

barbican

main gatehouse

keep

inner ward

outer ward

N

feet
0   50   100

could not function for long without its locality, or vice-versa. Castleguard was a regular form of military service. There was also the duty to work on buildings and earthworks. In the case of the Normandy castles seized by Philip, we have a list of services and duties drawn up by his clerks. One of them, Chize, had twenty-one parishes to depend on. One village had the duty of finding wood for a particular fireplace in the castle, or alternatively of serving the kitchen with water, and attending on the knights in the courtyard with basins of water, so they could wash their hands. The man who did this was paid in loaves and wine, and had the perquisite of collecting kitchen scraps. The janitor, responsible for the keys, was paid in fixed

dues on merchandise going through the town. Some tenants owed cartage service, discharged by providing oxen to pull the catapults and other engines. They also had to carry palisading to the castle. The peasants might not like neighbouring castles, but little towns tended to spring up in their shadows for protection, and their inhabitants were often responsible for keeping the walls upright and in repair.

In peacetime, townsmen were allowed to cultivate strips right up to the castle wall or the edge of the moat. But when war came the ditches had to be cleaned out ruthlessly, and the lean-tos which had accumulated against the walls pulled down. These townlets were the first to suffer if a castle were regularly invested. Indeed all the neighbourhood suffered. The besiegers first wasted the land before concentrating on the castle. The usual expectation was that this would do the trick, and compel surrender without a fight. No one enjoyed a siege, which was slow and hideously costly in lives, money and property. If a castle were well stocked and in good repair, with a loyal constable and a garrison in good heart, the odds were that the besiegers would simply go away. The metrical chronicle written by Jordan Fantosme, about the rebellion of 1173–4, shows how easily the king of Scotland and his baronial allies gave up if they met with resistance from the royal garrisons. He gives an intimate picture of Henry II, exhausted, just returned to London from France, getting the news that the Scottish king and the rebels had been forced to give up by the relieving army outside Alnwick: 'The king was leaning on his elbow, and slept a little, a servant at his feet gently rubbing them. There was neither noise nor cry – all his knights had gone to rest – nor any who was speaking there, neither harp nor viols nor anything was sounding at that hour, when the messenger came to the door and gently called.'

But if everyone tried to avoid a siege, sometimes they were inescapable. Siege-warfare was, increasingly, a matter for experts. John, for instance, had a corps of engineers or *ingeniatores*; a member of it was sometimes styled a *balistarius*, though strictly speaking this meant a crossbowman who used a

Helmsley Castle.

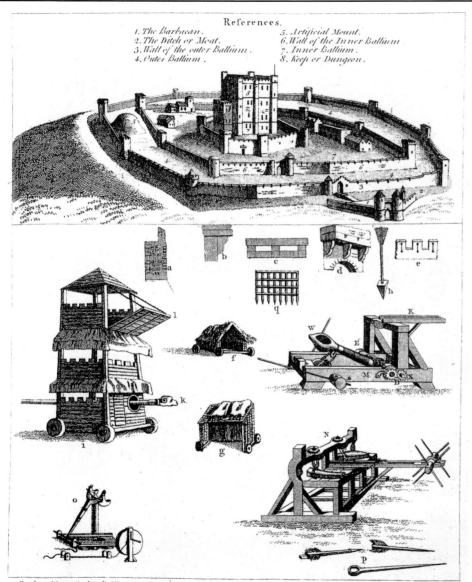

a. Section of the Wall of the Ballium. b. A Section. c. A Plan & d. A Perspective representation of a Machicolation. e. Crenelles & Oilets
f. The Sow. g. The Cattus. h. A Dart called a Quarrel. i. A Moveable Tower of three Stages. k. A Battering Ram. l. A Bridge to
Let down for Storming. o. Catapulta acting by counterpoise. p. Darts for the Balista & Winch for bending it. q. Herse or Portcullis.

balista. The crossbowmen were the élite of the garrison. The weapon came into general use from the early twelfth century. Originally it was of wood and horn glued together, after 1370 of steel. Attempts to proscribe its use by the Lateran Council in 1139 were unsuccessful. The English were unusual in preferring the longbow; it had a much higher rate of fire – five to one – and the great advantage that the bowman could keep his eyes on the enemy while reloading. But even the English admitted that the crossbow was a superior weapon in siege-warfare, especially in defence. The first true arrow-slits for crossbows began to appear just before 1190, in the multi-storey fighting gallery of the Avranches Tower at Dover, and at Framlingham in Suffolk. Thereafter, crossbowmen rapidly emerged as a specialist class of professional soldiers. They might be of varied social standing. In a band of eighty-four mentioned in a Liberate Roll of 1200 under John, twenty-six travelled with three horses each, fifty-one with two and seven with one. Philip Augustus's *arbalisters* were even more skilled; so valuable, indeed, that a lot of them had their names listed individually. But at the top of the siege profession was the senior engineer. John inherited two engineers, Ulric and Ivo, from his brother Richard; the first was of sufficient social standing to hold his lands by knight-service. We know even more about the second, a sure sign of his importance, including the fact that he had a row with his new master.

The crossbow's range grew to 370–80 yards in the fifteenth century (in 1901 Sir Ralph Payne-Gallwey, using a fifteenth-century weapon with a steel bow, shot bolts across the Menai Straits over 440 to 450 yards). It was designed primarily to force besieging men and machines to keep their distance. (The besieging bowmen had wood screens, called mantlets, to protect themselves.) The earliest machines were wheeled battering-rams, with iron heads, on the Roman model; but these were already obsolescent by the late twelfth century. Far more useful, in practice, were various forms of penthouses, or cats, used to protect men throwing brushwood to make causeways across ditches, undermining, or piling combustibles against wooden sections of the walls. Artillery included the *petriaria*, which hurled huge rocks, catapults or scorpions for smaller stones, or the medium-sized *ballista* or mangonel which threw stones weighing around half a hundredweight. By the end of the twelfth century some projectile engines were as powerful as early cannon. At the siege of Acre, 1189–91, the French king had a *petriaria*, called like many other types of major engine or mobile tower a *malvoisin*, which broke down the main wall of the city with its continuous blows. At the same siege, one of Richard I's engines killed twelve men with a single shot; this impressed the Saracens, who brought the missile to Saladin as a curiosity. Big sieges consumed prodigious quantities of ammunition. In 1198 Evreux Castle was stocked up for war with 6,200 bolts and 4,000 arrows. Stones were specially quarried for the bigger engines. When they ran out, paving stones and millstones were hurled, and iron bars, darts and sharpened poles. In 1339, during a French attack on Edward III's Flanders castle at Thin, dead horses and cattle were flung over the walls. Other missiles included pots of quicklime or burning pitch, and flaming torches. But stories of boiling oil and molten lead are probably fictitious; both were too expensive. Fire was what the defenders feared most, for even supposedly fireproof castles were crammed with combustible materials. Next came mining: that is, digging tunnels with wooden supports, which were afterwards fired, causing subsidence. With gunpowder came the true mine. At St Andrews, Fife, a mining tunnel and a counter-mine have been preserved. But these date from the siege of 1546–7. Direct evidence of early siege techniques and weapons is rare. We have a sketch of part of a trebuchet in a thirteenth-century architect's manual. But no major siege-engine has survived.

A strong, well-defended castle usually fell, if it fell at all, to a combination of weapons and privation. Château Gaillard, taken in 1203–4, yielded to starvation, to a system of counterforts and ditches which provided the attackers with cover, and to a terrific array of *petriariae*, mangonels, mantlets, a very high siege-tower, and mining. The middle bailey fell when an audacious Frenchman climbed up a stone latrine outlet on the river bank, from which he made an entry through a chapel window – a classic case of exploiting a weakness created by he pursuit of comfort. The final inner bailey was breached by undermining and a huge *petriaria*.

Nothing in the history of British castles has quite the varied interest of the siege of Château Gaillard, but there were a number of ferocious sieges in the reigns of John and his son. Against a well-defended castle persistence was the supreme virtue. Rochester held out against John in 1215 for three months; fighting continued not only after mining breached the curtain but after the assault had penetrated the huge keep itself. The garrison finally surrendered only when they ran out of food. After even Rochester fell, wrote one chronicler, 'men no longer put their trust in castles'. But anyone with less obstinacy than John would have given up. The following year the French dauphin Louis, though armed with the very latest machines, failed to take Dover. An up-to-date castle rarely yielded to a direct assault, unless it were unexpected. That is why psychological weapons were often employed. The knights defending Bedford in 1224 were excommunicated, with bell, book and candle, by the Archbishop of Canterbury and other bishops, on behalf of the king. The king's men had a tower strong enough to carry *ballistae*, and high enough to command the interior of the bailey; even so, the knights held out against these spiritual and material forces for two months.

Excommunication was also employed at the siege in 1266 of Kenilworth, so foolishly handed to his son-in-law by Henry III. By then De Montfort was dead, killed at Evesham by the Lord Edward, who had escaped from the castle and was now in charge of besieging it. Even in such masterly hands, however, the castle defied all the king's forces for a year, and only surrendered on easy terms. The elaborate water-defences made mining impossible, and bombardment was confined to extreme range of the biggest machines. Eyewitnesses described how huge boulders hurled by both sides sometimes met and shattered in mid-air. Edward directed the attack to the double

Opposite: Siege equipment, and the defensive measures taken to frustrate it, became highly technical from the late 11th century on. By the end of the 12th century some projectile engines were as powerful as early cannon; one of Richard I's engines at the siege of Acre killed twelve men with a single shot.

Opposite: Stokesay Castle in Shropshire is a delightful example of a late-medieval fortified manor-house. The great hall goes back to the 13th century, the half-timbered gatehouse to Tudor times.

moat on the fourth side, where the water barrier was narrowest. He had two wooden siege-towers, one big enough to contain two hundred archers and eleven catapults. He also unleashed a night attack by water, in barges dragged overland from Chester. Kenilworth was one of the great sieges of history, and it profoundly influenced Edward's castle strategy in Wales, as we shall see in the next chapter.

With the intensification of castle technology, there was an insatiable demand for expert craftsmen, who were increasingly well paid and therefore figure more prominently in the records. We have already heard of Maurice, Henry II's engineer. At Westminster there was an architect-dynasty founded by Geoffrey, Keeper of the Palace under Henry I, and his son, Nathaniel; Geoffrey's successor, Ailnoth, also brought his son, Roger, into the business. These four worked on the palace, on the Tower, at Windsor, Woodstock and elsewhere; they were also, under Henry II, in charge of demolishing adulterine castles. In the north a prominent architect of the age was Richard the Engineer, employed by the Bishop of Durham at Bowes and Norham castles. In Wales, Ralph of Grosmont figures in references to the 'three castles', and probably built them. These men were all termed engineers in the accounts, a name deriving from their skill in designing, making, dismantling and transporting siege-engines, and directing operations from them. They were liable to field service; were, in fact, soldiers. But they could build castles and churches, too – in fact they turned their hand to anything involving mechanical ingenuity.

From the early thirteenth century many royal craftsmen begin to figure by name in the accounts, and there is a growing tendency to specialize. Master Nicholas de Andeli was head of a group of French craftsmen, probably employed at Château Gaillard, who did work at Knepp Castle and later accompanied John to Ireland on campaign; he was in charge of siege-engines at Cambridge Castle, Knepp and Bramber, Nottingham and Knaresborough. He served Henry III until his death thirty years later, and was described as 'the king's carpenter'. Most siege-engineers were carpenters by training, and it is carpenters who figure most prominently in the records. But there was also the *petrarius*, mason or stonecutter; the *quareator* or quarryman; the *mier* or *cementarius*, who were stone-masons; *fossatores* who worked on moats and dry ditches, and the miners, who were responsible for the vaults and rockwork of castles. The *hurdatores* made the 'hoardings' or projecting wooden archer-galleries. *Piccatores* were employed in demolishing hostile fortifications. The engineers were the highest paid, receiving daily wages, annual 'gifts' and sometimes lands; some had their own seals. This group of highly skilled specialists, directly attached to the king, sometimes moving about with him, sometimes detached for supervisory duties at a group of castles, were precursors of the royal engineers.

Mason-architects were also omni-competent. Henry III's chief artistic adviser, Edward of Westminster, who coordinated work on Westminster Abbey, came from a family of goldsmiths attached to the Exchequer and Mint. He was a clergyman, and unusual in taking no part in military works. But Henry of Reims, Henry III's master-mason at Westminster, and perhaps the greatest of his craftsmen, also designed and built the famous Clifford's Tower of York Castle, on a new quatrefoil plan derived from French models. His successor, John of Gloucester, was another all-rounder; together with Master Alexander, the chief carpenter, he surveyed and reported on royal works, whether castles, manors or religious foundations, all over the south and midlands. And his successor, Robert of Beverley, looked after the Abbey works at Westminster, built Holborn Bridge, and was 'chief surveyor' of the Tower, Windsor, Rochester, Hadleigh Castle and numerous royal manors. These men were well rewarded. John of Gloucester got two robes yearly, 'of good squirrel fur, such as the knights of our household receive', plus daily wages, and presents of timber, house-property and land.

The emergence of skilled craftsmen, equally adept at creating within a domestic as well as a military context, inevitably reinforced the tendency for castles to acquire more comfort than

Opposite: Longthorpe Tower, in Northamptonshire, has a magnificent painted room on the first floor of the solar tower, only uncovered in 1945. Surprisingly often, castles were richly furnished and decorated.

was safe. The rot set in at the big royal palaces, like Westminster, Woodstock and Clarendon, where there were few concessions to military needs, and where the latest architectural refinements were introduced. Henry III, who loved comfort and beauty, set the pace. From his father John, a great builder of manor-houses and hunting-boxes, he inherited a score or more, prototypes of the fortified manor-houses of the later Middle Ages. They usually had a moat, some kind of defensible tower, and a palisade. No royal house of this type and date remains, but in Stokesay Castle, Shropshire, we have a thirteenth-century fortified manor built by a junior branch of the Say family. Such houses Henry loved to adorn and modernize, thus bringing luxurious habits deep into the countryside, to the scorn or envy of austere castelans.

Palaces and manor houses, even if fortified, were insecure, partly because they made generous use of wood. For castles as such, wood was rapidly going out of use under Henry. There were anomalous survivals. Surprisingly enough, Pickering, though up to date in other respects, retained a ring of wooden spikes outside its walls well into the fourteenth century, since we know that the locals were obliged to keep it in repair. And there was a good deal of wooden building in Henry's new and strong castle at Montgomery. Wooden towers called brattices were still used as temporary fortifications, especially on bridges; and Henry erected a prefabricated wooden castle on the Ile de Ré in 1242, one of the last of its kind. But in 1270 the timber tower on the motte at Shrewsbury collapsed of old age, a sign of the times. It is significant that the barons' wars of this period brought no rash of wooden castles, as they had during Stephen's reign.

But if wood was disappearing from the externals of castles, Henry III was busy bringing it into the interior, in the form of wainscoting for the chief rooms. It is not easy to visualize what these thirteenth-century castles were like inside, since they are now either bare and ruinous, or submerged in later work. Domestic accommodation was more often rebuilt than defences, so few early halls have survived. Of those built before

1160, we have Berkeley, Chepstow, Eynsford, Monmouth and Richmond; for the years 1160–1216 we have castles at Christchurch, parts of Farnham, Leicester and Framlingham, and the hall-cellar at Newark. These walls were usually whitewashed, with the line of the stones picked out in red; and, from the mid-twelfth century, adorned with paintings. One of the earliest of these, described by Geraldus Cambrensis, was Henry II's hall at Winchester, which contained a sad and savage rendering of an old eagle attacked by its ferocious offspring, an analogy of his own relations with his rebellious sons. Medieval man was desperate for colour and lightness, especially in castles where windows were small. So it is a mistake for restorers to make the stone show bare internally. External whitewashing was the rule, too. We possess evidence of instruction from Henry III to have Corfe and Rochester whitewashed. He also directed that the gutterings on the White Tower be repaired, so that its whitewashed walls should not be discoloured by rainwater. Internally, the walls were sometimes plastered in addition, if possible with the fine quality material made by burning gypsum, found in quantity in Montmartre (hence 'Plaster of Paris'). In 1251 Henry got the dais of the castle hall at Nottingham covered in 'French plaster'; it began to be more widely used in England after gypsum was found near Purbeck, though it still kept its French name.

Henry's favourite decorative motif, in both his castles and his palaces, was gold stars on a green background. Green was the most expensive colour, and Henry always went for the best; his rich tastes are often reflected in the language of his writs – work, he commands, must be *decens, pulcher, sumptuosus*; and it must be done quickly, 'even if it costs £100', 'even if a thousand workmen are required every day'. In his great painted chamber, or state bedroom, at Westminster, 80 feet long, 26 feet wide and 31 feet high, he had the finest wall-paintings in England. Wainscoting went up to the level of the paintings. His bed was a vast canopied structure with green curtains. None of his castles could provide him with a bedroom of this size and grandeur. But he had elaborate paintings in his castle-chamber at Winchester, gardens at Winchester and Marlborough, his own mews (for falcons) and dovecotes at Nottingham. Even humble castles might be elaborately decorated. In 1945 at Longthorpe Tower, Northamptonshire, a splendidly painted room was discovered on the first floor of the solar tower. The family of Robert de Thorpe, who built it, had only recently risen from servitude: his father had been a villein. Such sumptuousness at this social level hints at the lost glories of great men's castles, with riotous colour and masses of gold paint.

From the thirteenth century on we are able to gather innumerable details about other aspects of castle life in England. King John ordered new kitchens to be built at Marlborough and Ludgershall, capable of roasting two or three oxen in each. Such kitchens were built of wood, as separate buildings; and, because of the fire risk, they only gradually became integrated with the main castle building. At Oxford, in 1232, Henry III's kitchen was blown down in a gale; and a wooden kitchen of this type has been found at Weolley Castle, Birmingham; it had a reed-thatch roof and a pentice, or covered wooden corridor, linking it to the stone hall. In great families, kitchens tended to proliferate, king and queen, or lord and lady, having one each; at Windsor, Henry III had two built, both near the Great Hall, inside a palisade. John Lewyn, the great northern military architect, devoted much ingenuity to castle kitchens, being a sensible man. Two have survived, at Durham and Raby Castles, both octagonal, with three huge fireplaces each.

Fireplaces had first made their appearance at Colchester Castle, *c.* 1090; followed by Rochester, 1126–39, and Castle Hedingham, *c.* 1130. The first hooded fireplaces began to appear towards the end of the century, with Hamelin's Conisbrough leading the way; and in the thirteenth century we get the three elegant fireplaces of Aydon Castle, *c.* 1280, foreshadowing the elaborate affairs of the fourteenth and fifteenth centuries. But central hearths, with canopies and escape louvres in the roof, continued to be built even in royal residences, until the end of the thirteenth century. Of course it

was easier to insert a louvre than build a chimney. The first genuine castle chimneys appear early in the twelfth century, at Hedingham, concealed in a buttress. By the mid-twelfth century we find cylindrical chimneys, as at Framlingham, *c.* 1150–60 (though these have Tudor brick extensions). Most such early chimneys have long since gone, though a fine one, *c.* 1330, survives at Grosmont.

We know little about castle roofs, since they have disappeared. They were, it appears, often magnificent, as in the Great Tower at Chepstow, or at Conwy. For all buildings there was a steady drift from thatching, the prime cause of fire, with castles leading the way. The London assize of 1212 laid down that 'whoever wishes to build, let him take care, as he loveth himself and his goods, that he roof not with reed, nor rush, straw nor stubble, but with tile only, or shingle or boards or, if it may be, with lead or plastered straw. . . .' This ordinance was indifferently enforced, since in the 1260s Simon de Montfort, threatening London, studied a plan to free cocks with flaming brands tied to their claws over the city's roofs. Oak shingles, too, were not fireproof; Ordericus Vitalis says that the great hall of Brionne Castle in Normandy, thus roofed, was set alight by red-hot darts. Making castle roofs fireproof was a very gradual process. As late as 1260 the constable of Marlborough Castle was commanded 'to remove the shingles from the roof of the king's great kitchen and cover it with stone . . . to take the thatch off the outer chamber of the high tower, and cover it with the shingles of the said kitchen and to crest it with lead'. By the fourteenth century stone slates and earthen tiles were both cheaper than fine oak shingles; and blue slates, which had the great merit of lightness, were slowly coming in from quarries in Devon, Dorset and Cornwall. Portchester, Taunton, Corfe and Sherborne castles were the earliest to get proper slates. Meanwhile, leaden gutters were being installed; and in 1240, at the Tower, they were carried down to the ground.

So the quest for comfort continued. More staircases were added. At Rochester, in 1254, Henry III ordered a new staircase to be erected, 'so that strangers and others might enter the chapel without passing through the king's chamber as they were used to do' – a curious glimpse into the lack of privacy enjoyed by mid-thirteenth-century monarchy. Staircases were, in fact, often placed outside, as at Manorbier and Stokesay, to avoid cluttering the interior or weakening the wall. Alas, from a military viewpoint, windows were to do this all too well. Decorative windows soon made their appearance even in highly professional buildings like Conisbrough and Chepstow Castle hall, where the windows are especially fine, with richly moulded rear-arches, and scrolled hoods with head-stops. The openings tended to get steadily larger. Soon they were filled with glass.

Glass first made its appearance early in Norman times in Canterbury Cathedral. In the reign of Henry III it began to supersede horn, or wooden shutters in rich men's castles. By the end of his reign, Henry had put glass into the windows of most of his halls and chambers – at Clipstone even into the windows of his privy, and the queen's. Sometimes glass was inserted only in the top half, with a shutter below. Or there were shutters of firwood, bound with iron, which fitted over the spaces internally, sometimes with glass as well. From quite an early date these glass windows were painted, and under Henry III such paintings became armorial, a motif he introduced in stone and paint wherever he could. At Windsor Castle he even seems to have installed double glazing, for he ordered that in each gable of the high chamber a 'white glass' window should be installed outside the interior window, 'so that when the inner window shall be closed, these glass windows may appear outside'. Such glass windows were regarded as luxuries; they were movable properties until, in the reign of Henry III, they were made into fixtures. At Alnwick, for instance, the Earl of Northumberland's glass windows were taken out during his absence and carefully stored, being replaced by shutters. Medieval glass was particularly fragile and could easily be shattered by high winds. And windows were normally barred. In September 1238 a madman climbed into Henry's chamber at Woodstock, with the intention of murdering him; after this, the king, a timid man, had iron bars put on all his chamber windows. He even had bars put across the vent of his privy at Westminster – though in doing this he may have had the fate of Château Gaillard in mind.

Many castles also had internal windows, peepholes called squints. They usually looked down from the solar or great chamber to the hall, to allow the lord or king to know what was going on there; or to the chapel, so that mass could be heard and seen without getting out of bed. There are good squints at Stokesay and Penshurst, at Broughton Castle, Oxfordshire, and Beverston Castle in Gloucestershire; sometimes, as at Great Chalfield, the squint is concealed by a mask, with holes in the eyes and ears. In Winchester Castle Henry was linked from his solar to the hall by a primitive kind of speaking tube, known as 'the king's ear'.

Sanitary arrangements were also becoming more elaborate. Medieval manners placed much emphasis on cleanliness of the hands. Fingers came before forks, which were still rare in the fourteenth century – it was noted that the hated Piers Gaveston had a set of silver ones 'for eating pears'. People washed their hands on entering the hall for meals (or on leaving). So lavers, the secular version of the church piscina, were usually to be found near its entrance. Good lavers are to be found at Dacre, Woodsford Castle in Dorset, Goodrich and Beverston. At Warwick, Aydon Castle, Devon, and Compton Castle, Devon, there are washing sinks with drains in the service quarters. At Battle Hall, near Leeds in Kent, the hall laver, c. 1330, consists, within a stone framework, of a cistern formed like the twin rounded towers of a castle, battlemented, and each with a leonine head as a spout. This laver was in a hall built by the king's mason, Thomas de la Bataile, who built the great hall in Caerphilly Castle; and it may be he modelled it on one built at Westminster for Edward I by Master Robert the Goldsmith, though this one had leopards for spouts.

For bathing the usual practice was simply to fill casks or barrels with water. But monastic houses were constantly raising the standards of bathroom fittings, for themselves and

Opposite: Framlingham in Suffolk, one of the largest and best preserved castles in England, has vast curtain walls punctuated by thirteen strong towers notable for their fine brick chimney-stacks.

Ludlow Castle was the administrative centre from which the Council of the Marches ruled Wales. It has fine 14th-century state apartments, updated in Elizabeth I's day, and a vast council room where Milton's *Comus* was first performed.

their rich guests; and kings, who often stayed at the big, main-road monasteries, were quick to follow. John had his travelling bath and his bathman, William, and Henry III was even more particular. Edward II had a new bathroom made at Westminster, and from the detailed accounts of it we gather that the bath had an oblong canopy, was partitioned off, and that there was a paved floor in front. The bath was level with the floor, covered in tiles, to make it easier to remove the water; and

there were mats 'to put on the floor and pavement of the king's chamber on account of the cold'. Of course Westminster was a palace, not a castle; but we must not suppose bathing arrangements were any less lavish in the biggest castles, which in some ways had to have more elaborate and ingenious water-systems than non-fortified dwellings.

Certainly, the lavatories (privies, or garderobes, as they were called) were much better than one might have expected. Most big castle chambers had a fireplace and privy each. Henry III, in a typical order, instructed his sheriff at Southampton 'to make in our castle at Winchester, behind the chapel of St Thomas the Martyr, a certain chamber for the use of the bishops, and a chimney (fireplace) and a certain privy chamber for the same'. Where practicable, the privy was placed as far away as possible, on account of the smell, at the end of a passage in the thickness of the wall, with access to the chamber by means of a right-hand turn. Sometimes, as at Woodstock, Henry III ordered double doors to reduce the smell further. Where the wall was not thick enough, the privy was corbelled out, like an external buttress, as at Stokesay, Broughton and Longthorpe Tower. Shoots were built for the discharge, sometimes barred, concealed by masonry screens or protected by grotesque masks, as at Conwy, Harlech and Beaumaris. Castles with a big garrison sometimes grouped the privies into a 'garderobe tower', facetiously called, at Richmond, the Gold Hole Tower. If possible they were sited over the moat, or near a stream, or even on an arch over it. Christchurch Castle, for instance, has a garderobe tower built over its millstream. At Winchester Castle, Henry III ordered a garderobe tower to be built 'in the fashion of a turret', with double vaulting and a ventilation shaft. At Ludlow Castle, the early fourteenth-century double-garderobe tower survives to its full height of four storeys, over a plinth containing the shoot apertures – two on each face. Another good garderobe tower, with three storeys of privies, is at Middleham Castle, Yorkshire. In the garderobe tower at Langley Castle, Northumberland, there are no fewer than twelve privies, with a pit below, into which all discharged and through which a stream could be diverted to flush it out. Sometimes, as in the archbishop's palace at Southwell, *c.* 1360, the privies were placed well away from the main buildings in a circular house, with a central pillar as a shaft; but few castles had the space for this arrangement. Privies were single, or in pairs as at Thornbury Castle. A few privy seats remain: there is a stone seat at Longthorpe Tower, and a plank-like seat, slotted into the wall, at Bungay Castle. Privies had to be light, as people often read books there, following a recommendation in the popular *Life of St Gregory the Great*; and it was often the only really private place in the castle.

But some problems proved insuperable to medieval man. At Caernarvon a stone water-channel, lined with lead, runs around the Eagle Tower (completed in 1317) and carried water to the garderobe shaft for flushing; and there was a rainwater flushing device at Denbigh Castle. In the big castles, pits were built to a great depth – Henry III was particularly insistent on this point – and the *mudator latrinarum* was well paid to clear them out. He was known as a gong farmer (medieval man called privies gongs, jakes, withdraughts or draughts). But nothing availed. Complaints were numerous, even in the best-regulated castles; Henry III objected bitterly to one of his privies, built in what he termed 'an undue and improper place' and wanted it remedied, 'even if it costs £100'. It is a symptom of the failure to master the problem of smell that portable close-stools came into general use in wealthier families towards the end of the Middle Ages.

Smells of a different kind tended to infest all parts of a castle, especially the hall or refectory, unless it was 'strewed' often enough. Among herbs recommended as suitable for strewing were basil, haulm, camomile, costmary, cowslip and paggles, all kinds of daisies, sweet fennel, germander, lavender, lavender spike, lavender cotton, marjoram, mandeline, penny-royal, roses, red mints, sage, tansey, violets and winter savoury. Henry III provided mats for the first time, but only in his chapels, not in his halls; and Matthew Paris says the Londoners were shocked when they heard that Eleanor of Castile, bringing wasteful Spanish fashions in her train, actually put carpets on the floor of her bedroom.

Despite everything, castles were still very uncomfortable (and deathly cold) places at the end of the reign of the fastidious Henry III. It was left to his son, the brilliant Lord Edward, to introduce a completely new epoch in castle-building, which greatly improved their comforts as well as revolutionizing their military structure.

CHAPTER THREE

EDWARDIAN
SPLENDOUR IN
WALES

It was the decision of the great Welsh marcher lords, like Gilbert de Clare and Roger Mortimer, to side with the crown which enabled the Lord Edward to win the Battle of Evesham in 1268 and put down the Montfort revolt. The crown–marcher alliance also made possible the final conquest of Wales, which began to preoccupy Edward shortly after he became king in 1272. The Welsh were not a formidable fighting power, except as guerrillas. A Flemish observer with Edward's army noted: 'In the very depth of winter they are running about bare-legged . . . I never saw them wearing armour . . . Their weapons were bows, arrows and swords. They also had javelins.' Nevertheless, in the mid-thirteenth century Llewelyn the Great contrived, for the first time in Welsh history, to maintain bodies of armoured cavalry, siege-engines and even a small fleet. Against such a force the Anglo-Norman castles were vulnerable.

It was a sign of the times, therefore, that in 1268 Gilbert de Clare, richest of the marchers, began to build an immense new castle at Caerphilly in Gwent. It was also significant that the Welsh made prolonged and desperate attempts to harass the workmen and to take and burn the castle before it was defensible. Nevertheless by 1277 the castle was finished, and it opened a new epoch in British castle-building. The so-called 'Edwardian castles', of which it was the precursor, were based on the combination of three elements: the replacement of the keep by a rectangular or polygonal curtain, broken by symmetrically placed towers; an outer curtain to provide two linked defensive lines, one inside the other; and the creation of an immensely powerful gatehouse, on the castle's most vulnerable side, in which all the latest defensive technology was installed. All these elements had existed before, but they were first combined in Caerphilly, and it is tragic that we possess virtually no documentary evidence – since it was a private castle – about its design and building.

Caerphilly was not only the earliest concentric castle in Britain, it was also remarkable for its size and its water defences. Covering thirty acres, it is easily the biggest castle in Wales, and the terrifically high standards of its masonry and cementation ensured its survival, virtually intact, despite 'slighting' under the Commonwealth. The technical experience gained in the Kenilworth waterworks was put to good use. The castle stands on an island surrounded by an artificial lake, created by a great screen wall or dam, heavily defended, which controls the input of water from a stream; this wall also serves as a formidable barbican protecting the approach from the east. An equally large and powerful outwork protects the approach on the west. The castle proper is rectangular, surrounded by two lines of curtain-wall, the inner having a tower at each corner and two large gatehouses. The towers project so far from the corners that they command the outside of the walls from end to end. From these, drawbridges lead to the outwork and barbican. The final stronghold is the east gatehouse of the inner wall, which once included a splendid suite of state rooms. The castle defences combined all the latest devices: sluices to regulate the water-level, a mural passage in the inner wall at a level of fifteen feet to permit the rapid circulation of crossbowmen, multiple postern-gates to aid sorties and supply, and some thirty portcullises. Huge buttresses reinforce the outer works.

Edward I was away on crusade most of the time Caerphilly was being built; but when he returned in 1274 he undoubtedly visited it – he was soon turning the Tower of London into a concentric castle – and approved of what he saw. In 1276 he decided to treat the indigenous Welsh princes as rebels, and go for an outright conquest, using a series of strategically linked castles of the new type to pacify the territory once and for all – just as the Conqueror had used the motte-and-bailey to hold England. This inaugurated the biggest programme of castle-building in the whole history of the English crown. The programme stretched over more than a quarter of a century, but it was concentrated in three main stages, corresponding with the campaigns of 1277, 1282–3 and 1294–5. There were four groups of castles. The first were the royal border castles of Chester (the King's main sea-and-land base), Shrewsbury, Montgomery and St Briavels, all of which were remodelled and strengthened. Then came three captured native castles, Dolwyddelan, Criccieth and Bere, which were completely rebuilt (other Welsh castles were remodelled). Four new 'Lordship' castles, Denbigh, Hawarden, Holt and Chirk, were built; legally they were in private hands, but the building was to a royal design, supervised by the crown and to some extent financed by it. Finally, and most important, there were ten new royal castles: Builth, Aberystwyth, Flint, Rhuddlan, Ruthin, Hope, Conwy, Harlech, Caernarvon and Beaumaris.

Edward, who has a strong claim to be considered the ablest of England's medieval kings, was an expert in castle-construction, as he was in every aspect of warfare – indeed, in any art or science pertaining to kingship. He surveyed every site personally, and was usually present when the work began. The first task of the workmen was almost invariably to clear ground 'to set up the king's tents', and build a palisade round them. We have a little glimpse of Edward, during the building of Beaumaris, sitting at rest 'in the castle', after the day's work, and listening to an English harpist, Adam de Clithero, who was paid for two nights' harping.

But of course Edward did not design and build the castles himself. For this he enlisted the services of a man now regarded as one of the greatest architects of the Middle Ages. James of St George came from Savoy, with which Edward had a family connection, for Count Amadeus of Savoy, in 1246, had done homage to Henry III in return for a lump sum and a pension. Edward's best friend and companion-in-arms, Sir Otto de Grandson, came from Savoy. Of him the king said 'there was no one about him who could do his will better'; and it was Otto whom he chose to be his chief executive officer in Wales. It was very likely Otto, too, who introduced Edward to James of St George when the King visited Savoy on his way back from the crusade in 1273. James, like Otto, came from the shores of Lake Neuchâtel. He was the son of an architect and had worked in partnership with his father, and then on his own, between 1261 and 1275. For Count Peter of Savoy he had built the castle and town of Yverdon, on the lake, which strikingly prefigures his

later Welsh castles. He also built the comital palace at St Georges-d'Esperance, from which he derived his cognomen, and several other castles.

Edward was impressed by James's work and when in 1277 he decided to conquer Wales with castles, James was summoned, and thereafter served Edward for over thirty years. He was soon awarded the title 'Master of the King's Works in Wales', and, under the supervision of Otto (and Edward himself), he was effectively the chief professional officer for the whole Welsh operation. He got the unprecedented fee of three shillings a day, plus a pension of 1s 6d a day for his wife Ambrosia if he died. He was also awarded masonry contracts on his own account, and leased royal manors at nominal rent. In 1290–3 he was Constable of Harlech, one of the castles he designed and built. James, of course, was a siege-engineer as well as an architect. He was the chief engineer, for instance, on the Gascon Campaign, 1287–9, and at the siege of Stirling in 1304; indeed, he very likely designed the three new monster-castles on the shores of the Forth, with which Edward planned to hold down Scotland, but which were never built. What Edward liked about James was not only his professional skill but his sharp sense of economy: it is noticeable from the accounts that building costs tended to get out of hand the moment he left the site.

The prodigious effort behind Edward I's Welsh castle programme illustrates his extraordinary capacity for mobilizing the resources of the entire kingdom. Those involved came from literally every English shire, from Northumberland to Sussex; but they also came from the Vaud, the Valais and Viennois; money and raw materials came from all over England, Wales and even Ireland. Getting labour was not always easy, but Edward possessed legal powers to obtain it. This right to spirit men from one end of the country to another to build castles derived not from burgh-work, which was local, but fyrd-service, as updated by Henry II's Assize of Arms. In the rebellion of 1173–4, for instance, Henry had levied 500 carpenters in Norfolk to make siege-engines for use against their earl's

castles. For his campaign in Wales of 1212, John had levied a total of 7,630 men. Such levies occurred under Henry III, with specific commands – to bring 'good axes' and food for forty days (the legal maximum he could enforce). Edward merely carried the system a little further.

Of course the men were paid. At the first castle to be built, Builth, the accounts show that a master mason got 7½d a day; his deputy 3s a week. The men included four masons at 2s a week, five at 1s 8d, three at 1s 6d. Ten workmen clearing earth, and stonebreaking, which was presumably unskilled, got 1s or 9d a week; four mortar-makers, ten mortar-carriers and four sandthrowers also got 9d. Four water-carriers and thirty-four hodmen got 7d a week, thirty diggers and twenty barrowmen a penny more. Two carpenters got 3d a day each, a third 1s 8d a week. Two smiths, who sharpened the tools, got 2s and 1s 2d respectively, two foremen 1s 2d and three carters 10d. There were also thirty-six women on the site, at 6d a week each the lowest paid. The total workforce was 140, and they worked a seven-day week.

The organization Edward and James created had its failures, but it was often able to operate with a speed unusual with comatose medieval administration. When Hope Castle was smashed up by the rebels in 1282, there were 340 craftsmen at work on the repairs within a week, and within a fortnight the number, including diggers, had swollen to well over 600. Of course, there was always the chance of bonuses, 'by the king's gift', for diggers and others who worked particularly hard. And whenever the king was present in person, it rained silver coins. On the other hand, from the Flint accounts, we learn that over four months no less than £9 7s 6d was deducted from wages for bad work and absenteeism. A horn, costing 7d, was sounded morning and evening to mark the regulation hours. Work discipline, and other matters, were settled in the workmen's own courts. In 1305, for instance, Walter of Hereford petitioned to be allowed to hold his own free court for the workmen at Caernarvon Castle, 'as he had always done', and this included his right to deal with breaches of their contracts.

Opposite: Chirk Castle on the Welsh Borders was begun by Edward I as a major fortress, to which its squat round towers bear witness. In the late 16th century it was turned into a comfortable private house and has been lived in ever since.

Flint, in North Wales, had a unique design based around a large, cylindrical keep made up of two concentric shells. It had three storeys with an external diameter of seventy-five feet. Powerful in its day, it is now a mere ruin.

The cost of this massive deployment of labour and resources was, of course, enormous, and it continued to increase. Builth cost a mere £1,650, spread over five years. Aberystwyth, built over twelve years, cost at least £4,300. At Flint the bill was around £7,000, and at Rhuddlan £9,500. The 'big four' (Harlech, Conwy, Caernarvon and Beaumaris) were larger, more elaborate and correspondingly more costly. More than £20,000 was spent on Caernarvon, and in the building of Beaumaris the Wardrobe had to find £6,736 for the first six months alone – an unheard-of sum for such a brief period. In total, the king's castle programme in Wales cost £93,000, that we know of, and the true cost was nearer £100,000. It outstripped even Edward's capacity to gouge money out of his subjects – it also imposed a perceptible strain on the economy as a whole – and this helps to explain the ultimate failure of his Scottish campaign, and in particular his inability to carry out the necessary programme of castle work there.

On the other hand, Edward would have argued that castles with town-colonies attached, as at Conwy, Caernarvon and Beaumaris, for instance, ought to pay their way quickly.

Rhuddlan in particular must have proved a good investment for the crown, since it began to flourish once the castle was built. In any case, Edward would have added, castles in the long run were a cheap substitute for campaigning warfare. A country, even a poor one like Wales, held firmly down by castles was bound to turn in a profit to the crown; and its national income would rise as peace replaced endless harrying. Nothing could be more costly than a big, well-organized campaign of the type Edward mounted. For the 1277 campaign, he had 15,540 foot soldiers, including 9,000 Welshmen – he could always recruit more Welshmen than his opponents – and the feudal levy of 800 cavalry. Except for the last group all had to be paid for. It was the best army raised in England since the Norman Conquest, and the most expensive to equip and maintain. The campaign cost £25,000. It included equipping a fleet of 60 ships, with 350 crossbowmen on board as marines; and such expensive items as the 2,500 bowmen drafted to Hope to protect the workmen rebuilding the castle. The 1294–5 campaign was even more costly, because Edward, working with his customary energy and speed, had put three armies into the field within a matter of weeks, with a total foot-strength of over 31,000.

Of course it might be said that Edward got the worst of both worlds, since his castle-building in the 1270s and 1280s did not prevent further revolts. The answer was that Edward was distracted by other problems besides Wales – the reformation of the English judicial system, the church, Gascony, Scotland. He could not always garrison and equip his new castles up to full establishment strength, partly because money was short, partly because they were not finished. The castle system was never really completed, but by the early 1300s with the coming into service of Conwy, Harlech, Caernarvon and Beaumaris, consti-tuting a steel land-and-sea grip on the fastnesses of north-west Wales, the Welsh 'problem' was effectively solved for a hundred years. The castle programme also had profound consequences, chiefly beneficial, on the Welsh economy and the general level of civility. Anxious to make the best use of his powerful fleet, Edward shifted the power centres away from inland hills and the upper or middle reaches of the rivers, and towards the coast. Old mountain castles were abandoned, and even those nearer the sea were replaced by new castles with direct access to shipping. A good example was Rhuddlan, which replaced the old hill-castle of Dyserth. Rhuddlan was one of the new castellated boroughs, and to enable it to be supplied directly by ship the River Clwyd had to be rendered navigable. So a new 'cut', or canal, three miles long, was constructed under the direction of the master *fossator* William of Boston (the best diggers came from the Fen country). William went to see the king at Woodstock in June 1277, to get his orders, and the king spent most of the autumn at Rhuddlan to direct the works personally. At one time there were 968 diggers on the payroll at Rhuddlan, and an average of sixty-six were employed, six days a week for three years, on the canal. It proved a complete success and as a result made the new town prosperous.

Rhuddlan, built by Edward I, 1277–82, is a powerful, concentric castle with strong round towers and a wide, sea-fed moat. It is less well preserved than most of Edward's Welsh castles.

Denbigh was a Welsh
'lordship' castle, privately
owned by Henry de
Lascy, Earl of Lincoln, but
built with assistance from
Edward I as part of his
strategic plan for
garrisoning Wales.

As a rule, the new royal castles like Rhuddlan had a town attached to them. Private castles sponsored by the king were invested with a lordship, formed of confiscated Welsh lands. At Hawarden, for instance, the lordship went to Edward's close friend Roger de Clifford. Roger presumably paid for the new castle there, but it was designed and built with the advice of James of St George and, though now ruinous, its links with Caernarvon can still be detected. At Denbigh, work on the new castle began within a few days of the grant of the lordship to Henry de Lascy, Earl of Lincoln. Here, entries in the royal accounts make it clear that there was a close connection between the king's works, properly speaking, and castles built by feudatories as part of his scheme. Workmen used at Hope were switched to the Denbigh site to begin operations; and the beautiful symmetry of the castle, let alone the striking original-ity of the gatehouse with its triple towers, make it plain that James was the architect. The pattern was repeated at Holt, built as a new foundation in 1282, and awarded to John de Warenne, Earl of Surrey. Little now remains, since the castle was demolished in 1675–83, to provide building materials for Sir Thomas Grosvenor's Eaton Hall; but old plans and drawings, showing a pentagon, with four towers surmounted by watch-turrets, as at Harlech and Conwy, indicate James's work again. Chirk, given to Roger Mortimer, was another new marcher lordship held by knight-service. This castle, too, was conceived by the royal works department; in fact it closely resembled Beaumaris, though with a single curtain. Like the other lordship castles, it was never completed according to plan (though it is the only one of all the north Wales castles to be continuously inhabited), and the pattern suggests that, though Edward provided royal support for the initial foundation-digging and the building of the curtain to a defensible height, he left the completion to individual owners, who tended to run out of money. (At Denbigh, work on the castle seems to have stopped when De Lascy's only son was drowned in the well.)

Edward also remodelled three of the native castles which came into his possession. Criccieth, Llywelyn the Great's

Criccieth was a small Welsh-built castle of Llywelyn the Great, remodelled by Edward I with a strong, two-towered gatehouse. It had a constable, ten crossbowmen and four maintenance men (plus chaplain).

Right: The ground plan of Goodrich, in Herefordshire, placed firmly on the edge of a ridge of rock overlooking the Wye. Its ranges of sandstone buildings are remarkably unified and well preserved.

Far right: Conwy, like other formidable royal castles built by Edward I, had a fortified town colony attached to the castle and was designed to be supplied by sea if the land approach was cut off by the Welsh.

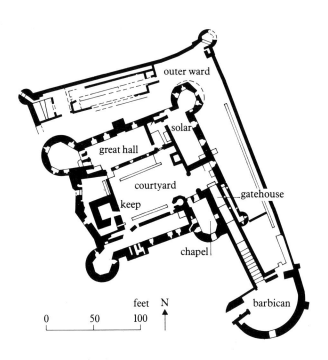

outer ward

solar

great hall

courtyard

keep

gatehouse

chapel

feet   N

0   50   100

barbican

castle, now quite ruinous, was gutted and given a completely new inner ward, with a strong, twin-towered gatehouse. It was a small establishment, with a constable (paid £100 a year to maintain it), ten crossbowmen, a chaplain, armourer, mason, blacksmith and carpenter. A similar case was Castell Y Bere, where £262 5s 10½d was spent in the 1280s setting up a new curtain-wall. At Dolwyddelan, the birthplace of Llywelyn the Great and a hill stronghold on the edge of central Snowdonia, Edward's building activities, again directed by James, seem to have concentrated on making it fit for his habitation, possibly for symbolic reasons. The defences of the castle were merely altered and improved; but James supplied a new range of state rooms, and built a new bridge and water-mill.

Royal expenditure on lordship and native castles is mostly lumped together under the heading 'divers other places'. Many English-held Welsh and border castles, though not directly connected with Edward's campaigns, were brought up to date during his reign, and possibly with his assistance. One case was Goodrich Castle in Herefordshire, superbly situated on the edge of a ridge of rock overlooking the Wye, and commanding an ancient crossing of the river. Its rock is divided by a natural chasm, which forms the moat; thus the castle is very compact, and the ranges of its sandstone buildings remarkably unified and well preserved. Under Edward it got a new keep, new curtain-towers, a great hall, gatehouse and barbican, though the last is ruinous. Edward also had a hand in the reconstruction of Kidwelly, in Dyfed, an old Anglo-Norman fortress which probably holds the record as the most fought-over castle in Britain. Edward in effect gave it to his nephew Henry of Lancaster by arranging his marriage to the Kidwelly heiress in 1291. The castle was then completely rebuilt on concentric lines, with an outer curtain defended by four strong towers and two gatehouses. The main Edwardian gatehouse, in particular, is a formidable affair – it has been compared to 'the awesome form of the pylon of an Egyptian temple' – and suggests the hand of the ubiquitous James.

The ten royal castles built by James vary considerably in design and appearance (Builth, Aberystwyth and Hope are very ruinous), but they have certain features in common. All had access to the sea or tidal rivers, to take full advantage of Edward's complete naval supremacy and the economics of water transport; wherever possible, as at Beaumaris, they had docking facilities, or at least a water-gate. Secondly, they each embodied new and radical solutions to the problem of defence. At Builth, for instance, the strength of the castle lay in its powerful earthwork, formed by a wet moat and a huge counterscarp bank encircling the whole site. At Flint the design culminated in a huge, cylindrical keep, built like a French *donjon*, isolated in one corner of the castle and surrounded by its own moat. Its walls were twenty-three feet thick.

Harlech, built by Edward I's great military architect, James of St George, on a superb natural site overlooking Cardigan Bay, proved almost impossible to take by assault. In 1294 thirty-seven men held it against the entire Welsh army.

Wherever possible, James adopted the concentric design, which had the inestimable advantage that the defenders on the inner ring could deny access to the outer wall even after it had been breached. But sometimes natural and artificial defences were in conflict. Thus at Conwy, chosen because it had a sheltered tidal harbour and a huge jutting slab of rock, the natural site for a castle and its attendant town, there was simply no room for James to develop the concentric principle. Indeed, he did not even have room to set up the powerful main gatehouse he normally preferred, and the gateways are simply built into the curtain wall, being defended mainly by the adjoining wall-towers. But this did not mean Conwy was a weak castle. Quite apart from its natural strength, now obscured by the two bridges, the railway and the levelling on the Gyffin Estuary, the castle bristled with traps for aggressors. Access was artfully contrived to be as difficult as possible. On the town side (the weakest), entrance could be made only after climbing a steep stairway, crossing a drawbridge and breaking through three gateways in succession, all in the face of direct fire by walls and towers on every side. The approach from the estuary to the east gate was commanded by a barbican, which stood high above it, and by a tower which stood out in the estuary. The inner gateway of each entrance was defended by a machicolated parapet, stretching across from one flanking tower to the other. All eight towers have beam-holes for wooden hoardings, enabling bowmen to cover every inch of the curtain, and they are linked by a continuous wall-walk. Hence this large and powerful castle could be, and in fact was, defended by a comparatively small garrison of thirty: fifteen crossbowmen, a chaplain, a smith, an artificer, a carpenter, a mason and ten others, chiefly watchmen. The castle had no less than 142 arrow-slits, made by John Flauner at a cost of 1s 2d each. But of course it was also a royal palace, with suites to accommodate the king and queen and their principal attendants. These rooms alone cost £320 for the masonry and £100 for carpentry, and by the time the castle was completed in 1291–2 the total cost had risen to over £14,500.

Harlech, perhaps James's favourite castle, was also placed on a superb natural site, for in the thirteenth century the waters of Cardigan Bay were over half a mile closer and lapped the foot of the immense crag on which the castle rests. Hence there was a harbour built into the crag, so that the castle could be supplied and reinforced by sea. This was guarded by walls which, as it were, constituted part of the outer bailey extending down the cliff. The approach to the upper fortress from the water-gate was a steep path cut into the rock, defended at a point two-thirds up its course by a gate with a ditch and drawbridge, and terminating in a postern gate under the command of the south-west corner tower. The inner bailey is, in effect, a narrow terrace between two walls. On the eastern, or vulnerable, side, facing higher ground, the castle had a very powerful front. There are two drawbridges and two gateways, all under fire not only from the walls and towers in front but from the wall-walk of the outer bailey on the right flank. The outer gate was defended by a two-leaved door, and passage of the gatehouse proper was guarded by a timber bar, three portcullises, two doors and eight machicolations. Hence it was the real stronghold of the castle, and though the wall-walk is otherwise continuous, the gatehouse was a self-contained defensive unit which could be held even against a force which had broken into the heart of the castle.

So long as they could be supplied by sea, Conwy and Harlech were virtually unassailable. In the rebellion of 1294, thirty-seven men defended Harlech against the entire Welsh army, and even as late as the 1640s Harlech was the last of the royalist fortresses in Wales to fall to parliament (bad roads prevented Cromwell from getting his siege-train there). Both castles fell to Owen Glendower in the early 1400s, Conwy through a treacherous carpenter who betrayed the castle while the garrison was at church, Harlech because the French fleet cut off supplies. Harlech had defied Glendower with a mere forty men, the famous 'Men of Harlech', and in 1409 it needed the ferocious John Talbot, with a force of 1,000 professional soldiers, to retake it for the king – a good example of the

Kidwelly Castle, Dyfed, was given powerful new defences under Edward I, including a formidable gatehouse. It is believed to hold the record as the most fought-over castle in Britain.

economies of manpower which a well-designed castle could achieve. Even in the Civil War its garrison was only fifty strong.

Royal castles, however, might have symbolic as well as military importance. Conwy, for instance, was the nearest equivalent to a North Welsh capital. It was the burial place of Llywelyn the Great, the site of his palace and it contained a Cistercian monastery which had the status of a national church, like Westminster Abbey. All were completely demolished and covered by the massive fortification of the new castle and town, and the heavy cost of uprooting the abbey and putting it elsewhere was amply compensated, in a political sense, by the ocular eclipse of the native dynasty and its institutions. Caernarvon was invested with even more symbolism. Edward was fascinated by the magic of monarchy (as well as its practical duties) and he exploited to the full the 'divinity that doth hedge a king'. Caernarvon was the ancient centre of the kingdom of Gwynedd, the site of Roman, Norman and Welsh castles. Edward's capture of it in 1283 was the culminating point of the

war. He determined to build an imperial capital there, as a suitable setting for his royal progresses and as a headquarters for his viceroy, Otto de Grandson, who was paid £100 a year for holding Caernarvon and an additional £1,000 a year 'for keeping the land of Wales'.

Hence it is no accident that Caernarvon, though designed and built by James, and in all military essentials following the same pattern as his other big castles, has superficially a very different appearance. The towers are polygonal rather than round, and there is a very striking patterning of the walls with bands of different coloured stone. Byzantine influence is apparent. Like Byzantium it had its 'golden gate', the water-gate of the walled town, whose name survives in its Welsh version, Pryth y Aur. James designed the great Eagle Tower, which contained the royal suite and the viceregal lodgings, to be surmounted by three turrets, each adorned by an eagle. The eighteenth-century traveller Thomas Pennant relates a story that Edward even found a genuine Roman eagle statue in the nearby ruins of Segontium. Certainly he was much taken with the imperial theme, not least because Otto himself claimed to be of imperial stock. In 1284 he contrived to have his son Edward born in the castle – the first royal child to be born in Wales since the last princes of Gwynedd – though Caernarvon was then only half built, and the queen would have been more comfortable in Rhuddlan. For this occasion he had the robes specially sent up from London.

But Caernarvon was also designed as a fortress – as Dr Johnson put it, 'an edifice of stupendous majesty and strength'. Like Conwy, its site made true concentricity impossible; in fact it resembles an hour-glass, with a narrow waist and two bulging ends. But it has two splendid gatehouses and nine powerful towers, many with turrets projecting high above the battlements. The Eagle Tower is over 120 feet high and has the essentials of a keep, such as a chapel. In fact it once had its own water-gate and dock, which meant it could still be supplied from the sea (which also provided an escape-route) even if the rest of the castle fell. Along and inside the walls were two tiers

Caernarvon was the keystone of Edward I's military strategy in the conquest of North Wales. Dr Johnson, on a visit there, called it 'an edifice of stupendous majesty and strength'.

of mural passages pierced with arrow-loops, and on the south side there were three tiers of fighting platforms. Fully garrisoned, then, the castle had stations for a large number of archers, with tremendous firepower. And the King's Gate, or principal gatehouse, though built after James's death (1316–20), clearly follows his original plan and is the masterpiece of Edwardian military architecture. It was approached by a drawbridge which worked on a pivot between the moat and a pit. The outer passages were protected by four portcullises and two doors, and commanded from above by seven sets of machicolations. If set on fire, the portcullises could be drenched with water. The entrance passage was under fire from a number of arrow-loops on both sides, and its centre portion was commanded by six doorways, through which heavy missiles could be thrown down. There was also an inner passage, designed to have a portcullis and door at both ends. The castle, then incomplete, was penetrated by Welsh rebels in 1294, and there is evidence that this massive and ingenious gatehouse was James's response to the defects in design thus uncovered. Certainly, the gatehouse did the trick. Owen Glendower lost three hundred men trying to take it in 1401. He tried again in 1402 and 1403, the last time with heavy siege equipment, but he was repelled by a garrison of only twenty-eight.

Caernarvon remained in royal service as the administrative centre for North Wales until well into the seventeenth century and the town flourished accordingly. But though building continued in the castle for half a century, at a cost of over £20,000, it was never exactly finished according to plan. It was the same tale at most of the Edwardian castles. The last years of Edward's reign, when he was totally obsessed by Scotland, was a period of financial stringency; and his son lacked not only the money but the will to finish his father's splendid legacy – he never once revisited the castle of his birth. Beaumaris, the last of the Edwardian castles, is the tragedy of an unfinished masterpiece. On a flat site with sea access, it expressed the idea of concentricity and covering firepower to perfection. Edward must have been delighted with James's design for 'the new

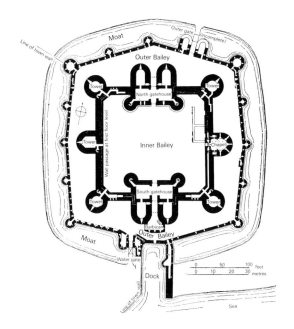

Left and far left: Beaumaris, last and most elegant of Edward I's Welsh castles, expressed the idea of concentricity and covering firepower to perfection. It was never completed according to plan, however, because money ran out.

castle at Beau Mareys' and he pressed the work ahead at a tempo phenomenal even by his standards. During the summer of 1295, under the protection of the fleet, about 1,800 diggers were at work on the site, plus 450 masons and 375 quarrymen – coins from their wages still occasionally turn up in the neighbourhood. Some 2,300 trees were felled to provide timber, and among other items we hear of 2,428 tons of sea-coal (for the forges) and 105,000 assorted nails.

Yet by the winter of 1295–6, when a great many of the workmen were, unusually, kept on, the financial pressures were already acute. We know this from the survival of a remarkable letter to the Exchequer written in February 1296 by James and his clerk of works, Walter of Winchester. 'We write to inform you', it says, 'that the work we are doing is very costly and we need a great deal of money.' Although it was outside the normal season, it continued, James still had over 1,000

The ground plan of Caerphilly, the earliest concentric castle in Britain, and the largest in Wales. Covering thirty acres, it is notable for its powerful water-defences and the high standards of its masonry.

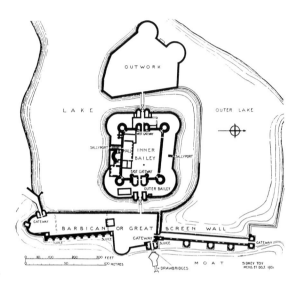

finish the castle they needed to employ 400 masons, 2,000 minor workmen, 100 carts, 60 waggons, 30 boats bringing stone and sea-coal, 200 quarrymen, 30 smiths and carpenters in addition – plus the garrison and payment for materials. It continues: 'As to how things are in the land of Wales, we still cannot be sure. But, as you well know, Welshmen are Welshmen, and you need to understand them properly. If, which God forbid, there is war with France and Scotland, we shall need to watch them all the more closely.' There is a desperate postscript to the letter: 'And, Sir, for God's sake be quick with the money for the works, as much as ever our lord the king wills – otherwise everything done up till now will have been of no avail.'

In fact expenditure in 1296 fell to £100 a week and the work at Beaumaris never recovered the sense of urgency which marked its first six months. Work continued spasmodically for many years, and the cost eventually rose to £14,400; but in 1343, when it was surveyed, it was still unfinished, and the surveyors reported that £684 6s 8d would be needed to remedy matters. There is no evidence that this money was ever forthcoming, and in its basic structure the castle is substantially the same today as when work was abandoned early in the fourteenth century. Of course the castle was roofed, furnished, lived in and defensible. Indeed it probably fulfilled its designer's purpose as well as any of the Edwardian castles. It has a square inner bailey with walls fifteen feet thick, six towers and two powerful gateways, each with three portcullises and two doors. The outer bailey has twelve towers and two gatehouses, with a dock at the south gateway where the moat meets a 'cut' from the sea. The gap between the inner and outer curtains is narrow, so that the inner can control the outer; and, in addition, the outer towers are built out of line with the inner ones, thus exposing the flanks of an enemy advancing from the outer to the inner gate. The gatehouses are opposite each other, as at Caerphilly; and, as at Harlech, their defences were planned so they could be held as easily against the inner as the outer bailey. The real stronghold of the castle was the north gatehouse,

carpenters, smiths, plasterers and navvies on the payroll, plus a garrison of ten men-at-arms, twenty crossbowmen, all mounted, and a hundred infantry. Although more than £6,000 had been provided the previous year, the men's pay 'has been and still is very much in arrears, and we are having the greatest difficulty in keeping them because they simply have nothing to live on'. To keep going, £250 a week would be needed throughout the coming season. They add: 'If, however, you feel we cannot have so much money, let us know, and we will put the workmen at your disposal according to whatever you think will be the best profit of our lord the king.' They reported that parts of the castle were already twenty-eight feet high, even the lowest being twenty feet; they had begun ten of the outer and four of the inner towers. 'Four gates have been hung and are shut and locked every night, and each gateway is to have three portcullises . . . at high tide a 40-ton vessel will be able to come fully-laden right up to the castle gateway; so much we have been able to do in spite of all the Welshmen.' Nevertheless to which could be isolated from the curtain-wall by shifting movable bridges. To cut down manpower there was a mural gallery as well as a wall-walk. But some of the defences, notably the north gatehouse, were not completed; nor were the towers built up to the planned height.

Beaumaris was built to palatial standards. It had five separate suites of noble lodgings, presumably for the king, the queen, the heir-apparent and his consort, and the constable (or viceroy). The main hall in the north gatehouse, with its five huge windows (facing inwards of course), must have been a splendid apartment. Naturally the comforts, even luxuries, of these Welsh castles have vanished almost without a trace. But they were once very prominent. Edward campaigned as hard as any medieval monarch, but he liked to surround himself with magnificence and ease, and he took his wife (who had her own Spanish ideas about comfort) wherever he went. The royal couple seem to have insisted that gardens be laid out at any new castle they chose to inhabit. At Rhuddlan, under the heading of 'the Queen's Work', the well was prettified and provided with a wooden roof, and encircled by a fishpond, lined with four cartloads of clay from the nearby marches, and equipped with seats on its circumference; the courtyard was laid with 6,000 grass turves and fenced with the staves of old casks. Rhuddlan also had a special building for the queen's goldsmith, but his duties were not solely decorative since he made the brass parts

of war-machines. The queen had another lawn laid out at Conwy, and we are told that one of her squires, Roger le Fykeys, saw that it was watered. A great many other interesting details emerge from the copious royal accounts. At Caernarvon, one Hova, a smith, was paid for making a dozen iron spikes to prevent pigeons and seagulls from perching on the head of Edward's statue over the King's Gate. Other birds were more welcome. In the middle of the castle's millpond a nest was built for swans, and it is likely that swans – royal birds – were to be found in the water defences of all these castles.

There are still swans in the moat at Beaumaris, and in general it is remarkable how much of Edward's work in Wales has survived. He did a tremendous amount of building at Westminster and the Tower, but it was soon concealed by later work. His great religious foundation, Vale Royal in Cheshire, has gone. There is little to show, either, for his titanic efforts in Scotland. But in Wales only his castle at Builth has vanished. Flint, Aberystwyth and Hope are ruins. But Rhuddlan and Harlech are substantially intact, and Conwy, Caernarvon and Beaumaris are complete, so far as the stonework is concerned. They form a substantial testimony to the determination of a great king, and to the architectural skills of a great designer. They also mark the transition from the austere fortresses characteristic of the Norman–Angevin age to the castle-palaces of the later Middle Ages.

CHAPTER FOUR

THE LAST OF THE FEUDAL CASTLES

Like his grandfather, Edward III was a martial man, who spent a great deal of his life in the saddle, and a sumptuous, if not extravagant, builder. He liked to be present when the foundations of a new castle were laid, and he plainly had his favourites: a clerk, dealing with refortification work at Newcastle, added 'which lies near to the king's heart'. Like his grandfather, who had James of St George to realize his schemes, Edward III had his own building impresario, William of Wykham. Wykham's origins were humble, and he seems to have begun life as keeper of the king's hunting dogs at Windsor. But he quickly impressed the king (an impatient man, like all the Plantagenets) by the extraordinary speed with which he could organize and carry through vast undertakings. He was also in orders, which meant that the king could reward him with benefices rather than cash. Soon he was 'our beloved clerk'; in 1359 he was appointed 'chief keeper and surveyor' of Windsor, Leeds, Dover and Hadleigh (all important castles) and of twelve southern manor-houses, given plenary powers to 'ordain and dispose' of all building in those places, and in addition was in charge of the new castle being built at Queenborough. He occupied the office, in fact, which soon developed into the Clerkship of the King's Works (later the Office of Works, and now swallowed up in the Department of the Environment). As such in 1356–61 alone he handled personally over £9,000 of the king's money, and immense stocks of materials. In time, he became the king's Secretary, 'who stays by his side in constant attendance on his service', Lord Privy Seal, and finally, in 1367, Lord Chancellor and Bishop of Winchester, holding an immense combination of offices and benefices from which he financed his own building schemes at Winchester, Oxford and elsewhere.

Wykham was not so much an architect (though he clearly knew a great deal about it) as a man who could be relied on to assemble massive quantities of labour, materials and cash in the right place at the right time. The pity is that so little of the work he and Edward did together has survived. In 1361, for instance, Edward founded a new town and fortress at Queenborough, called after his wife Philippa, to dominate the narrow passage between Sheppey and mainland Kent which was then one of the chief sea-routes to the Thames. The castle, designed by John Box, may have been influenced by certain symmetrical castles built by the Emperor Frederick II in southern Italy in the previous century; it also prefigures the artillery forts Henry VIII was to build in the 1540s. In essence, it carried the principle of concentricity to its ultimate conclusion, based on a circular plan. The outer bailey was concentric with the keep, but passages on each side connected the keep with the outer world, and could be held even if the outer bailey was lost; the inner bailey had six circular towers ranged round a circular courtyard. This elegant exercise in functional design cost £25,000; but the town never flourished and the castle was demolished under the Commonwealth. A few mounds and Edward's church are all that remain.

At Windsor, Edward and Wykham completely transformed the castle, turning it into a splendid fortified palace and installing the latest military technology and domestic amenities. Some of Edward's work, such as the great wooden building, modelled on the lantern at Ely Cathedral, which he set up to accommodate his feasts for the Knights of the Garter, which he founded, has gone completely. What remains, and it is very considerable, is now largely obscured by Hanoverian restoration and refacing; but apart from St George's Chapel (built by Edward IV) and the great terrace (set up by Elizabeth), Windsor retained the face and basic structure Edward III gave it until the end of the eighteenth century. He spent £50,000 on it, easily the highest figure for any single building operation by the crown in the whole Middle Ages. And Edward carried this through while he was spending £1,000 a year fortifying and garrisoning Calais, which he had acquired in 1347, some £29,000 on Westminster and large sums on a number of fortified manor-houses, palaces and hunting-boxes, some of them new.

This intense and prolonged building activity stretched the national resources, especially of skilled labour, almost to breaking point. Edward exploited his powers of compulsion more ruthlessly than any of his predecessors. From the 1340s, he constantly issued commissions of impressment, as well as powers to purvey materials at fixed (i.e. low) prices. These orders grew even more frequent after 1349, when the first of a series of outbreaks of bubonic plague, known as the Black Death, cut the population by up to a third and made labour of any kind scarce and costly. One chronicler wrote that 'almost all the masons and carpenters throughout the whole of England were brought to that building [Windsor Castle], so that hardly anyone could have any good mason or carpenter except in secret'. Craftsmen and labourers seem to have been as reluctant to go to Windsor as they were to march into the wilds of Wales. One group of Yorkshire masons under impressment for Windsor were forced to don distinctive red clothing (like convicts) 'lest they should escape from the custody of the conductor'. The royal clerks or knights armed with Letters Patent charging them to impress and purvey were also authorized to pursue and arrest 'contrariants'. Any 'contrariant and rebellious' workman could be locked up or forced to provide securities for good behaviour.

Of course in a seller's market for labour private men and clerical foundations could and did outbid the crown; and pay more promptly too. The Statute of Labourers, 1351, constantly repeated and reinforced, was supposed to control wage-inflation. But a royal proclamation of 1361 complained that 'great numbers of carpenters, masons and other craftsmen, workmen and labourers, hired upon the king's works in divers places, finding their wages thereby diminished, and that they can take more in the service of men of religion and other masters than in the king's service, have departed from the king's works . . . whereat the king is much moved'. Two years later, another royal proclamation asserted that 'almost all' the craftsmen engaged in work on the royal castles at Windsor, Hadleigh and Queenborough had 'secretly withdrawn', having been tempted by 'excessive gains and gifts . . . contrary to the statute'. Again it was 'religious persons and other masters, clerks and laymen' who were to blame; the king's works were

Opposite: Windsor, now the largest inhabited castle in Europe, has a history stretching back to the Normans. Greatly enlarged by Henry II and Edward III, it was expensively restored in Georgian times.

Page 78: Leeds Castle in Kent was given by Edward I to his beloved Queen Eleanor and, with its superb moat, has feminine beauty as well as great intrinsic strength. Restored and grandly furnished, it is now a conference centre.

Page 79: Carisbrooke Castle.

Right: Carisbrooke, with its mighty late-medieval gateway, has always been the largest and strongest fortress on the Isle of Wight. Its defences were strengthened in Tudor times and the Roundheads kept Charles I prisoner there.

Far right: Corfe, one of the most appealing ruined castles, was a Norman creation which was refortified under Charles I with an artillery bastion, and underwent a major siege in 1643.

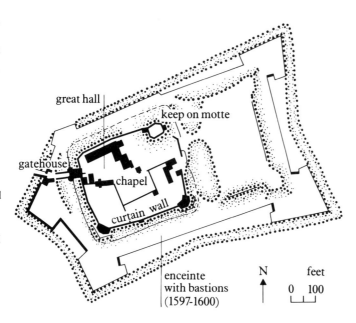

great hall

keep on motte

gatehouse

chapel

curtain wall

enceinte with bastions (1597-1600)

N feet

0 100

Spanish allies. This was the first of the periodic invasion scares which, right up to the early 1940s, were to leave such a substantial mark on the English coastline.

The worst year was 1377, when the French attacked the Isle of Wight and sacked Rye and Winchelsea, the latter a fortified new town built by Edward I. There was another bad scare in 1385, when a fleet was actually assembled on the French coast, but never sailed. Two of its ships were captured on their way to the rendezvous, and found to contain timber for prefabricated palisades; the timber was impounded and promptly used to strengthen the defences of Sandwich. These scares continued at intervals until the middle of the fifteenth century. Naturally the south-east was the most seriously alarmed. The crown had its hands full maintaining the defences of Calais, which was itself a severe impediment to a successful French invasion. Its elaborate water-works, sluices, walls, castle and satellite forts are worth a chapter in themselves, but they lie outside the scope of this book. They were enormously expensive but the entire political nation was in agreement that Calais was an English 'jewel', 'the brightest jewel in the crown', it was said, and no cost must be spared to hold it. Accordingly, under Edward III, £1,000 a year, on average, was spent on its defences, rising steadily to £1,700 a year under Edward IV. No other English fortress, not even Berwick, the key to Scotland, absorbed such large, regular sums.

Hence, with the money draining away on Calais, the crown could not afford a new defensive system for the south-east. Queenborough blocked one route to London, but if it was intended to guard the whole Thames estuary it was sited in the wrong place. The best the crown could do was to put its castellans on the alert everywhere, and to bring as many castles and town defences up to date as it could afford. Precautions were taken as far afield as Conwy, Caernarvon and Beaumaris (a French fleet was active off the coast of Wales in the 1400s). Rochester, still sound but out of date, was refortified. The decaying castle of Southampton was modernized, 1378–88, at a cost of nearly £2,000. Money was also spent on the royal castles

thus being subjected to 'hurt and hindrance' and he was 'moved to anger'. Angered the king may have been but he was fighting a losing battle. Indeed, he was eventually forced to break the law himself, as we know from his instructions to the Clerk of the Works at Windsor, and even to Wykham, authorizing them to pay excess rates. In time, the higher wages became general and attempts to enforce the statute were abandoned.

One reason why the king found himself competing for labour was that large numbers of private individuals were building or modernizing castles, and they were doing this partly in consequence of Edward's decision to enforce his claim to the French crown. In the 1340s and 1350s he was generally successful; but in the late 1360s, and especially in the 1370s, he lost command of the sea, at any rate from time to time, and England's coasts were exposed to attack by the French and their

Penshurst, the finest 14th-century manor-house in England, with a Great Hall fit for a king, was fortified during the invasion scares at the end of Edward III's reign. Towers were added in the 15th century.

walls. To this period, 1375–81, we owe the massive defence works at Canterbury which radiate from the Westgate, itself a formidable item of military architecture. And, in addition, a number of wealthy landowners and retired generals in the area received royal licence to fortify their manors or build themselves castles.

One example is Scotney Castle in Kent, which was fortified by Roger Ashburnham, as a direct result of the sackings of 1377. The ensemble at Scotney as it is seen today contains only a fragment of the fourteenth-century castle, with a seventeenth-century house attached; it is a romantic, contrived landscape, composed of buildings, ruins and nature, in the eighteenth-century picturesque fashion. But originally it comprised a formidable defensive area, though on a small scale: the moat was made to circle two islands, where people and cattle could find safety, the eastern one girdled with a curtain and four circular towers, one of which stands to its full height (though minus battlements and with a seventeenth-century conical roof). There was a similar scheme at Penshurst, though without water. In essence, Penshurst is the finest fourteenth-century manor-house in the country, with an unaltered great hall fit for a king. It was built by Sir John de Pulteney, an enormously rich draper, who was Lord Mayor of London four times between 1331 and 1337. He got a licence to crenellate in 1341, but his house actually had no fortifications at all; these were the years of Edward III's victories. Protective walls were built later during the invasion scare; and a second licence to crenellate was issued in 1393, by which time the house belonged to Sir John Devereux. A later owner, the Duke of Bedford, Henry v's brother and regent to his son, added towers and further stretches of high wall, by which time the house was completely fortified, though never a fortress.

Another refortified house was Leeds Castle, Kent, built at the junction of three roads, and originally with a triple barbican to overlook them. It has a complicated building history, and many of the apparently medieval defences were put up in the nineteenth century. Edward I acquired it in 1272, and made it

at Carisbrooke, on the Isle of Wight, which got a powerful new gateway, at Corfe, the strongest castle in Dorset, also updated, and at the ancient castles of Portchester and Winchester. In Cornwall in 1386 the Duchy authorities were even directed to refortify crumbling Tintagel and Trematon, lest 'our enemies of France and their adherents' should 'take and hold some fortress in our realm of England, and in particular on the sea coast, from which they can make war and ravage our said kingdom'.

England was growing increasingly nationalistic in the second half of the fourteenth century, and making the south-east secure was something of a national effort, as well as dictated by self-interest. The prosperous towns of Kent, and Sussex and Hampshire did not want to share the fate of Rye. So citizens played their part, alongside the crown, in strengthening town

Bodiam was built by one of Edward III's generals in the late 14th century during a French invasion scare. Ingeniously restored by Lord Curzon around 1920, it is the perfect example of a late-medieval courtyard castle.

Opposite: Bolton, in
Yorkshire, is a
well-preserved
14th-century
rectangular-style castle,
with high walls, a massive
five-storey tower at each
corner, and a sturdy
turret at the centre of each
of the long sides.

over to Queen Eleanor as part of her dower. He also remodelled the gatehouse and built a new wall with D-shaped turrets. Leeds is on an island, with elaborate water-defences, and it was these that were developed in the late fourteenth century to meet the French threat. At Cooling, also in Kent, John de Cobham got a licence to fortify his house on the north Kent marshes in 1381 – the French had attempted to sail up the Thames two years before. Most of the defences he erected between 1381 and 1385 (the accounts survive) have gone, but the splendid gatehouse is still there, bearing a copper plate on which he signalled his patriotism:

Knouwyth that beth and schul be
That I am made in help of the cuntre
In knowyng of whyche thyng
Thys is chartre and wytnessyng.

There were other patriots around, many with money made in the French wars. Sir Edward Dalyngrigge, one of Edward III's generals, married a wife who brought with her the Bodiam estate in Sussex. This is situated on the Rother, then navigable, and in 1386 Sir Edward was given licence to crenellate his manor-house there, and so block a French route of entry. The licence states:

The King and all to whom, etc, greeting. Know ye that our special grace we have granted and given license on behalf of ourselves and our heirs, so far as in us lies, to our beloved and faithful subject, Edward Dalyngrigge, Knight, that he may strengthen with a wall of stone and lime, and crenellate and may construct and make into a castle his manor house of Bodyham, near the sea, in the County of Sussex, for the defence of the adjacent county, and the resistance to our enemies, and may hold his aforesaid house so strengthened and crenellated and made into a castle for himself and his heirs for ever, without let or hindrance of ourselves and our heirs, or of

our agents whatsoever. In virtue of which, etc, the King at Westminster 20 October.

The licence, as usual, provided simply for fortifying an existing house. But Sir Edward found this impracticable, abandoned his manor, and built an entirely new castle half-way up the hill. Thanks to Lord Curzon, who restored it in the 1920s, Bodiam is one of the best-preserved examples of a late medieval courtyard castle. Sir Edward demanded comfort and was rich enough to provide it for himself; so the castle had the full range of suites for his family, a chapel, quarters for his men and his servants, and ample facilities of all kinds. Curzon said he had counted thirty-three fireplaces and twenty-four lavatories built into the walls, all with drainage.

The castle has been criticized on the grounds that the walls are too thin, and not much use against cannon. Certainly, on the only two occasions it was attacked, in 1484 and 1643, Bodiam surrendered quickly, but this proves little. In some ways it was an ingenious castle. Rectangular in shape, it had a powerful circular tower at each corner, with a gatehouse in the middle of the north side and square towers in the middle of each of the other sides, the south square tower having a postern. To cross the very wide moat, fed from the Rother, an aggressor had to overcome a barbican and an outwork, both within the moat. The approach was by a timber bridge, at right angles to the gateway and exposed to flank fire from the castle walls. The entrance was from the bank by a drawbridge. To reach the barbican you had to turn right on the outwork and cross a second drawbridge; and from the barbican a third drawbridge led to the main gateway of the castle. Unfortunately, all this elaborate system is gone (Curzon was only able to describe it after draining and excavating the moat), and the present approach is simply by a straight causeway, probably built in the sixteenth century. But the castle defences themselves remain: the gateway was defended by machicolations, loopholes, three sets of barriers, one at either end and one in the middle, each consisting of a portcullis and door (one of the

The ground plan of Nunney, in Somerset, a spectacular and splendidly preserved French-style courtyard castle, built by Sir John Delamere, a veteran of the Hundred Years War. It is, in effect, a keep with a hollow core.

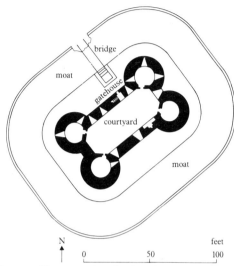

bridge

moat

gatehouse

courtyard

moat

N

feet

0   50   100

in the 1320s, they included 78½ quarters of corn of two years storage and 34 of three years; 10½ quarters of wheat malt; 71½ quarters of new beans and 41 of old beans; 7 bushels of beans and barley mixture; 2 tons of pilcorn; 9½ quarters of oatmeal; 7 bushels of oatmalt; 64 new and 14 old carcases of salted meat; 81 oxhides; 40 mutton carcases; 20 new and 52 old hams; 1,856 stockfish, plus large quantities of wine, honey and vinegar.

Other private castles were built at Sheriff Hutton and Wressle in Yorkshire, at Shireburn in Oxfordshire, at Chillingham in Northumberland, Maxstoke in Warwickshire and Amberley in Sussex. These are, or were, courtyard castles; but sometimes the towers of the courtyard were brought so close together, in the French fashion, that the courtyard became little more than a well. This happened at Nunney in Somerset, a spectacular and splendidly preserved castle built by the French war-veteran Sir John Delamere. Except that it has a hollow core, this structure is more like a keep than the centre of a concentric castle. Another French-style castle in this part of England is Old Wardour in Wiltshire, built on the model of the Château de Concressault by yet another veteran, John, 5th Lord Lovell. It is superbly situated by a wooded bank over an eighteenth-century lake, and resembles Nunney, though not rounded, in that it is like a keep or even a hexagonal house, with a hexagonal courtyard in the middle. Both Wardour and Nunney contained luxurious accommodation. What, exactly, was their purpose? Nunney was licensed as early as 1373, and does not seem to have been inspired by the invasion scare; Wardour, 1393, fits in with the scare years, but is well inland. One is tempted to believe that both were primarily testimonials to the wealth and experiences of the old campaigners who built them.

Some of these military adventurers were immensely rich, their money deriving from loot and the ransoms of high-born prisoners. The fortune of Sir John Fastolf, who built Caister Castle in East Anglia, is itemized in an inventory made at his death in 1459, which lists £2,643 in ready cash, 98 ounces of gold plate and no less than 14,813 ounces of silver. He could serve a banquet to over a hundred people off silver and silver-gilt, and

original portcullises, made of oak, plated and shod with iron, can still be seen); the passages of the main gateway (and postern) are vaulted, the bosses of the ribbing having, in many cases, six-inch holes, to provide painful surprises for intruders. Granted that the cannon of the 1390s were not yet of much use against stonework, this would have been a difficult castle to take in its own age.

Bodiam was only one of a number of late fourteenth-century rectangular castles, many built by rich veterans like Dalyngrigge, which combined strength with a high level of comfort. Bolton, in Yorkshire, is another well-preserved example, with high walls, a massive rectangular five-storey tower at each corner, and a powerful turret in the middle of both the long sides. There was also a strong gatehouse. The courtyard system in the middle provided ample room for a multitude of cellars, storerooms, brewhouses and bakehouses. The bigger they were, the longer the castle could hold out (and the more profitable the commercial services it could provide in peacetime). When the contents of Caerphilly were inventoried

he had over 200 gallons of fine red wine in his cellars. Such men not only built expensive new castles, they also retained on their payrolls large numbers of mercenaries to defend them.

It was this practice, which has been termed a bastard kind of feudalism, that was one powerful element in the anarchy which marked in England the middle decades of the fifteenth century. The old knight-service system had virtually broken down. Neither king nor lords were now followed into battle by men whose relationship to them was based on feudal services deriving from the ownership of land. They hired killers, and then in turn their power and wealth attracted the loyalty and services of neighbours – 'good lordship' as it was called. Of course such a system could only flourish when the central monarchy was weak, and it was precisely in the minority and feeble majority of Henry VI that the country reverted to the baronial gangsterism of Stephen's reign. Then the private castles flourished again, and the groans of the oppressed were heard in the land. Sometimes these criminal lords were brought to book. In 1448 parliament charged William de la Pole, Duke of Suffolk and the great power in East Anglia, with controlling the appointment of sheriffs 'to be applied to his intent and commandment, to fulfil his desires and writings for such as him liked'; those who would not 'be of his affinity' were set aside, and legal suits he favoured were 'furthered and sped', and 'many of your true lieges by his might and help of his adherents disinherited, impoverished and destroyed, and thereby he has purchased many great possessions by maintenance, and done great outrageous extorsions and murders'. It said that 'man-slaughters, murderers and common, openly noised misdoers' had been drawn to the duke, 'seeing his great rule and might' and had been supported by him 'in suppression of justice' and 'to the full heavy discomfort of the true subjects of this your realm'. Suffolk was killed, perhaps by pirates, in 1450. Another gangster was James Fiennes, Lord Saye and Sele, owner of Broughton Castle, Oxfordshire, and a power in the home counties, who was largely responsible for provoking the popular indignation which eventually led to Cade's rebellion.

Left: Caister Castle, Norfolk, was built by the famous Sir John Fastolf in the 1430s, and still has its towers – nearly one hundred feet high – its gatehouse and some walls. Home of the family who wrote 'The Paston Letters'.

Right: Warwick was the chief midlands stronghold of the 15th-century Earl of Warwick, 'the Kingmaker'. Its French-style donjon, known as Caesar's Tower, rises 133 feet from the foot of its plinth.

Far right: Tattershall is a five-storey brick castle built in the mid-15th century by the immensely wealthy Lord Cromwell, Henry VI's Treasurer. It towers 120 feet above the Lincolnshire countryside.

Such men, operating from castles and fortified manor-houses, with the connivance or even active assistance of the supposed lawful authorities, aroused violent opposition. Fiennes was executed, along with his puppet sheriff of Kent, who married his daughter.

The mercenaries who served these lords were loyal only so long as the pay was forthcoming. This had its effects on castle architecture. Increasingly, the lord's part of the building was isolated from the rest, so that it could be defended against mutinous or treacherous followers. This was true, for instance, of Bodiam, and most of the late fourteenth-century castles mentioned above; and it was a common feature of all remodelled castles in the fifteenth century. Bodiam, too, had a mess-hall with kitchen, as well as separate lodgings, for the retainers. Such 'livery and maintenance' lodgings, modelled on the arrangements for students at Oxbridge colleges, were built by most of the great lords. One of the earliest examples is at Dartington Hall (1388–1400), built by Richard II's half-brother, John Holland, Duke of Exeter, to accommodate his house-retainers. Another is at Amberley, Sussex, where a two-storey lodging was built for the mercenaries on the payroll of William Rede, Bishop of Chichester.

In some cases the lord felt safer (and could live more grandly) if he built himself a great tower, or donjon, on the French model. Rosemond's Tower, at Pickering, is a good example. There is another at Ludlow. At Warwick, seat of the all-powerful Beauchamps and later the Nevilles, there was a costly facelift at the end of the fourteenth century, and two such towers were built. Each contained many tiers of well-lighted rooms, with fireplaces, latrines and mural bedrooms. Caesar's Tower is trilobed, 133 feet high from the foot of its massive plinth; all except the fifth of its six storeys have strong stone vaulting, and so are fireproof. The lowest was a prison (hence 'dungeon'). Storeys two, three and four were family rooms; the fifth was an ammunition store and the sixth a guardroom, leading to two tiers of ingeniously designed battlements. Guy's Tower is essentially the same, but has no prison. The towers at Warwick, though self-contained, are part of the perimeter defences of the curtain. At Raglan the principle is carried still further. The immense Yellow Tower of Gwent, probably built by Sir William ap Thomas around 1440–45, which proved almost impervious to artillery even in the mid-seventeenth century, has its own separate moat and drawbridge, at an angle in the perimeter, and is a castle in its own right.

One feature of these towers of 'bastard feudalism', whether built as part of new structures or added to old ones, is that they are often made of brick, like the defences of Calais, which had no stone of its own. The finest of them all, at Tattershall in Lincolnshire, was, like Bodiam, rescued and restored by Lord Curzon. Its builder, Henry VI's Treasurer, Lord Cromwell, was one of the richest men in the kingdom. Much of his wealth was ill-gotten, for in his will (1455) he left his executors with the task of restoring, 'for conscience's sake', some £5,481 6s 8d, which

he must have extorted; and at Tattershall he built and endowed a magnificent collegiate church where perpetual prayers for his soul were to be said. The great tower, which is intact, was put up on the west side of the inner bailey of a thirteenth-century castle. Virtually everything except the tower has long since gone, but the total defences were once formidable. Including the vaulted basement, the tower has five storeys, and rises 120 feet to the top of its turrets. The three upper storeys were Cromwell's private quarters, each having a large hall with chambers at the sides. There are wide spiral staircases, fire-places of great magnificence, traceried windows, corridors with vaults and decorated with sculptured armorial bearings, and much other evidence of grandeur. Indeed Cromwell built more for display than for security, for though the tower had two tiers of battlements and was undoubtedly planned to be defended, it had three entrances, all weak, the floors are of timber and its windows are large.

Sometimes, and more in the English tradition, fifteenth-century brick towers take the form of gatehouses. At Herst-monceux in Sussex, Roger de Fiennes, Cromwell's contemporary and Treasurer of the Household, built himself a large rectangular brick castle (licensed to be crenellated 1441); this has a moat and high walls, with octagonal towers projecting at the corners and semi-octagonal towers at intervals in the curtain, but the main defences, behind a counter-balance drawbridge, were powerful towers of the gatehouse, equipped for artillery and with a double fighting-platform on top. Another powerful brick gatehouse was set up, as part of a new rectangular castle built around an old defended manor-house, at Kirby Muxloe in Leicestershire. The builder, Lord Hastings of Ashby Castle, got his licence here in 1474, and employed as one of his master-masons John Cowper of Tattershall, who may well have worked on Cromwell's tower as a young man. Not much is now left, apart from the north-west corner tower and the gatehouse half-way up its second storey. It was defended by a moat, drawbridge, and portcullis and two-leaf doors at either end of the gateway, flanked by octagonal turrets enclos-ing spiral stairways. The workmanship throughout is of very high quality, as it usually is in these fifteenth-century brick castle-mansions.

At the same time, Hastings was refortifying and restoring a twelfth- and fourteenth-century fortified manor-house at Ashby-de-la-Zouch, not very far away. Here he raised a high curtain round the weak south side of the building and built a magnificent tower house in the middle of it. Its main rectangular body has four storeys, with a small east wing divided into seven low storeys. The main part, stacked up, was a set of store-rooms, then kitchen, then great hall, with a great chamber on top – almost a reversion to a twelfth-century stone keep. It was still considered 'a place of considerable strength' in 1648; hence its 'slighting'. Hastings came to a similarly violent end. He was one of the most active of the baronial ruffians. The year he began his Ashby tower, he entered into a bond with two lords, nine knights and forty-eight squires, who swore to aid him against all persons in the kingdom, and to raise as many men as they could, armed at his expense. In 1483 the Duke of Gloucester, later Richard III, broke up a meeting of the Privy Council at the Tower and ordered Hastings's immediate execution. His head was hacked off on a log. We have the accounts for Hastings's building work at Kirby Muxloe from October 1480, when the first forty cartloads of wood were delivered at the brick kiln, till the day six months after his execution, when all work ceased abruptly; presumably his assets had been confiscated by then, and the money to pay the wages had run out.

Of course these bastard-feudal chieftains were not the only section of society to defend themselves with stone and brick. Society was no more secure in the fourteenth and fifteenth centuries than it had been earlier, in some ways less so. The later Middle Ages in England were marked by rising anti-clericalism. The pope was hated because it was thought he sided with the French. Clerical wealth and privilege aroused endless resentment, and many high ecclesiastics were iden-tified with government mismanagement and intolerable

Opposite: Herstmonceux is an outstanding 15th-century brick castle, moated and equipped for artillery but also with luxurious living accommodation. It is well restored and until recently housed the Royal Observatory.

Right: Ashby-de-la-Zouch, with its formidable ninety-foot tower, was the stronghold of Lord Hastings, a baronial ruffian of the Wars of the Roses who was executed by Richard III in 1483.

Far right: Wells, next to the cathedral, is the best preserved and most romantic of all the bishops' fortified palaces. From the early 14th century on, prelates were often attacked by angry mobs.

taxation. Since they could not be tried in the ordinary courts they were often lynched. Bishop Stapleton of Exeter was murdered by a mob outside his London house in 1326; Archbishop Sudbury of Canterbury, Chancellor to Richard II, was dragged from the chapel of the White Tower in London in 1381 and butchered, while Bishop Ayscough of Salisbury, secretary to Henry VI, was seized in the Priory Church at Edington, and stoned to death. The murder of Becket in 1170 had been universally unpopular; but from the fourteenth century such crimes against prelates brought public rejoicing. So, to defend themselves, bishops and abbots crenellated, turreted and moated their dwellings. In 1329, for example, Bishop Burghersh was licensed to turn his palace at Lincoln into a fortress; two years later the Bishop of Wells did the same (his splendid moated palace is still there). Everywhere bishops refortified their own castles, and monasteries which had hitherto been totally undefended built themselves walls. One of the most completely fortified religious houses, Ewenny Priory in Glamorgan, was of course in an area traditionally considered insecure (there are a number of fortified churches, for instance, in the Gower Peninsula). But it is notable that its walls were completely rebuilt, a tower added to the south gate, and a new north gatehouse set up, in the early fourteenth century, by which time south Wales was regarded as pacified. More striking still are the strong, crenellated gatehouses added to the buildings of many English abbeys and priories, which now felt themselves to be objects of possible attack – at Butley Priory in Suffolk, and at such famous royal foundations as Battle, Ely, St Albans and Bury St Edmunds. It is significant, for instance, that Thornton Abbey in Lincolnshire got its licence to crenellate in 1382, the year after the Peasants' Revolt. Hence a great many of the surviving late-medieval gatehouses are monastic, and such stone or brick gateways became part of the architectural idiom of Oxbridge colleges. For the most part they were not defensible against an army, but they provided some degree of protection against mobs or gangs of baronial marauders.

Hever Castle is a
14th-century fortified
manor-house, once the
home of the tragic Queen
Anne Boleyn. From 1903
it was sensitively restored
and embellished by the
American millionaire,
Waldorf Astor.

It was against such casual enemies that many secular buildings were fortified or refortified at this time. An outstanding example is Hever Castle in Kent. Its first licence to crenellate came around 1340, but the moating and main defences seem to have been planned after a further licence was issued to Sir John de Cobham (also active at Cooling) in 1384. Here the motive may have been protection against the French, but the defences were well kept up throughout the fifteenth century, no doubt against such Kentish predators as Lord Saye and Sele – especially after the castle was acquired by Sir Geoffrey Boleyn, a successful hatter and Lord Mayor of London, in 1462. The three-storey gatehouse is massive, and the building well-preserved (and expensively restored by the Astors after 1903). But it could not have withstood cannon-fire.

The sort of assault a semi-fortified manor-house of the later Middle Ages had to face is well described by Margaret Paston in her account of the seizure of Gresham by Lord Moleyns in 1448. She says that about a thousand of his followers turned up

> arrayed in manner of war, with cuirasses, coats of mail, steel helmets, glaives, bows, large shields, guns, pans with fire, long cromes to draw down houses, ladders, and picks with which they mined down the walls, and long trees with which they broke up gates and doors, and so came into the said mansion, the wife of your beseecher at that time being therein, and 12 persons with her – the which persons they drove out of the said mansion, and mined down the walls of the chamber wherein the wife of your said beseecher was, and bare her out of the gates and cut asunder the posts of the houses and let them fall, and broke up all the chambers and coffers in the said mansion and rifled and bare away stuff, array and money to the value of £200.

In short, not a regular siege but a case of breaking-and-entering in great force. The 'guns', one imagines, would have been hand-guns, not cannon.

But cannons were coming in, in increasing power and growing numbers. It is a paradox that technology was producing ever-proliferating luxury in castles and, at the same time, ever deadlier means of blowing all to bits. The fourteenth century produced some significant craftsmen, especially carpenters. William Hurley, who built the lantern at Ely and Edward III's magnificent Round Table structure at Windsor, also designed the hall at Caerphilly, and constructed a variety of massive siege-engines at the Tower. In 1338, for instance, we have records of him dismantling a 'great engine' at the Tower and taking it to the siege of Dunbar, accompanied by four expert carpenters and three smiths. Another famous carpenter

Kirby Muxloe in Leicestershire was an old fortified manor-house, updated during the Wars of the Roses with a powerful brick gatehouse. The workmanship throughout is of very high quality.

Opposite: Scotney Castle
is the remains of a
14th-century moated
tower, part of a large
manor-house fortified to
resist the invading French
after they sacked Rye and
Winchelsea in 1377.

was William Herland, who partnered John Box in the building of Queenborough. His son Hugh, called 'the disposer of the king's works touching the art or mystery of carpentry', made the roof of Westminster Hall in his old age, next to the Ely lantern the finest surviving work of any medieval carpenter. But he also did a great deal of military work, especially in Kent during the panic. His colleague, Richard Swift, discovered by the Black Prince, was equally active with siege-engines but was not above making two 'petites canons' as toys for the infant Richard II in 1377.

Carpenters had been the traditional engineers, siege experts and makers of war-machines. But in the fourteenth century with the coming of gunpowder they began to yield place to the smiths. Greek fire, in use since the seventh century, contained no gunpowder and was not a true explosive. Formulae for making gunpowder had existed in China since the eleventh century, but it was not until the thirteenth century that the Chinese used it for firearms; and, as it happens, the earliest surviving record of a Chinese cannon belongs to a period when they were already becoming common in Europe. It was in Europe, early in the fourteenth century, that gunpowder was first used to discharge missiles. Like the true concentric castle, it may have been a case of a number of established discoveries being brought together. Recipes for a substance incorporating saltpetre, sulphur and charcoal are found in Europe about 1300, and the first records of cannon appear a generation later, at Metz (1324), Florence and England (1326), and Spain (1331). In England, we first hear of a royal smith, Henry Lewes, at the Tower in 1275, but he was helping the royal armourer and the crossbowmakers. It was not until the reign of Edward III that Walter the Smith, in conjunction with Reginald of St Albans, a craftsman from the Wardrobe, made the first English firearms. Edward ordered them for the Crécy campaign, 1346-7, and actually used them at Calais. They were 'ribalds', made of wood bound with iron hoops. By the end of the reign, however, guns made entirely of metal were being cast in the Tower forge, and the smiths had taken over completely. Of course the Tower

smiths – especially the great fifteenth-century dynasty, the Clampards – made a great many other articles to order: weapons of all kinds, hooks, hinges, screens, bars, window-frames, iron doors and portcullises for castle gateways, chains for drawbridges and harbour defences, and fire-irons and candelabra for royal palaces. Much of their time was spent on producing masses of iron clamps and crampons for strengthening castle walls and towers. Great quantities of such ironwork were shipped from the Tower workshops to Queenborough. A big branch workshop was opened up in the king's name at Calais. But, increasingly, the royal smiths specialized in hand-guns and cannon.

The first cannons were very small, weighing only between twenty and forty pounds. Manuscripts of about 1326 show one resting on a trestle, and discharging a 'quarrel' or heavy arrow. But they quickly grew in size; by the time of Richard II guns of up to 600 pounds were being made for forts and castles. In England cannons first became of real military importance in the rearmament against the French invasion threat which led to the castle-programme described earlier. Thus, in 1365, the Wardrobe Accounts recorded that two 'great guns' and nine small ones had been issued from the Tower to Queenborough. In the 1360s Southampton walled up all its great gates and posterns, except five, and ordered that 'all the doors and windows of the houses towards the sea should be walled up three feet thick or more at the cost of the lords'; gun-ports, which can still be seen, were then inserted. In 1380 the Archbishop of Canterbury was licensed to build the new West Gate, the earliest known fortress designed to be used with guns. Its gunslits look like inverted keyholes, and were designed to be used to harass besiegers' bombards. Other 'invasion scare' castles with purpose-built gunslits were John de Cobham's Cooling, Dalyngrigge's Bodiam and the new west gate at Winchester. The Archbishop of Canterbury, not content with his new fortifications in his cathedral city, refortified for artillery his old palace, Saltwood Castle, where (it is supposed) the murder of Becket was plotted; here he had Henry Yevele, the great architect and military

Cooling Castle, in Kent, was a manor-house strongly fortified during the French invasion scare at the end of Edward III's reign. Its powerful outer gateway with flanking towers is perfectly preserved.

engineer, construct for him a new great gatehouse, with gunslits just like Canterbury's, together with massive water defences.

With the fifteenth century cannons really began to win sieges, if not yet battles. Henry IV was the first English king with a practical knowledge of guns and what they could do. He had fought with the Teutonic knights, with the Genoese against the Moors and with the Hungarians against the Turks – and it was in these great East–West conflicts that cannon were first used on a big scale. Henry, who knew how cannon were cast and produced, stepped up the Tower's programme. In 1405 his big guns quickly reduced the Earl of Northumberland's strong castles at Berwick, Alnwick and Warkworth. The captain of Warkworth, having boasted he could hold it against all comers, surrendered after only seven terrifying shots. Henry V inherited his father's expertise and enthusiasm. For the siege of Aberystwyth in 1406 he had a gun-train shipped round from Bristol; and he used cannon to take Harlech. Guns were probably more trouble then they were worth in a field action; Henry had none at Agincourt, and the French battery there did them no good. But Henry used big cannon against Harfleur in 1415, and it was his siege-train which enabled him to take all the important French castles in Normandy, and so annex the province – something the Black Prince had never been able to do. Conversely, it was the French predominance in artillery – they had bigger and better guns, and more of them – which made possible their reconquest of Normandy in Henry VI's reign. When they took Caen in 1450 they had twenty-four bombards, each so large, it was said, that a man could sit inside its barrel without lowering his head.

The development of really powerful cannon gave central authorities in all the states of western Europe an opportunity to establish their power over feudal or bastard-feudal lords, who tended to lack the resources to acquire siege-trains or to build fortresses capable of withstanding them. We have seen how, in the twelfth century, Henry II effectively raised the cost of military technology, made cheap castles obsolete, and so turned the castle system from a promoter of anarchy into an instrument of royal supremacy. By the mid-fifteenth century artillery had produced a big and expensive jump forward in the arms race, with the added advantage (to the monarch) that the manufacture of gunpowder, and the casting of large cannon, might be enforced as a royal monopoly. In France and Spain, for instance, the crown seized its chance eagerly; there, cannons formed a central basis of the new despotism. In England, however, the crown missed its cue, at least for a time.

In theory, of course, cannon might have made the Wars of the Roses impossible. When royal cannon were deployed in force, anarchy melted away. Thus, in 1464, the Earl of Warwick, acting for the crown, made short work of Bamburgh. When Sir Ralph Grey refused to yield the castle, the Earl sent an order through his herald: 'We will besiege this castle seven years if necessary. For every gunshot which hurts a wall of this royal stronghold, this jewel, a Lancastrian head will fall.' He had five great guns, called London, Newcastle, Edward and Richard Bombartel, and Dijon. The last, made of brass, sent a large ball right through Sir Ralph Grey's own chamber, knocking him unconscious beneath the debris of his stone ceiling. The garrison took this opportunity to capitulate, and, when Sir Ralph came to, he was taken to Doncaster, tried and hanged.

But of course the siege-train belonged to Warwick, who was an expert artilleryman and one of the first to see the real possibilities of big guns. Cannon made him a kingmaker. The Lancastrian monarchy was too poor to establish a monopoly in the new military technology. There had been, in any event, a steady decline in royal revenues since the palmy days of Edward III, and during Henry VI's minority capacious noble hands were thrust into the royal till. Lord Cromwell, who as Lord Treasurer was one of the greediest, told the King and Parliament in 1433: 'Daily many warrantis come to me of paiementz . . . of much more than all youre revenuz wold come to, thowe they were not assigned afore . . . the which warrantes, yf I shuld paye hem, youre Household, Chambre and Warderope, and your Werkes, shuld be unservid and

unpaid. . . . ' Thus cannon, which should have worked to the advantage of the central power, in fact did the opposite.

Nor was this all. Lack of royal money also altered the internal balance in the number and strength of fixed fortifications. Cannon were of growing importance, but they had by no means yet rendered castles obsolete: witness the long defence of Harlech, a thirteenth-century design. Castles played a tremendous part in the conquest and loss of Normandy. But castles demanded even more money than cannon; so here again the penniless crown was disadvantaged. A king who, like William I, built a modern castle in every county town and at every important bridge crossing, and had it garrisoned with an adequate force under a loyal captain, was the absolute master. Again, Henry II ensured that all modern castles were either in his own hands, owned by trustworthy friends, or 'watched' by royal strongholds of at least equal power. This system lasted until the reign of Richard II, but broke down increasingly under the Lancastrian kings. They spent a lot of money on the northern castles, like Lancaster, Leicester, Pontefract, Bolingbroke and Tutbury. The great gatehouse at Lancaster, with its semi-octagonal towers, is a visible survivor of this policy. They also kept up a few major royal strongholds, chiefly in the south: Dover, Portchester, Pevensey, Southampton, Queenborough, Windsor and Nottingham. But many more of these strongholds were allowed to go to ruin; they were not even kept up as progress-houses or hunting boxes, let alone fortresses. The position deteriorated rapidly under Henry VI. Even when he came of age, he showed interest only in the educational foundations that he had established at Eton and King's, Cambridge. So the royal castles no longer provided a comprehensive system protecting and enforcing the crown's authority. In Wales, the Scottish borders and the Channel these castles still constituted a thin defensive line. But in the heart of England they left a vacuum. Hence, for the first time since the reign of Stephen, the midlands, parts of the south-west, East Anglia and much of the north were dominated by private castles. This was the military background to the Wars of the Roses.

The royal position improved radically under the Yorkists; and it was completely transformed under Henry VII who, by his multiple inheritances, his confiscations and his good housekeeping, acquired for the crown fully one-fifth of all the revenues of England – a position it had not held since the days of the Conqueror. So he and his successors were then able to take full advantage of the political consequences of gunpowder technology. Not only that: they were able to invest in the first post-gunpowder castles, as we shall see. But in the meantime, the castle still lingered on, if not in all England, at least in the north; and it is to the Borders that we now turn.

Opposite: Portchester, in Hampshire, was one of the enormous forts built by the Romans to resist sea-invaders in the 3rd century AD. The walls, still intact, are ten feet thick and twenty feet high, but the keep built in one corner is Norman.

CHAPTER FIVE

CASTLES AND
TOWERS OF
THE BORDERS

Barnard Castle was refortified early in the 14th century by Anthony Bek, the great Bishop of Durham, who added a magnificent hall at the same time. It has a fine rocky site overlooking the River Tees.

Previous page

left: Bamburgh, in the later Middle Ages, was a key defensive point on the north-east coast. In the 1890s it came into the possession of the armaments millionaire, Lord Armstrong, who remodelled it somewhat drastically in 'pseudo-baronial' style.

right: Warkworth Castle.

It is a curious fact that, while England's borders with Wales were the scene of endemic fighting from the time of the Normans onwards, the Scottish border was comparatively quiet until the end of Edward I's reign. This is not to say that castles were rare in the north. On the contrary. In Northumbria, which Sir Nikolas Pevsner calls 'the castle county of England', there are a great many of all kinds. The area never had an Iron Age, in fortress terms, and fortified sites date from Roman times; but many continued to be occupied until the sixteenth century. And, at all periods, houses were being turned into fortified towers, towers into keeps, new castles built and old ones brought up to date. The tendency was to add to the level of fortification as the Middle Ages progressed, and the Border threat grew.

A typical case is the Bishop of Durham's Norham Castle, on the upper Tweed. Of course the Bishop had his great castle in his palatine city. But his manor at Norham built about 1160 was originally only a fortified house, or hall-keep, protected on two sides by the river and on the others by a ravine and ditch. It had, of course, two wards, but the man-made defences were limited. Then, in the fifteenth century, it was considered necessary to turn the main defence into a ninety-foot tower keep. In Prudhoe Castle, by contrast, the original keep – perhaps the oldest of the Northumberland keeps – remains. This was built by the D'Umfravilles; and when the Percies took it over they found it unnecessary to add to its size. But they put up a fine gatehouse, with perhaps the earliest oriel window in England, and added a strong barbican in the mid-fourteenth century.

The Percies were not, originally, a Northumberland family. When William de Percy (called Aux Gernons, or 'Whiskers', hence Algernon) came with the Conqueror, he settled at Spofforth in Yorkshire, where he was given eighty-six manors. There he built Spofforth Castle, the family home for 300 years until their possessions in Northumberland grew so large that they moved to Alnwick. Spofforth is not really a castle at all, but a ruined strong-house, delightfully situated overlooking a stream and sited on a rocky outcrop. The house was licensed for

crenellation under Edward II, when the threat from the north first became acute, and most of the existing building dates from that time. Here, Hotspur was born, and one can still gather from the ruins an impression of what a wealthy lord's house was like in the north before security disappeared.

Aydon Castle, in Northumberland, was being crenellated and strengthened at almost exactly the same time as Spofforth. It had a position of great natural strength, but was comparatively lightly defended, without a keep or strong tower, until a licence was issued in 1305. Here is another early example of a fortified house rather than a castle. Haughton Castle, also in Northumberland, is a case of a hall-house being made into a castle, though a little later (1373). It is oblong, with four angle towers and a fifth, higher tower in the middle of the south front. The towers were added as part of the fortification, but the original house remained as the core. The same thing happened

Spofforth, the original home of the warlike Percies, and birthplace of Hotspur, is a ruined stronghouse, delightfully sited on a rocky outcrop overlooking a stream.

Opposite: Alnwick, the chief castle of the Percies, was expensively restored in the 19th century. On a beautiful river site, it is remarkable for the stone soldiers (18th-century replicas of the originals) placed on its battlements to puzzle enemy scouts.

at Featherstone, on the South Tyne, where the West Range is as early as the thirteenth century, but a strong tower with a tunnel-vaulted, fireproof basement was added after the disasters of Edward II's reign.

But in Northumberland the fourteenth century produced splendid new castles, as well as the refortification of older houses – at least a dozen in fact. While, farther south, the concentric castle and its modifications were being developed, up north they clung to the old-style keep, though they tended increasingly to fashion it into a tower-house. Chipchase, for example, has a large-scale tower-keep of the mid-fourteenth century (now accompanied by a Jacobean mansion with Georgian additions); it is fifty-three feet long by thirty-eight feet square, with a vaulted basement and three solid storeys above. Belsay Castle, even more impressive, is an oblong tower too, but with two wings in an L-shape. It is also equipped, as many northern strongholds were from this date, with bartizans or corner-turrets at the top.

Of course these bigger castles tended to be on ancient, or at least old, sites, where the defences were naturally strong and where wells could be sunk. Barnard Castle, refortified early in the fourteenth century by Anthony Bek, the great Bishop of Durham, was a Norman castle on high rocks overlooking the Tees, with a great round tower of sandstone ashlar before the bishop got possession, refortified it and built a magnificent hall. Bamburgh is also a natural site for a castle, formed by the precipitous outcrop of Whin Sill, rising to 150 feet, and giving the building one of the most impressive silhouettes of all English castles. There had been a fortress on the rock for centuries, and in the twelfth century it acquired a Norman keep and three baileys. Then, in the fourteenth century, it was massively fortified by the crown, and turned into one of the strongest castles in the north.

At Alnwick, the new headquarters of the Percies, the site was less strong, though the view of the castle from the river below is exceptionally fine. Here there was a Norman castle, much altered, when the Percies took over in 1309. They built a strong new curtain-wall, powerful wall-towers and an exceptionally ingenious gate and barbican, perhaps the best of its kind in England – certainly the most difficult to take, if we exclude the principal royal castles. Alnwick is also notable for its stone soldiers, or apotropaic figures, on its battlements. These are, in fact, eighteenth-century replicas, but such *tromp l'oeil* devices were common in medieval times to puzzle enemy scouts, provided the battlements were high enough (as at Caernarvon). They are also found at Raby and Hylton in County Durham and Bothal in Northumberland. Alnwick and Bamburgh formed, with Dunstanburgh, a trio of big, powerful castles which, in the later Middle Ages, held the key to the English north-east and its coast. The first two have suffered from injudicious restoration. Bamburgh was acquired in the 1890s by the armaments millionaire, Lord Armstrong, and drastically rebuilt in what he imagined to be baronial style; as one architectural historian put it, 'the acme of expenditure with a nadir of intelligent achievement'. Alnwick was rebuilt twice, first in the 1760s, when it was 'gothicized' in the Strawberry Hill manner; then in the 1850s and later, much more fundamentally, when the 4th Duke of Northumberland spent £250,000 on modernizing and beautifying it inside and out.

On the other hand we do possess two outstanding and unspoilt examples of great fourteenth-century Northern castles. Dunstanburgh, the third of the trio, has been uninhabited now for centuries. It is on an immensely strong natural promontory of basalt, sticking out into the sea, which enabled walls to be dispensed with on much of the perimeter. Even today, it cannot be approached by car: there is a mile-and-a-half-walk over moorland rolling down to a wild sea, with the spectacular silhouette of the castle growing gradually nearer – a view made famous by one of Turner's finest paintings. There may have been an earlier fortified house here, but the chances are that Thomas, Earl of Lancaster picked on this spot for the first time, when he decided to build a great fortress after the English disaster of Bannockburn. The fortified area, over eleven acres, is enormous, enough to protect all the people and cattle

of the district against a raiding Scots army. The architect, Master Elias, the mason, had worked under James of St George, and it is not surprising that the main defence lay in the huge gatehouse, which also contained the great hall and the other state apartments. The castle was modernized in 1380–4, when another head of the House of Lancaster, John of Gaunt, was lieutenant of the Scots Marches, and it remained one of the main fortresses of north-east England until the coming of the Tudors.

Warkworth, though also ruinous in parts, is an even better preserved example of what a major late-fourteenth-century castle looked like in the north. It had a long history, including two sieges by Scottish kings, before the Percies got it in 1332 and made it their favourite residence. They were at work on its defences throughout the rest of the fourteenth century and towards the end Hotspur's father, the redoubtable Earl of Northumberland who figures so prominently in Shakespeare's *Henry IV Part One*, built a completely new tower-keep. This has been acclaimed, by Pevsner and others, as one of the finest achievements of any medieval architect in England. It is of great size, capable of accommodating the earl and his family, a sizeable body of armed retainers and enough stores for a long siege. It is completely self-contained, and could have been defended for months even if the outer defences of the castle fell. Yet within its powerful walls there is a considerable degree of comfort and, even more remarkable, light, let in by a central lantern and ingeniously placed interior windows. In short, the architect, by carrying a little further the principles of the 'collapsed courtyard house', which we have seen illustrated at Nunney and Old Wardour, has gone a long way towards resolving the perennial conflict between ease and security. As a workmanlike late-medieval fortress–palace, Warkworth is without equal.

Of course, we must lament the times, and the misjudgements, which made such structures as Warkworth and Dunstanburgh necessary. We shall have something to say in the next chapter about the events which led to Edward I's intervention in Scottish affairs, and the consequences for Scotland. Here it is enough to note that the results for the borders, on both sides, were disastrous for more than 300 years. Nature had always made this a poor area, at any rate by the standards of southern England – or even southern Scotland. In the Middle Ages the countryside had to support many more peasants than it does now. In Tudor times the population of Liddesdale, Teviotdale, Redesdale and Tynedale was about three times as high as at the end of the eighteenth century. The social structure was primitive, even pre-feudal in some ways. In Tynedale and Redesdale the institution of gavelkind, which divided landed inheritances equally between the sons, led to a proliferation of small, uneconomic farms. Hunger had a tendency, even at the best of times, to breed violence, raiding and spoliation, and so more hunger.

The consequence of English invasion, and Scots counter-invasion, was the institutionalizing of violence. On both sides the raid, hitherto an anti-social but understandable product of hunger, became a feature of public policy. The area ceased to be policed in the normal way and became a perpetual theatre of national revenge. Raiding, whether for oneself or for the rival crowns, became a profession, almost the only one, as poverty increased and farming for the market became more hazardous. Time made matters worse, not better. Certainly, under the Tudors, English crown policy became systematically ruthless. At Berwick, their great fortress, grain had to be imported from Yorkshire and butter from as far away as Suffolk; but government showed no desire to encourage local production by putting down violence. On the contrary Henry VIII, for instance, deliberately incited the English border clans to mount tribal raids. On his orders the Earl of Northumberland agreed 'to let slip them of Tynedale and Redesdale for the annoyance of Scotland'. The king commanded his official, Sir William Eure, 'to let slip as many under his rule as should do the Scots three hurts for one'. In 1534 an expedition into the Scots borders led by Sir Ralph Eure and Sir Brian Layton destroyed 192 fortified towers, bastels and churches. The Earl of Hertford, later

Opposite: Warkworth is the fortress-palace of the fighting Percies of Northumberland; it was cleverly designed to provide, in addition to strong defences, comfortable living accommodation for the Earl and his family.

Protector Somerset, commanded a similar expedition in 1544. Even under the peaceable Elizabeth, the Earl of Sussex, after the Northern Rising of 1569, harried deep into Scottish territory, though the two countries had a peace treaty and were nominally allies. The Scots also mounted raids, chiefly to steal cattle and, above all, horses. They went south of the Tyne on many occasions, and into Weardale and Westmorland. As late as 1596 some of them broke into Alnwick Castle, trussed up the watch, and stole all the horses.

Except in periods of total war there was a system of a kind. The entire border area was divided into three marches, East, Middle and West. The Scots Eastern March ran from the sea to the Hanging Stone on the Cheviot, embracing the coast up to the Lammermuir Hills and all eastern Berwickshire. It was dominated by such clans, or 'names' as the Homes of Home Castle, and the Wedderburns of Fast Castle. On the English side the East March consisted of north-east Northumberland, the area around Norham Castle and most of the Durham palatinate, with the River Aln forming the southern boundary. Herons, Selbys and Greys were the big 'names'. Berwick was the capital.

The Scots Middle March was the rest of Berwickshire, and Roxburghshire, administered from Kelso and Jedburgh. On the English side, there was the rest of Northumberland, plus Tynedale and Redesdale, and Belingtonshire in the Palatinate. Alnwick was the administrative centre, and there were also garrisons at Harbottle and Chipchase, ready to 'let slip' such obnoxious 'names' as the Ogles, Collingwoods, Fenwicks or Widdringtons. On the western side the Scots March included the areas administered from Kirkcudbright and Dumfries, and Annandale, dominated by the Maxwell clan of Caerlaverock Castle, and the Johnstones of Lockwood. The English West March was run from Carlisle, and garrisons kept at Askerton, Bewcastle and Rockcliffe. The big 'names' were the Lowthers, the Carletons, the Salkelds and the Musgraves.

It is significant that wardens of these marches first appeared in the early fourteenth century, when the whole security

Far left: Norham Castle was a fortified manor-house of the Bishops of Durham, reinforced in the 15th century by a ninety-foot tower-keep. It played a key role in the defence of the East March against the Scots.

Left: Illustration from Holinshed's 'Chronicle' showing English troops rounding up Scots cattle in retaliation for a raid. The innumerable Pele towers and fortified houses and churches of the Borders were the products of 300 centuries of ruthless border raiding, which lasted from the early 14th century to the union of the two crowns under King James I and VI of Scotland in 1603.

position deteriorated. On the Scots side the chief officers and their subordinates were always local nobles or lairds, for the crown could not afford to pay anyone. This was part of the trouble. On the English side, too, the biggest families, such as the Dacres, Cliffords, Percies and Nevilles, were always prominent in the warden system; but gradually, and especially under Elizabeth, the crown insisted that the key posts be paid by 'inland men', on salary and allowances, whose personal interests did not conflict with those of the state.

The duties of wardens were similar to those of sheriffs, but also included national defence, and the administration of a complex system known as the *Leges Marchiarum*, or Border Laws, drawn up by the agreement of both sides but qualified by many local by-laws. In some ways they were more savage, in others milder, than the common law of either country. In general they reached back to a much earlier age. The punishment for many forms of wounding was a cash compensation; slaughter was not a capital offence until the 1560s. On the other hand, a thief could be 'forbidden by sound of trumpet from all places' – this was 'putting to the horn' of outlawry. Every man had to be able to find sureties at all times, and this meant he had to have a 'name', that is belong to a clan which took responsibility for him. But sometimes a whole name would be put to the horn, and it then became what was known as a 'broken clan'.

Opposite: Caerlaverock, near Dumfries, dominates the invasion route into Scotland from the south-west. Built in the 1290s, it is triangular-shaped with a massive gatehouse at its apex and a deep moat.

Broken men, or clans, had no alternative but to live by crime, and they usually infested remote areas where the law could not easily operate. The worst was Liddesdale. The area of Longton and Canonbie, on the West March, was a kind of no man's land, infested by broken Grahams, Armstrongs and Bells. In 1551 a joint commission, almost in despair, reached back into the Dark Ages for a solution and built an earthwork, known as the Scottish Dyke, to hem in these dangerous men.

Though killing was lightly punished, other offences were 'border treason', high treason or felony, all punished by death. These included (in England), harbouring, aiding or accompanying a Scot engaged on foray and supplying arms and other listed commodities without licence. Receiving stolen goods, or 'recetting' was heavily punished, as was intermarriage with the Scots, selling them horses, 'trysting', crossing the border without a licence and moving stock across it. But it was one thing to proclaim laws, another to enforce them. The warden could order a 'Warden Rode' or raid, to hunt down a malefactor or extract revenge; all able-bodied men were obliged to respond to his call for a day and a night. Such raids, unlike harryings, did not require the sovereign's consent, because of the need for speed in recovering stolen goods. Sir Robert Cary, a famous Middle March warden, has left an account, in his *Autobiography*, of such a raid, which he carried out personally with his two deputies, sixty gentlemen and a hundred lesser men, the last armed with spears, bows, steel hats and jacks (protective jackets). This raid was directed against the Armstrongs, who despised fixed defences and took refuge in the wilds of Tarras Moss. Carey built a 'pretty fort' to hem them in, then invested the Moss on two sides, recovered the cattle and captured five leading members of the clan.

In addition to the raid, really a measure of desperation or last resort, there were guard duties of watch and ward, which applied to all hale men. Bishop Ridley, born in the tower of Wilimostewick, near Haltwhistle, recalled: 'In Tynedale, when I was a boy, I have known my countrymen watch night and day in their harness, such as it was, that is in their jacks, and their spears in their hands.' Permanent watch was kept on fords, passes and all fortified buildings; strangers were challenged, and if their explanations were unsatisfactory, 'taken before bailiffs and constables to be tried'. If raiders were known to be out, the full watches or 'plumps' were called out, forty men replacing the normal two. There was a network of beacons and signal stations, controlled from Carlisle on the English side and from Home Castle in Scotland. These were often piles of logs, 700 feet up the hillside; or grates suspended from stone lanterns on the roofs of houses and castles. One fire burning meant raiders were coming; two, coming fast; four, in great strength. The regulations stipulated that: 'Every man that hath a castle or tower of stone shall upon every fray raised in the night give warning to the countrie by fire on the topps of the castle tower in such sort as he shall be directed from the warning castle, upon paine of 3s 4d.'

The system depended on the existence of towers or castles every two or three miles. Then a pursuing posse could be collected swiftly. Such squadrons carried burning peats on the points of their lances – 'hot trod' (trod meant track). The law allowed 'parties grieved to follow their lawful trod with hound and horn, with hue and cry, and all other manner of fresh pursuit, for the recovery of the goods spoiled'. This was also called 'going the dog' (i.e. with bloodhounds). Failing to follow a lawful fray was punished with fines, even imprisonment. To obstruct a pursuer on 'lawful trod' was a crime. A thief, taken 'with the red hand', might be lawfully slaughtered on the trod, provided it was 'hot'. But a pursuer could 'forefeit his trod' by not abiding by the rules.

The system radiated from the various big castles. Indeed, castles were essential not merely for defence but to act as prisons. On the Scots side the strongest prison was the vast and gloomy fortress of Hermitage, which dominated the wildest stretch of the frontier and was frequently hung with hill mist. This rectangular brown sandstone tower-house, still intact except for roof and ceilings, is a kind of Dracula-place in Scottish legend and history, associated with the wicked Lord

Hermitage, the most frightening of the old Scots border strongholds, is in Scottish legend one of Dracula's haunts, associated with the wicked Lord Soulis. It was Sir Walter Scott's favourite castle.

Soulis, believed to be possessed by the Devil. Of course Liddesdale, the most criminal of the dales, invited rough justice. Here, in 1342, the Knight of Liddesdale, Sir William Douglas, disposed of Sir Alexander Ramsay, a friend of the English, by starving him to death in the castle pit. It was Sir Walter Scott's favourite castle, and he chose it for the background of his portrait by Sir Henry Raeburn. The building, he said, was partly sunk in the ground, 'unable to support the load of iniquity which has been long accumulating within its walls'; and he reported that 'its ruins are still regarded by the peasants with peculiar aversion and terror'.

In truth it was the existence of Hermitage which enabled any law whatever to be enforced in this part of the world, for at least it was difficult for malefactors to escape, or to be rescued, once they were in there. Carlisle was the main prison–fortress on the English side. Its prison-rooms in the keep can still be seen and they are remarkable for the touching, if primitive, carvings which poachers, raiders and victims of the Wars of the Roses fashioned on its soft sandstone walls. But escapes from Carlisle were frequent. In 1596 the castle housed Kinmont Willie, a leading Border ruffian, who was believed, at least by the Scots,

to have been seized in defiance of local law and custom. After spies reported that the castle was 'surprisable', Sir Walter Scott of Buccleugh and his supporters worked out details of a raid, under cover of a horse-race at Langholm (such sporting meetings were the usual occasion for conspiracy). So two hundred raiders assembled at Morton, a tower belonging to Kinmont, and equipped themselves with ladders and 'instruments of iron for breaking through the cells and forcing the gates if need had been.' They crossed the River Eden, which was in spate (it was April) and landed on Sauceries Flat in Carlisle, now a park. Stones were hacked away from the postern to allow the bolt to be moved and the raiders rushed in, sounding trumpets. They knew where to find the prisoner, who does not seem to have been chained or locked in a dungeon. Lord Scrope, the warden, ruefully reported that the watch 'by reason of the stormy night were either on sleep or gotten under some covert to defend themselves from the violence of the weather'. He suspected collusion and blamed 'the viperous generation' of Grahams, 'those caterpillars'.

But the focus of Border warfare and social life was not so much the big castle as the pele tower or fortified house, of which there were hundreds. The word 'pele' has caused some confusion. It comes from *pilum*, a stake or palisade, and whether spelt pele or peel it covers a variety of defensive buildings. Originally there were thorn circles, called lodges, for cattle. Then came wooden palisades, with 'bratiches' or timber screens added. These were slowly replaced by walls of turf and clay, reinforced by timber, with a ditch or 'fill-dyke' around. This whole fortified area was known, from the *piles* or pales, as a pele. Then towers of turf and clay, or timber, were built within the stockade – the cattle on the ground floor, humans above, in a room reached only by a ladder. These structures began to be made with stone, a common practice by about 1550. When stone was also used to replace the outer stockade, the area was known as a barmkin, and the tower became the pele. But in this usage it may originally have signified timber rather than stone: the Scots privy council instructed all substantial men to build barmkins of stone and lime sixty feet square, and lesser men to build 'peles of great strength' to house their stocks and neighbours. Only in the seventeenth century did a tower belonging to a pele, or a tower within a barmkin, get itself called a pele; and it was some time, too, before barmkin began to stand for courtyard, as opposed to the wall which surrounded it.

This type of fortified building already existed in England in the thirteenth century, as we can see at Dally, Tarset Castle, Shortflatt and Shield Hall. But the breakdown of security in the fourteenth century forced substantial farmers and squires to build many more. A list, dating from 1415, of all the Northumberland castles contains over a hundred names, most of them of a pele type – Raw Pele, Highshaw, Iron House, Black Middlings Pele, Barty's Pele, Shillar Hill, Evistones, Branshaw, Rattenraw, Shittleheugh, West Woodburn Pele and many others which still exist. An alternative to the stone tower, which was really a miniature keep, was the small fortified house, longer, narrower and lower, and called 'bastels', after the French *bastille*. Such bastels as Akeld, near Wooler, Gatehouse in North Tynedale and The Hole in Redesdale have walls about five feet thick, compared with ten in many towers. Such buildings rarely had a barmkin; the entrance was by external stone steps, and stock was usually kept in the vaulted basement floor, or pend.

After the 1569 rising the Earl of Northumberland and his lady sought refuge in such a place, in Liddesdale, owned by Jock o'the Side, and found it 'a cottage not to be compared to any dog-kennel in England'. Some years later, across the border also, Christopher Lowther found the houses of the Grahams 'but one little stone tower, garretted and slanted, or thatched, some in the form of a little tower not garretted, such be all the lairds' houses in Scotland'.

South of the border, the typical tower was a solid square mass of local grey stone, forty feet by fifty, and much smaller within. The earlier towers were grander, built of dressed stone, sometimes six storeys high. But as more and more families found it necessary to build one, they shrank to three storeys or

less, and undressed stone was used. There were slits in the walls, or perhaps one window. The essential was that the pend should have a stone vaulted ceiling, and thus be fireproof. The next floor was the main one, of hall, dining-room and kitchen, and was reached by a trapdoor in the vault of the pend, or a ladder outside. The men slept on this floor, which had a huge fireplace, and a chimney tapering into the roof. The window was shuttered (not glazed), with a window seat or 'shot window'. Above were bedrooms, then a steep-pitched roof, with thatch or, better, stone slabs. On it was a 'clan bell' or a grid for the alarm beacon. The corners were equipped with stone bartizans, or wooden structures, from which missiles could be dropped or flung. There might be a spiral staircase in the thickness of the wall, arranged as a 'turnpike', clockwise, so that the sword-arm of the defender, but not the attacker, would be free – unless he was left-handed. There were often two doors, the outer of oak studded with nails, the inner an iron yett, reinforced by a heavy wood beam which extended several feet into the wall on either side.

Tower and tower-houses are still common on both sides of the border. There is an excellent example of the smaller type of tower at Smailholm, between Melrose and Kelso. It is built of blue whinstone, on top of a hill, with rocks on three sides and water on a fourth, and dates mainly from the fifteenth century. The tower has four storeys and walls nine feet thick. There is only one window in each wall. The defences include an iron yett, with a bolt three inches in diameter, a tiny barbican before the inner door, and a partially destroyed barmkin wall, with a little chapel within. Of the larger types of tower-house one of the finest is Cocklaw Tower, near Chollerton in North Tynedale. This massive tower is forty by fifty feet, and entered through a door in the south wall, which is fifteen feet thick, and built of great ashlar blocks. A door on the right of the entrance leads to a spiral staircase in the thickness of the wall, and opposite is the guardroom, with a dungeon below. As usual, the only entrance to the dungeon is by a trapdoor.

Even in the sixteenth century the border lairds and squires

who lived in these little fortresses had a way of life which was medieval in its austerity, though their lands might be extensive. Sometimes, in addition to the tower, the owner had a farm-house for himself, and separate quarters for the servants, using the tower only in times of active raiding or war. Carey writes of one of the Grahams having 'a pretty house, and close to it a strong tower for his own defence in time of need'. It was rare to have glass in the windows. The walls were plastered and whitewashed, and sometimes they, and the tables, were decorated with carpets from Turkey and Persia. The floors were still strewn with moor grass and rushes, sweetened with heather and thyme, even in the reign of Elizabeth. Chairs were uncommon, and bedsteads come in only with the Tudors. Chests, settles and stools figure in inventories and wills, together with blankets, tablecloths, cushions and pillows. Other examples of 'insight', as household possessions were called, are rare.

Across the border, in Scotland, the lairds dressed scarcely better than their men. The food was meat, cheese, barley (in broth); bread was rare, and usually made of pease, beans and barley. But the gentry, on both sides, drank wine. Mary Queen of Scots, after her defeat at Langside, wandered in this region for three night, 'like the owls', and complained that she got only sour milk and oatmeal – no bread. In some areas the poverty was even more acute and their inhabitants reviled by outsiders. The people of Liddesdale were termed 'limmer' thieves – that is, all able-bodied inhabitants were thieves by profession. Liddesdale men talked of people beyond the passes, or 'swires', as foreigners. They, like the Armstrongs and Grahams, thought of themselves as neither English nor Scots, and treated all strangers as enemies. There was not a single road in Liddesdale until well into the nineteenth century. Redesdale and Upper Tynedale were not much better. Until 1771 the Newcastle Company of Merchant Adventurers forbade its members to hire labour from these dales, on pain of a £20 fine.

Yet even, or perhaps especially, broken clans could provide formidable fighting bands, otherwise they would not have survived at all. In about 1550 the Grahams were said to be able to put five hundred men into the field; fifty years later, their leader, Rob Graham, properly bribed, could gather 'two or three thousand men useful to England'. The Armstrongs topped the 3,000-mark of armed men at times. Such men formed the nucleus of English raiding parties and *chevauchées*, and took the lead in storming tower-houses. Sir Ralph Eure, under Henry VIII, left a description of the taking of a tower with a border band. He said they 'went to a tower of the Lord Buccleugh, called Mosshouse, and won the Barmkin and gat many nags and nolt and smote very sore the tower and took thirty prisoners'. His men smashed the barmkin gate with axes, 'scumfishing' those in the tower by heaping damp straw against the walls, then lighting it. They 'wickered' the door by piling brushwood against it, burning it, then wrenching open the yett with crowbars. Carey often scaled towers with ladders. On one occasion he used a party of Carlisle burghers 'to get to the top of the tower and uncover the roof'; then twenty of them jumped down. But, as with any other kind of castle, surprise made all the difference. We have an eyewitness description of the taking of Lockwood Tower, Annandale, in 1547:

We came there about an hour before day; and the greater part of us lay close without the barmkin. But about a dozen of the men got over the barmkin wall, and stole close into the house within the barmkin, and took the wenches and kept them secure within the house till daylight. And at sunrise, two men and a woman being in the tower, one of the men rising in his shirt, and going to the tower head, and seeing nothing stir about, he called to the wench that lay in the tower, and bade her rise and open the tower door and call up them that laid beneath. She so doing and opening the iron door, and a wooden door without it, our men within the barmkin brake a little too soon to the door. For the wench, perceiving them, leapt back into the tower, and had gotten almost the wood door to. But we got held of it so that she could not

Opposite: Prudhoe, in Northumberland, is an ancient castle of the D'Umfravilles, with a fine gatehouse added by the Percies. It has the first stone keep in the area and the earliest oriel window in England.

get it close to. So the skirmish rose, and we leapt over the barmkin and broke open the wood door. And she being troubled with the wood door left the iron door open: and so we entered and won the Lockwood.

Not surprisingly, in these wild parts, a clergyman preferred to become a participant rather than a helpless spectator. The church and church property were frequently attacked. Senior clergy threw their weight behind authority. Wolsey, as Archbishop of York, put Tynedale, 'that evil country', under interdict. Richard Fox, Bishop of Durham, used the 'greater' excommunication against the robbers of Tynedale and Redesdale. Gavin Dunbar, Archbishop of Glasgow, published a solemn, 1,500-word curse, damning the Scots reivers. Clergy were sometimes on the lists of men 'known' to the authorities. In the remoter dales, thought Fox, the clergy were an infamous lot: 'They keep their concubines. They are irregular, suspended, excommunicated and interdicted clergy, ignorant almost entirely of letters, so that for ten years they cannot read the words of the mass. . . . And some are not ordained at all . . . in profaned and ruined places, with vestments torn, ragged and most filthy . . . and the said chaplains administer the sacraments to thieves, without compelling them to restitution'.

The truth is that the clergy took on the colouring of the people among whom they lived. In areas where the king's writ ran they followed the lead of the bishops and even took part in the watch, as the Border Law obliged them to do. More, they built towers themselves. Vicar's peles are still found at Alnham, Elsdon and Corbridge. The one at Corbridge has three storeys, each of a single room. The lowest, the cellar, is vaulted; then there is a parlour; then a study-bedroom. The door on the ground floor leads directly to the cellar, lit only by narrow slits. Behind this door, which is made of wood, fireproofed by iron plating, there is a straight stair up, with a stone hand-basin at the top. The main room has a good fireplace, a window with stone window-seats, a privy and wall-presses. The bedroom has no fireplace, but a unique stone book-rest. There is a

defensive parapet on the tower, with square turrets at the corners and embrasures fitted with shutters. In addition many church towers were made defensible in the later Middle Ages. One such is at Burgh-by-Sands, Cumbria (c. 1330), though the top of its three storeys has been destroyed. As with almost all stone border towers, the bottom storey is vaulted, to make it fireproof. It is entered by the west end of the church, and protected by an iron yett with oak panels. There are other fortified church towers at Newton Arlosh, not far away, and at Great Salkeld, a few miles north of Penrith. The last has a tower built at the end of the fourteenth century, five storeys high, with an embattled parapet; the basement and the first storey are vaulted, and the entrance is barred by a yett. Higher up there was living accommodation. Of course, the fact that a priest lived in his church tower does not make it a fortified one; in many such cases there is no trace of defences. But in Bedale, Yorkshire, the upper part of the tower was a fortified priest-home; and it had a portcullis, which barred access to the spiral staircase leading to the upper floors.

If even priests had to defend their bedrooms as far south as the Lake District, Lancashire and Yorkshire, we are not surprised to find that castles of all kinds continued to be maintained and modernized there long after the south and the midlands had been 'reduced to civility'. Cumbria, indeed, in addition to royal castles of Norman origin, like Carlisle and Penrith (once a Neville stronghold), has numerous fortified buildings of all types, though many of them date, in their origins or present form, from the Scots threat of the fourteenth century. Thus Brougham Castle, just south of Penrith, at a point where the rivers Lowther and Eamont meet, has a typical keep of the reign of Henry II. But it was radically reconstructed early in the fourteenth century, with a new outer gatehouse, so that the keep and inner and outer gatehouses combine to produce one of the most formidable entrance-systems of the time – very similar to the contemporary entrance-keep at Dunstanburgh. This castle was held by the Cliffords for four hundred years, and it was the last of their line, Lady Anne

Clifford (1590–1676), who devoted her long life and formidable energy to keeping up the castles of Cumbria; for, in addition to Brougham, she restored and repaired all the Clifford castles. These included Brough, high in the Pennines, built on an old Roman station, and surely one of the most magnificently situated of all British castles, and Appleby, Pendragon and Skipton. In the outer gatehouse at Brougham she erected a slab, to commemorate her work, which quotes Isaiah: 'And they that shall be of thee shall build the old waste places; thou shalt raise up the foundations of many generations; and thou shalt be called, The repairer of the breach, The restorer of paths to dwell in.' Of course she did it from caste and family pride, as well as for aesthetic satisfaction. The slab also lists her titles: 'Countess Dowager of Pembrook, Dorsett and Montgomery, Baronesse Clifford, Westmerland and Veseie, Lady of the Honour of Skipton in Craven, and High Sheiffesse, by inheritance, of the Countie of Westmerland'.

Pendragon Castle, which she restored, has a pele tower going back to the twelfth century; and there is another at Dovenby Hall, near Bridekirk, though it is covered by a Georgian front. Appleby Castle, too, has a twelfth-century tower, though it is really a keep, since this was a formidable castle, on a splendid site at the top of the town, overlooking a steep bank of the Eden, with moats marking the inner and outer baileys. Of the other great Cumbrian families the chief was the Dacres. Their principal house, in the sixteenth century, was Naworth Castle, near Carlisle, which is now a very agreeable and imposing medley of architectural styles, including a nineteenth-century tower by Anthony Salvin. But the heart of the castle is, as one would expect, a fourteenth-century tower, built in fear of the Scots, which is still equipped with a yett, now rare south of the Border. The original Dacre stronghold was at Dacre itself, and the castle there is still intact and lived-in, though it is not so much a castle as (again!) a fourteenth-century pele tower, with strong projections or buttresses at each corner, one of which contains the staircase. As usual with well-built pele towers, this has a tunnel-vaulted, fireproof basement.

Among the best Cumbrian peles there is Sizergh Castle, of a type consisting of the tower itself, a hall range, and then later enlargements. This has belonged to the Strickland family since 1239, though evidently everything was pulled down to make way for the new tower, in the 1330s, when Edward III was resuming the war against the Scots. This is one of the largest of the pele towers, sixty by forty feet, and its walls are nearly ten feet thick at the foot, tapering to 5½ feet – though the upper windows, as often happened in such cases, were enlarged in the fifteenth century to let in more light, the worst Scottish threat having receded. The same thing happened at the splendid Isel Hall, the oldest part of which is the fourteenth-century pele tower, which had elegant windows punched in its walls under Henry VIII. Another fourteenth-century pele tower house is Yanwath Hall, two miles south of Penrith, on a bluff overlooking the Eamont. This tower has three storeys, including a hall-floor, now lit by Tudor windows; and it has four turrets, with the original fourteenth-century moulded octagonal chimney-stack, a great rarity. Of course, lower ranges were added later, to enclose a courtyard, and it is now a sizeable castle, with spectacular views of the Cumbrian fells from the top of the pele. One agrees with Thomas Marshall, the seventeenth-century historian of Westmorland that Yanwath 'hath a delicate prospect when you are at it, and hath the grace of a little castle when you depart from it'.

Cumbria's worst years were undoubtedly in the fourteenth century, especially under Edward II, when no undefended house was safe. But it has a long coast-line and Scots raiders from Galloway, arriving by boat, posed a threat until long after. In the grounds of Naworth Castle, for instance, there is a sixteenth-century bastle-house; this is a strong, stone structure, with room for cattle on the ground floor, and living quarters above with barred windows – the most elementary type of defensible house, the castle reduced to its barest essentials. And Cumbria was right to fear attack, for the raiders sometimes penetrated much farther south, especially into those parts of Lancashire and Yorkshire which could be attacked by

advancing down the wild axis of the Pennines.

In north Lancashire regular castles are rare. There is of course Lancaster, and the remains of a small castle at Clitheroe. But the number of pele towers testifies to the long continuance of raids. Piel Castle itself is a keep, rather than a pele; but its date (licensed 1327) indicates the Scots threat. At Hornby Castle there is a magnificent pele tower, which goes back to the end of the previous century, when Edward I was already looking north, though its top is from the time of the Tudors (a huge 'baronial' front was added in 1849–52). Some castle–houses, like Gawthorpe House, were built round pele towers; Broughton Tower is also built onto a pele, sixty feet high, with the distinguishing tunnel vault and spiral staircase. Other fourteenth-century pele towers are at Borwick, Broughton-in-Furness, Dalton-in-Furness and Gresgarth. But there are also a number of fifteenth-century towers, Turton Tower, for instance, Wraysholme Tower, and Greenhalgh Castle in Gardstang. Many of these defensive structures were kept in repair until comparatively modern times, and it is evident that parts of Lancashire were not considered secure until well into the seventeenth century.

On the other side of the Pennines, in North Yorkshire, big castles, as we have already noted, are common. But the Scots, at times, were able to penetrate this defensive system, and wealthy landlords continued to defend their property in stone long after great castles like Bolton, Sheriff Hutton, Danby Castle and Snape Castle, began to crumble – though the last, it must be said, was rebuilt by Lord Burghley's eldest son, Thomas Cecil, in Elizabethan times. More typical was Nappa Hall, near Askrigg, a manor-house built about 1460 by Thomas Metcalfe, with two towers and a hall between them. The big tower had four storeys, battlements, and a high turret containing the stairs. Mortham Tower, near Rokeby Park, is built around a fourteenth-century tower-house; it has *tourelles*, that is turrets corbelled out from the wall, and upright window-openings, unglazed, instead of battlements, and a staircase in one corner. Another fourteenth-century pele tower is Gilling

Castle; and there is a fine fifteenth-century pele, Crayke Castle, built by the Bishops of Durham on an old motte-bailey site. Gilling, though less charming than Mortham, was certainly stronger, being eighty feet square; it is now, like so many fourteenth-century peles, incorporated in a grand array of domestic buildings dating from Elizabethan times to the eighteenth century.

Generally speaking, from the crushing of the Northern Revolt (1569) onwards the north of England and the English Borders began slowly to relax their guard. The decisive moment came in 1603, when the two crowns were at last united, without bloodshed. To be sure, this brought an outburst of last-minute violence, known as the Ill Week. But James, though he could not handle the English parliamentary system, was extremely skilful and persistent in putting down baronial brigandage and general lawlessness, and he successfully defused the frontier. He abolished the wardenships and set up a commission, which ordered all strongholds to be demolished. It was said that some thirty to forty towers of the Eliots alone were razed to the ground. The Scots Privy Council commanded that 'all iron yettes' be hammered into 'plew irnis' (plough coulters); men were told to 'put away all armour and weapons' and to keep no horses worth above fifty shillings sterling or £30 Scotch. The regulations were enforced by Jedburgh Justice (i.e. hanging without trial). Sir George Home, the Earl of Dunbar, was put in charge of pacification on both sides of the Border. In 1606 he hanged '140 of the nimblest and most powerful thieves in all the Borders'. Other troublesome people were half pushed, half persuaded, to join the new 'plantations' in Ulster. Some had no choice in the matter: thus 149 Grahams were exiled, most of them to the Ulster glens; and the hard core of the Armstrongs, also, were shipped from the Solway to Belfast Lough. Some of the bigger border lords took a leading part in pacification, consolidating their estates in the process, and becoming leading nobles of the kings – this was how the Scotts, Dukes of Buccleuch, rose, and the Howards, Earls of Carlisle. It was rough justice, but when had the Borders known anything else?

Far left: Sizergh, in Cumbria, is one of the largest of the north-country pele-towers. Measuring sixty by forty feet, its walls are ten feet thick at the foot, tapering to five and a half feet. The Stricklands have lived here since 1239.

Left: Dunstanburgh, a vast castle of John of Gaunt, occupies a wonderfully strong natural site on a promontary overlooking the North Sea. Though very ruinous, and uninhabited for centuries, it has great dramatic power.

By 1611 the commissioners could report 'perfect and settled peace and quietness'.

Farther north still, however, Scotland continued to live in the age of the castle and the tower-house. Long after the Border problem was solved, new and very strong towers were being built by Scottish lairds. Coxton Tower near Elgin, for instance, set up in 1644, was completely stone-vaulted; except for the door and window-frames it did not contain a scrap of wood, and so was completely fireproof. The axes of the vaults were reversed in each room above the other, to spread the stress; and it was complete with a yett, machicolations and gunloops. It says a good deal for Scottish conditions that in the mid-seventeenth century a man still found it desirable to build a house capable of outfacing anything short of an army; and to Scotland we now turn.

123

CHAPTER SIX

THE
SCOTTISH
INHERITANCE

Huntingtower, a delightful Scottish castle, originally comprised twin towers, roofed over in the 16th century to form one fortified house. Inside it is notable for its brilliantly painted timbers.

Previous page
left: Castle Campbell, near Dollar, the original home of the great Clan Campbell, occupies a spectacular site in the Ochil Hills. Its romantic beauty belies its name of 'Castle Doom'.

right: Neidpath, overlooking the Tweed near Peebles, is a 15th-century tower-house. Ruinous but still roofed, it gives a clear idea of a working castle of a typical late-medieval Scots laird.

How many castles there are in Scotland is more a matter of definition than anything else. According to one calculation there are 1,185 castles and fortified houses, and this does not include known sites where virtually all traces of habitation have disappeared, or hundreds of baronial-style houses of the nineteenth and twentieth centuries which call themselves 'castles'. But it does include medieval towers and tower-houses. The biggest groupings are to be found in the border counties of Wigtown, Kirkcudbright, Dumfries, Berwick, Peebles, Roxburgh and Selkirk. What is striking about the historic castles in Scotland is not merely their quantity but the number which have survived into modern times and the high proportion which are still inhabited. To understand the reasons for this we must examine Scottish history.

The eastern coast and the lowlands of Scotland were penetrated by the Norman invaders, and their miscellaneous French and Flemish allies, almost as quickly as England itself. And, as in England, they introduced a feudal system based on motte-and-bailey castles. But in the twelfth century the Scottish ruling class (outside the Highlands and Islands) was almost exclusively recruited from families of Norman, Breton and Flemish origin. The Scottish royal house, under David I, who began his reign in 1124, his grandson Malcolm IV, William the

Lyon, Alexander II and Alexander III, who died in 1286, identified themselves completely with the French-speaking nobility and its feudal institutions. In 1212 Walter of Coventry called the Scots royal house 'French in race and manner of life, in speech and in culture'. These five kings all looked to the south and to the southern, foreign ideal. Two of them had English wives, and all, like David, who was Earl of Huntingdon, had English lands and titles. They created a new monarchy, on Anglo-Norman principles, based on four institutions: the spread of feudalism, the reform of the church on the lines William the Conqueror had followed in England, the plantation of burghs, and the personal royal control of government machinery.

Even the geographical balance of the kingdom tipped towards the south. David I frequently held his court in his castles of Roxburgh and Carlisle (the latter was Scottish until the time of Rufus). The earliest sheriffdoms were established from castles built at Roxburgh, Berwick, Edinburgh, Haddington and Linlithgow. Scotland as a whole was divided into 'governed' areas, where writs issued by the king would probably be obeyed, and 'ungoverned' areas, which he claimed in name but could not rule in fact. The governed areas were being progressively extended – first from the Lothians to Stirling, a great step forward; then up the east coast as far as Inverness. Primitive castles were built as administrative centres, as the Norman and Angevin kings did in Wales and Ireland. At the end of the thirteenth century, the sheriff was still essentially the head of a military district, enforcing castle-guard, which was the main service due, under feudal rules, from landholders. Royal and baronial burghs were set up as part of this civilizing process, and to provide manpower for the castles attached to each burgh. But until the reign of Alexander III, in the second half of the thirteenth century, Scottish kings behaved more or less like the English palatine Earls of Chester. In short, in administrative and institutional terms, Scotland was heading in the same direction as England, but was still a couple of centuries behind.

To some extent there was the same time-lag in military technology. Stone castles were rarities in Scotland until the thirteenth century. Where wood could not be obtained, turf and clay were used for defensive earthworks and walls. Where stone castles were built, they often occupied ancient natural defences, as at Dunbar, where the castle is on a headland, and its ruins are almost indistinguishable from the rocks on which it is built. Such sites, common on both west and east coasts, remind one of Tintagel: that is, a Dark Age defensive position surviving into feudal times almost in defiance of the principles of medieval architecture. Most Scottish castles built before the middle of the thirteenth century were simple towers. There was, for instance, a stone tower at what is now Traquair House, near Peebles and Innerleithen. This has a claim to be the oldest continuously inhabited house in Scotland, for the original

tower, which is near Ettrick Forest, was a royal hunting lodge under Alexander I. At Traquair, William the Lyon signed the charter which founded the abbey of Glasgow and endowed it with lands. The tower, now the north-east corner of the house, was an integral part of it until at least the reign of Mary Queen of Scots, for she stayed in the great chamber there, and it contains some of her fine embroidery; but by that time the house had grown into almost a French-style château, which was further added to in the reign of Charles I. The magnificent gates, according to Sir Walter Scott, were finally closed after 'the Forty-five', the owners swearing they would never be reopened until a Stuart was crowned again; and shut they remain. So the building is a microcosm of Scottish history.

Such primitive towers as originally constituted Traquair House were only slowly replaced by sophisticated castles. At Dirleton in East Lothian, a little past North Berwick on the Edinburgh coast road, a twelfth-century castle was built by the De Vaux family, who arrived in Scotland under the auspices of King David. William de Vaux, a favourite follower of William the Lyon (1165–1214), built the original castle, on a small craggy knoll at the east end of a long, low ridge of gently rising ground. Apart from its natural defences, it was not formidable, being chiefly of wood – certainly nothing to compare with such an implacable structure as Conisbrough, then rising in the north of England. But in the thirteenth century, when the richer lords were changing to stone, Dirleton was rebuilt in the French fashion. There are affinities with Coucy, in France; for the wife of Alexander II (1214–49) came from Coucy, and her seneschal was made lord of Dirleton. So the castle, already founded on solid rock, acquired massive walls of fine ashlar, a group of three towers at the south-west, plus two large round towers at the south-east and north-west corners. This rebuilding made it a formidable fortress. It was not, to be sure, on anything like the same scale as its English contemporary, Kenilworth, and unlike the latter it certainly introduced no innovations in military technology. But it indicated that the gap between England and Scotland was narrowing.

Threave, on an island in the River Dee near Castle Douglas, is a four-storey tower with enclosing walls, built by Archibald the Grim, one of the Black Douglas Earls of Nithsdale.

Opposite: Edinburgh's
castle, built on a huge
basalt rock 450 feet above
sea-level, has been
fortified since the 7th
century and bears traces
of military architecture
from every age.

In later ages the Scots looked back on the comparatively peaceful reigns of Alexander II and Alexander III with nostalgia, as an Augustan period; afterwards, 'Our gold was changyd into lede'. English people still regarded the Scots as strange and primitive. Henry III's daughter, Margaret, who became Queen of Scotland at the age of eleven in 1251, hated it, and complained piteously at what she regarded as her horrible experiences in Edinburgh Castle. But the English connection was close, and growing closer. Most of the earls and magnates of her husband also held lands of Henry III or Edward I, and were sometimes more active in England than in Scotland. There was a large group of Anglo-Scottish families. The house of Steward, or Stuart, itself was descended from the Breton family of FitzAlan, which was just as celebrated in English history, and originally came to Scotland from Shropshire. Henry III played a paternalist role in Scottish politics, as a sort of over-king; not surprisingly, for the Scottish monarch himself held land in England of the English crown.

But in this ambiguity lay the trouble. Alexander III, Edward I's brother-in-law, and a good friend of the English, died in 1286, leaving no direct heirs. The heir of the blood was Margaret, his grandchild, daughter of the King of Norway. The plan was to marry her to Edward I's heir, and so unite the kingdoms; but the 'Maid of Norway' died en route, leaving two competitors to the crown, John Baliol, a major English landowner and the eighty-year-old Bruce, grandfather of Robert Bruce the king, who had served England as a judge. Edward I was appealed to and agreed to act as arbiter, provided both competitors acknowledged him as superior lord of Scotland. The Scots grudgingly accepted this as the alternative to civil war, and they had no complaints about Edward's choice of Baliol, who undoubtedly had the better claim. But Baliol, once chosen, had to swear fealty to Edward I for the realm of Scotland, held of him as superior lord. This involved Edward's right to hear appeals from the Scots king, with forfeiture as the punishment for failure of the Scots crown to acknowledge appellate jurisdiction. The situation was analogous to the dispute over the Duchy of Aquitaine, which Edward held of the French king. In both cases a clash was inevitable, and the attempt of the superior lord to enforce his rights led to war. The truth is that the strict principles of feudalism were incompatible either with the institution of sovereign kingship or with national frontiers.

Edward I's attempts to assert what he regarded as his undoubted rights in Scotland led to a dramatic epoch of castle-building and siege-warfare over large areas of Scotland. The gap between Scottish and English military technology narrowed almost to vanishing-point, as Edward's repeated invasions familiarized the Scots nobility with the latest hardware and engineering. At one time all the lowland castles were under Edward I's control, and in 1296 he took many more north of the Forth, from Auchterarder to Elgin and from St Andrews to Aberdeen. That year he stormed and took the town of Berwick, and began to build a new fortress there, laying the first stone with his own hands. John Baliol submitted and left Scotland for good; all the Scots nobility performed homage to Edward, the proceedings being recorded in the Ragman Roll; but next year William Wallace began the struggle for Scottish independence, and thereafter Edward never had quite the same grip on the Scottish heartlands, though he captured Edinburgh, Stirling, Lochmaben and Jedburgh in the campaign of 1298.

Doubtless Edward's original intention was to repeat the strategy he used in Wales, and transfix Scotland in a vice of impregnable stone concentric castles, with burghs of English settlers attached. Certainly he tried hard enough, to the limits of his resources. Indeed, the Scots nationalists did not regard castles as neutral instruments of war, which might be held by them just as strongly as by the English invader. On the contrary, they regarded castles as practical symbols of foreign rule, and their usual policy was to 'slight' them. In this their instincts were manifestly sound. Where Edward failed was that he was too old, and too short of money, to press forward his castle-building policy vigorously enough. Indeed, he really

lacked the cash to build any new stone castles on the scale of his Welsh masterpieces. Of course he had a French war on his hands too; and bitter disputes with the church in England, and some of his subjects, over money. He was never able to give to Scottish strategy the same undivided attention he gave to Wales in the 1280s. In Wales he built carefully designed stone castles on strategically selected sites; in Scotland he built mainly in timber on sites others had chosen.

There were some flashes of his old vigour. At Dumfries, he vastly strengthened the existing castle by throwing up an outer ditch and wall. The royal accounts show that 276 ditchers were recruited for the works, plus eighty carpenters (though only fifteen masons, significantly). Adam of Glasson was the 'engineer', and working under him was a Cistercian monk, Brother Robert of Holmcultram, the chief carpenter. Edward inspected the works in person and, as usual, handed out cash gifts to the workmen – ten shillings to the carpenters, sixteen to the ditchers, five to the masons. At the siege of Bothwell Castle, in 1301, he took personal charge. This powerful castle had been built by a Scottish baron, Walter of Moray, and it had a massive circular donjon keep, with its own separate moat and drawbridge. (The present ruins bear the marks of the Scottish slighting in 1336, to prevent it again falling into English hands.) Edward had 6,800 men at this siege, and a huge detachment of skilled engineers and carpenters, plus twenty masons. The carpenters first made a bridge for the passage of the army to the site; then a formidable siege-tower, known as the Belfrey, constructed in Glasgow and brought, dismantled, the eight miles to Bothwell in thirty wains, or hay-wagons. He also had three big *balistae*, and twenty-three skilled miners from the Forest of Dean. The castle surrendered after three weeks.

Edward grumbled, according to the Lanercost Chronicler, that 'whatever he gained in summer he lost in winter'. So the only solution was to strengthen the castle infrastructure. In 1300 he had captured Caerlaverock, the newest and most formidable castle in south-west Scotland. This was a great prize, for it dominates Dumfriesshire and stood astride the natural invasion route into Scotland for anyone entering across the Solway Firth from Cumbria. Next to the eastern land-route, along the coast-road to Edinburgh, this was the quickest and most obvious way to take the Scottish lowlands. The English came across the Firth and built castles in Galloway to protect their bridgeheads. One such was Tibbers Castle, put up by Sir Richard Siward, a Scot in English service, in 1298. Caerlaverock also dates from the 1290s, and was probably of English construction: but it fell into Scottish hands.

Even today, Caerlaverock is hard to get to and very wet and marshy, with a moat stocked with rare wild geese and duck. It is a very strong building in fine deep-umber sandstone, in a striking triangular shape, with two giant towers and the gatehouse at the apex. This castle changed hands between the English and the Scots more often than any other (with the possible exception of Berwick), and it thus bears traces of many centuries. The gatehouse with its towers, and the bottoms of the towers at each end of the triangular base, belong to the original castle Edward beseiged. Edward entrusted the castle, after he had taken it, to the Maxwells, the leading local family. But they sided with the nationalists, when convenient, and declared for Robert Bruce in 1312 when Edward was dead. Over the centuries the Maxwells clung on to their possession, whether English or Scots were overlords; they did much building in the fourteenth century, and at the end of the fifteenth they added bartizans, which turned the gatehouse into a tower-house, following the Scots principle of building upwards, rather than the English habit of spreading out into a courtyard-style manor-house. In the 1630s Robert Maxwell, 1st earl of Nithsdale, built within the castle what was termed 'that dainty fabrick of his new lodging', with windows and columns in late-Renaissance style, not the only grim Scots castle to introduce a whiff of Italy in the seventeenth century. To judge by the initials carved in its soft stone, Caerlaverock was an early cynosure of Romantic ruin-fanciers, who recognized that here was perhaps the finest medieval castle in Scotland.

In accordance with his new all-weather policy, Edward spent

the winter of 1301–2 at the castle of Linlithgow, reconstructing it and fortifying it on a grand scale, and turning it into a palace too. He inspected the site with none other than James of St George, and afterwards the two men drew up an indenture, or letter of intent, for the work which James undertook to do; he was appointed 'souerayn ordenour des oueraynes que nous auoms deuisees a fair entour la fermete de Linliscu' ('high-commissioner of the works which we have commanded to be carried out in the fortress of Linliscu'). The work was carried through as quickly as Edward's money would permit, a hundred regular foot-soldiers being impressed, doubtless to their disgust, as labourers (at Dumfries Edward had even used women diggers).

The campaign of 1303–4, Edward's last big military effort and perhaps his most heroic, culminated in the siege of Stirling, the final military spectacular of his reign. Stirling has a strong case to be considered the finest natural fortress in Britain, stronger even than Edinburgh, though it springs from the same geological structure. It is a high, steep rock, with flat country all around, and though it slopes into the town of Stirling – its weakest side – it is otherwise abrupt, the views are magnificent, and its command over the roads and rivers of the area absolute. Even the modern approach, through the winding streets of the town, is very satisfying. Of course Stirling for centuries remained a fortress – it was a barracks as recently as 1964 – and little of the medieval castle survives, or rather is visible; its centrepiece is the superb Renaissance palace created by James v, built on three sides of a courtyard; chapel, hall and the palace rooms, consisting of two suites for the king and queen, each with gard-hall, presence chamber and bedroom. But the post-medieval defensive structure of counter-guard, nether-bailey and castle in the middle is not essentially different from the military problem which confronted Edward.

In his thorough and professional manner Edward concentrated first on getting his besieging army in the right places. The bridge over the Forth being denied to him by the Scots garrison (only thirty men, be it said), he had three prefabricated timber

Linlithgow was in turn a royal castle, a fortress-palace of Edward I, then a palace of the Scots royal family and the birthplace of Mary Queen of Scots. The ruins date from the 15th–16th century.

bridges made at Lynn, in Norfolk, under the supervision of Richard, his chief engineer at Chester. These are described as *major pons*, *medium pons* and *minor pons*, but each was defended by a bratice running over a drawbridge. They took three months to make, at a cost of £938 9s 6d, and were then loaded on thirty ships, led by two pilot ships carrying the carpenters' tools and chests of iron bolts for reassembly. It is interesting that Edward could not get work of this quality done on the spot. Indeed, sometimes in Scotland he could get no work done at all. Some sixty carpenters and two hundred ditchers he had ordered for work at Dunfermline Castle refused to come; they said he owed them so much in wages for work carried out at Linlithgow that they would choose exile rather than work for him again; and in the operations at St Andrew's Castle, six carpenters went on strike 'because they did not have their wages as they wished'. Edward not only had his bridges built in England, he took them back there, for storage at Berwick, after they had fulfilled their purpose.

For the siege itself the king assembled a collection of mangonels, catapults and other stone-throwing engines unique in British history. There were a dozen siege-engines big enough to have proper names: the Parson, the Vicar, Lincoln, Segrave, Kingston (the last two after commanders), Veweth Forester, Gloucester, and so forth. Among the engineers were Thomas of Houghton and both the Glassons, Robert bringing with him the engine with which he had taken Brechin Castle the autumn before. Kingston, named after the Constable of Edinburgh Castle, was brought by its engineer-in-charge, Robert of Bedford, from St Andrews. Another master-carpenter, Reginald, commanded Sir John Segrave's engine, Weland. The royal accounts list the thousands of yards of ropes and hawsers assembled for this great artillery concentration, and the tons of lead, for counterweights, stripped from church roofs for scores of miles around. Walter of Hereford, James's second-in-command, was in charge of the quarrymen making ammunition; and in the Stirling Forest, Sir Owen of Montgomery, a veteran of many Welsh sieges, had a gang of woodmen making mantlets and hurdles. Presiding over the whole siege-works, directly under the king, was James himself.

The siege began on 22 April 1304 and lasted twelve weeks. Edward and his second wife, Queen Margaret, lodged in the town, and the uxorious old man, always anxious to give his queen pleasure, had a special timber 'oriel' constructed to allow the queen and her ladies, safely out of shot, to watch the operations. Virtually every known method of warfare was employed, including Greek fire and, very likely, gunpowder. By the time the garrison was ready to surrender, on 20 July, Edward's carpenters had just finished making a new weapon, called a *loup de guerre*, or war-wolf. What precisely it was we do not know, but Edward was so eager to see this new engine in action that he forbade anyone to enter the castle until it had been fired at the walls.

For thirty Scots rebels to defy the military might of England for three months seemed to the king intolerable. Moreover, the capture of Stirling served nothing. The new settlement, in turn, was overthrown by Bruce's coronation in 1306 and further rebellion. At each phase in the struggle Edward responded with heightened savagery. At Berwick he hanged twelve Scots knights and put the Bishop of Glasgow in irons. He executed the Bishop of St Andrews and the Abbot of Scone, Wallace himself, the Earl of Atholl, Simon Fraser and Christopher Seton. Bruce himself he could not get his hands on, but Bruce's wife, sisters and daughters were taken from sanctuary into custody; one sister, Mary, was put in a specially constructed cage in a turret at Roxburgh Castle; the Countess of Buchan was fastened into a similar one at Berwick. The effect was to stiffen Scots nationalism (the fourteenth century saw the birth of nationalism in western Europe). With Edward dead, the Scots won Bannockburn and ravaged England down to Yorkshire; they followed this up with the Declaration of Arbroath, 1320, in which they stated: 'As long as there shall but one hundred of us remain alive we will never consent to subject ourselves to the dominion of the English. For it is not glory, it is not riches, neither is it honour, but it is liberty alone that we fight and

Opposite: Stirling, on a high, steep rock with flat country all around, is probably the finest natural fortress in Britain. In 1304 it was the site of Edward I's most spectacular siege, which lasted for twelve weeks.

Opposite: Tantallon in
East Lothian, perched on
high, wild and lonely
cliffs overlooking the sea,
and with a magnificent
medieval gatehouse, is
one of the most
impressive of all Scottish
castles.

contend for, which no honest man will lose but with his life.'

English pretensions were revived by the massacre of the Scots at Halidon Hill, outside Berwick, in 1333. Then followed a hundred years of fluctuating warfare – during which the Scots gradually drove the English out of the southern uplands, from Haddington to Dumfries – ending in 1460, when James II was killed regaining the castle of Roxburgh (Berwick was never finally retaken). As we have already seen, the effect on the Borders was tragic, for warfare there continued even when the rival kings were nominally at peace, or engaged in what Henry VIII termed 'rough wooing'. But the effects on Scotland itself were in some ways even more serious, for though the English could not maintain their presence in Scotland on a permanent basis, they could win battles, and ravage and destroy in their wake, as they did in France. In 1513 there was another 'official' war, leading to the great massacre of Flodden, in which James IV was killed. The Scots were again defeated at Solway Moss in 1542 and Pinkie in 1547. The English ravaging of the Scots Borders which we noted in the last chapter was sometimes followed by punitive expeditions deep into the central lowlands: in 1544 the Earl of Hertford plundered and burnt Edinburgh, Leith and Holyrood, Newbattle Abbey, Haddington, Burntisland and Dunbar, stealing 10,000 cattle and 12,000 sheep. The next year he sacked seven abbeys, sixteen castles, five market towns and 243 villages.

No wonder the Scots looked back to the time before 1287 as their golden age. In fact, life in the 'governed' parts of Scotland was better and more secure in the thirteenth century than it was 300 years later. The clock of progress was set back; or, rather, stood still, so that the distinction between governed and ungoverned areas persisted until the eighteenth century. This was despite military 'progresses' by the kings into the wilder parts, the surrender by the King of Norway of the Western Isles and the lands he held on the mainland, and the end of the Lordship of the Isles in the fifteenth century. There were many schemes for resettling the ungoverned lands and, in the reign of James VI, there were also plans to build colonizing burghs in

Kintyre, Lochaber and Lewis, with castles attached. But the independence of the highlands remained more complete than that of Ireland beyond the Pale.

One chief reason was the incompetence or misfortune of the Scots kings. Many of them came to the throne as infants, nearly always fatal for good government in the Middle Ages. The feudalism the royal line had promoted collapsed as a vehicle for unity and instead promoted faction. If a monarch survived his minority he risked being killed in battle against the English, like James IV. Of course the kings tried to reassert themselves. In the fifteenth century gunpowder and cast-iron guns (like Mons Meg at Edinburgh) came to Scotland, and were declared a royal monopoly; but here again the crown was unlucky, James II being blown to pieces when one of his cannon exploded at the siege of Roxburgh. The crown, as in England under Henry VI, was too poor to dominate the military scene. Most of the powerful castles were in private hands. There the nobles entrenched themselves, converting their government offices into hereditary tenures, and gradually acquiring inalienable rights of 'regality' (as well as the jurisdiction of 'pit and gallows' which they had always exercised). Scotland was not a united country, as is suggested by its division into diocese and shires, and the burghs and castles that were erected on the edges of the ungoverned lands were strongpoints, not administrative centres.

In these circumstances with the king merely first among equals, vigorous and successful families could compete with royalty, and this is reflected in the powerful castles they built from the fourteenth century onwards. Thus at Tantallon in East Lothian, the Douglases, Earls of Angus, built one of the greatest of all Scottish medieval castles. It is about two miles to the east of North Berwick, perched on high cliffs overlooking the sea, a wild and lonely spot which strongly recalls Dunstanburgh in Northumberland. Here, too, the sea-cliffs form natural defences of great power, and the immensely strong gatehouse, which is the main building of the castle, reminds us that Dunstanburgh and Tantallon were built in roughly the same

period (the Douglases often sided with the English, and may have had English technical assistance). But in addition the powerful, high fighting-platforms on either side of the gateway and the outer bailey with its vast earthworks – which spring vividly to the eye in aerial photographs – give more than a hint of the grim defensive system of Caerphilly. It needs no imagination to see that the family which controlled this castle could hold the road from Berwick to Edinburgh against anything less than a national army.

In the fourteenth century castles of comparable strength and importance were being built much farther north in Scotland, though they did not necessarily attain their mature form until much later. A case in point is Glamis Castle. Here we have a departure from the concentric-style castle, ultimately of Norman inspiration and commoner in the south, and instead a development towards the huge tower-houses which were Scotland's most characteristic form of military defence. Glamis is an old site, held by the Scots kings from a very early date. The old castle here was given by Robert I to John Lyon, Lord of Glamis, in 1376, on the occasion of his marriage to the king's daughter. Lyon at once began a major reconstruction, from which dates the earliest part of the present castle, the rectangular tower with a short wing attached to it at the south-east corner. It still occupies the central position among the accumulations of later centuries. The original medieval defences have gone, except for two wall-towers. The castle was much altered and expanded in the seventeenth century, again around 1800 and a third time during the Balmoral epoch. The central stairway was rebuilt (it winds round a large hollow stone newel, down the centre of which pass unseen the long cords and weights of the outside clock at the head of the stair-turret, making rumblings in the dead of night) and the upper parts of the tower above the fourth storey, with later roof and bartizans added. But an iron yett still defends the main entrance door at the foot of this stairway, and the heart of the castle remains the great tower which an independent Scots lord built to mark his growing power in the fourteenth century.

Cawdor Castle has essentially the same origins, a new strong tower built in the second half of the fourteenth century. It is true the licence to fortify dates from 1454, but the reason for this is that the tower was built by the crown, for Cawdor was a royal castle until James II gave it to the Thane of Cawdor, issuing a licence at the same time; a fortified tower should never be dated on the evidence of a licence alone. Cawdor Castle is rectangular, on a steep bank overlooking the little Cawdor Burn, which forms the western defence line, with deep dry ditches on the north and east, and the entrance guarded by a drawbridge over the ditch. The original square tower is in the centre, later ranges of building surrounding three small courts. The keep was originally of four storeys, the first and fourth (the two most vulnerable to attack) having stone barrel vaults. The Thane's alterations, from 1454, included a new, stronger doorway, with a yett, machicolations and bartizans on the top of the tower. Here, then, despite later alterations and additions, is one of the earliest of the big Scottish tower-houses.

Roughly contemporary with Cawdor is Borthwick, in Midlothian, south-east of Edinburgh. In some ways this is the most remarkable castle in Scotland. The 1st Lord Borthwick began to build it sometime after 1430, and the Borthwicks have lived there without a break ever since. More unusual still, the castle's original conception has not been substantially altered or added to in five and a half centuries. It is a massive two-slab tower, very grim and impressive, overlooking a wild and desolate valley, and protected on three sides by rivers and gorges. It has lost its original curtain-walls and flanking towers but in other respects it is intact. In fact it has had a fortunate history, being besieged only once, by Oliver Cromwell, who on 18 November 1650 summoned the then Lord Borthwick to surrender: 'If you shall necessitate me to bend my cannon against you, you must expect what I doubt you will not be pleased with' (the consequent damage can be seen). Whoever designed this castle was well in advance of his time; a hundred years later the same principles were being followed. Despite the simple plan there are an astonishing number of rooms,

Opposite: Glamis Castle lacks its old medieval defences but its rectangular tower, dating from the 14th century, is still the core, surrounded by later accumulations. Its gateway is still defended by an iron yett.

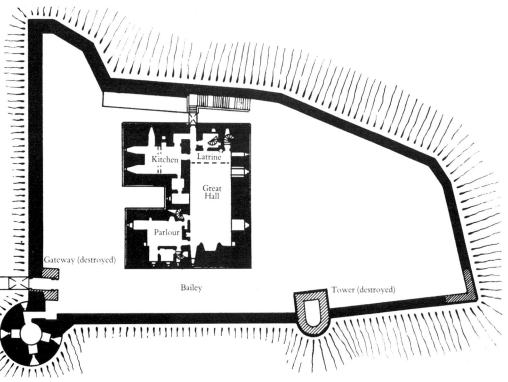

Kitchen

Latrine

Great
Hall

Parlour

Gateway (destroyed)

Bailey

Tower (destroyed)

At Neidpath, just outside Peebles and overlooking the Tweed, there is another fine fifteenth-century tower-house, this time a remodelling, by the Hays of Yester, of a former Border Fraser stronghold, built in the thirteenth century. It is a little ruinous, but still roofed, and gives a much clearer idea of a stark late-medieval laird's fortress than most Scottish castles of the period, which have been enlarged and modernized. It has none of the grim beauty and elegance of Borthwick: it is plainly a working castle. Such strongholds, uninhabited but still resisting the elements, are not uncommon in the Scottish lowlands and the hills of the south. There is a castle at Threave, on an island on the broad part of the River Dee in Kirkcudbrightshire, not far from the town of Castle Douglas. This is not, strictly speaking, a fifteenth-century castle, since much of the work in the four-storey tower is fourteenth century, though the outer enclosing wall dates from 1455. Its builder was Archibald the Grim, one of the Black Douglas Earls of Nithsdale; later it passed to the crown, who appointed the Maxwells as hereditary keepers. One's first glimpse of this fine stronghold, across the windswept waters, is not easily forgotten. One can see why Archibald sited it here: its role was both offensive and defensive, since it lies on the main invasion route from the south, and was a take-off point for plundering raids into England.

Of course, the Black Douglases were big people; Threave could, and doubtless often did accommodate a large raiding party. But every laird, even every bonnet-laird, had his tower, especially in such border areas. Not far from Threave, dominating a little valley south of Castle Douglas, is an excellent example of a minor fortress, Orchardton Tower, which has been well restored by the Department of the Environment. It dates from about 1450, and was built for the Laird of Orchardton, John Carnys. Carnys was a man of very modest means, and his tower is correspondingly rudimentary. It contains a ground-floor vaulted cellar; a main first-storey room which also served as a chapel, and a top-storey chamber or bedroom. The building served as a watchtower, for the sea could once be seen

passages and stairs. It is completely fireproof, all the principal rooms being stone-vaulted, and the topmost vaults are pointed, with a high-pitched stone slab roof laid on top. The stonework throughout is superb, the outer facing being of beautifully squared ashlar – 13,000 tons of it; and it has been estimated that the whole building must weigh at least 30,000 tons, for the tower is a good hundred feet high, and the walls are up to fourteen feet thick.

Far left: The ground plan of Borthwick, in Midlothian, a massive two-slab tower, very grim and impressive and intact except for its curtain walls and flanking towers. Overlooking a wild valley, it is protected on two sides by rivers and gorges.

Left: Orchardton Tower dominates a little valley south of Castle Douglas. It is a small, rudimentary fortress and watchtower, built in about 1450. At one time every community in south-west Scotland had such a strongpoint.

Craigmillar, only three miles from the centre of Edinburgh, is an impressive concentric castle with ten-foot walls. Built on a rib of solid rock thirty feet high, it is equipped with a complex defensive system.

from its roof; and it is a notable fact that a great many southern castles and towers are placed within easy reach of the sea, or a navigable river, but rarely on the shoreline itself. Carnys was not rich but he had armed followers; they lived in a range of outbuildings at the tower's foot, now ruinous; and the whole was enclosed by a defensible wall. At one time virtually every community in this part of the world had such a tower; but most have disappeared completely or are mere heaps of stones; what makes Orchardton unique is that it has survived virtually intact, though the top roof has gone.

At the other end of the socio-military scale were the so-called 'imperial clans', like the Campbells, who in the later Middle Ages were encouraged by the monarchy to expand into the ungoverned areas. Castle Campbell, their original home, is only a short distance from the town of Dollar, but its site, at the junction of two glens in the Ochil Hills, gives it one of the most spectacular situations of any castle in the British Isles. It was once called Castle Gloom, but the impression it leaves on the visitor is not one of gloom but of intense, almost overdone romance. There are dense woods, rushing streams and steep cliffs on all sides, and above the tree line the bare moorland. Below lie Dollar and the broad Forth Valley, with the Pentland Hills in the far distance. The castle is basically a fifteenth-century structure, with additions up to the seventeenth century; and it has a feature not uncommon in Scotland – a late-sixteenth-century loggia in its courtyard, bringing a touch of the Italian Renaissance to this rain-sodden upland site. Campbell is defended by its setting, notably by the sheer banks and tumultuous waters of the Burn of Sorrow and the Burn of Care which straddle it. But it is a formidable fortress all the same, built around a courtyard with the original tower-keep in one corner, and outer defences, now terrace-gardens, leading down to the glen bottom. The tower itself is particularly strong, impressive and well preserved and there is access to the roof, from which the views are tremendous.

Campbell is a case where increased wealth and grandeur led a rising family to expand its tower-keep into a massive courtyard-castle. This often happened to fifteenth-century towers. Crichton Castle, which overlooks the River Tyne in Midlothian, is splendidly situated in what is now a sheepfold sloping down to the water. The original builder was John de Crichton, who was given a barony by Robert III; but it was his son, the famous or infamous Sir William de Crichton, Chancellor of Scotland during the minority of James II, who constructed the fifteenth-century keep-gatehouse which is the nucleus of the present castle. Crichton spent his life engaged in a savage vendetta against the Black Douglases, and it was he who was responsible for the gruesome 'dinner of the black bull's head' in Edinburgh Castle. The castle later became attached to the Bothwell earldom, in its various incarnations, and thus passed through the hands of Ramsays, Hepburns and Stewarts. Forfeited for the third time in 1567, after the downfall of Mary Queen of Scots' lover, it was eventually granted by her son, James VI and I, to his kinsman, Francis Stewart, a man of considerable culture and taste, who completely refurbished the castle and added a magnificent Italianate courtyard, its chief decorative feature. Craigmillar, only three miles to the southeast of the centre of Edinburgh, has a somewhat similar architectural history, though it has always been a royal castle. Here, an L-shaped tower-house, built of reddish-grey carboniferous sandstone and sited on a verge of solid rock about thirty feet high, was expanded into a powerful concentric castle, with an inner and an outer curtain. The defensive system is not at all clear at first glance, and is best comprehended by studying the aerial photograph printed in the castle guide; but the walls are very sturdy – in places nearly ten feet thick – and the castle was a formidable military enterprise.

In some cases, however, the tower-house did not expand at all, but survived as a residence, more or less unaltered, from the fifteenth century to this day. At Comlongan, near Ruthwell in Dumfriesshire, there is a tower-house of an exceptionally pure and stark kind, built to a plain and simple rectangular plan. It is extremely difficult to find, but impressive and approached through a magnificent avenue of beeches. Each floor covers the

Doune is a big tower-house type stronghold on the main route from Edinburgh to the Isles, belonging to the great family of Moray. Prince Charles Edward used it as a military prison during the 1745 Rising.

western forts at Dunstaffnage and Inverlochy. The castle has not substantially changed from its original design. It is a big version of the tower-house type, with a large high-walled courtyard, two great halls (one for the retainers), and excellent battlements, from which there are splendid views of the River Teith. Moray was the illegitimate half-brother of Mary, and both she and James often stayed at Doune; a suite of apartments over the kitchen range is still called after her. It was garrisoned by the government as recently as 1689, and Prince Charles Edward used it as a military prison during the 1745 rising (it has a number of cells). It was ruinous in Walter Scott's day, but well restored by the 14th Earl of Moray in the 1880s, and is still in Moray hands.

Mary was also at Loch Leven Castle, in Kinrosshire; indeed, she was imprisoned there. The lake is not enormous – about nine miles in circumference – but it has a certain placid beauty and is now one of the most important wildfowl reserves in Scotland. The castle is on an island close to the shore and is not, one imagines, a particularly secure place, since the water is shallow. It is an early fifteenth-century tower, much added to in the sixteenth century. Mary was brought here in 1567, after she lost the Battle of Carberry, and escaped with the help of young Willy Douglas; he locked everyone into the great hall and dropped the keys into the loch, where they were found 300 years later. The courtyard wall encloses the greater part of the original island, now expanded by drainage. There is an arched gateway leading to the main tower, with the hall below and a solar, where the queen slept, occupying all the floor above. She signed her abdication there, being waited on by the 4th Lord Ruthven, from nearby Huntingtower Castle, north-west of Perth, on the River Almond. This is a delightful castle, notable for some fine painted timbers, a rare reminder that castles were often a blaze of colour internally. The castle, originally called Ruthven, was the scene of the 'Ruthven Raid' in 1582 when the young James was snatched out of the power of the Duke of Lennox and the Catholic interest. The Ruthvens were created Earls of Gowrie, but came to grief in 1600 in the wake of the

complete ground-floor plan of the house, and there are no concessions to comfort or elegance, or anything to detract from the impression of grim strength which is conveyed. Here the owners solved the problem of disfiguring accretions by building a quite separate house alongside the castle in the nineteenth century.

The sixteenth century was the golden age of Scottish castles, and it is astonishing how many of them were associated, in one way or another, with the desperate events revolving around the lives of Mary Queen of Scots and her son James. Actually, one of the most famous, Doune, the fortress of the Regent Earl of Moray, on the Callander–Stirling road, is not strictly speaking a sixteenth-century castle. It was first built by the brother of Robert III, Robert Stewart, Duke of Albany (duke, that is, of all Scotland north of the Forth), and another regent. Like Edinburgh, which was linked as part of a defensive system to Stirling on the one hand and the sea-defences of Leith on the other, Doune was what might be termed a 'strategic' castle. The hostile power of the Lord of the Isles led Albany to plant Doune on the main road up from Edinburgh, a staging post to the key

Loch Leven Castle sits on an island close to the shore of a lake near Kinross. Mary Queen of Scots was brought here in 1567 after she lost the Battle of Carberry, but she later escaped.

Right: Craigievar Castle, near Aberdeen, is often regarded as the perfect example of the Scottish tower-house in its mature, 17th-century form. It is of pink harled granite and has six storeys.

Far right: Crathes, near Aberdeen, is a splendid tower-house from the 16th century, the golden age of Scottish castles. It has a noble great hall on the first floor and well-preserved painted ceilings.

supposed 'Gowrie Conspiracy' against the king. James converted it into a royal castle (it eventually became the dower-house of the Duchesses of Atholl) and passed an act of parliament changing its name to Huntingtower.

Huntingtower is a good example of the change from the truly medieval castle to the sixteenth-century tower-house; for its original twin towers, once linked only by a curtain, were roofed over to form one house in early modern times. The sixteenth century brought greatly increased comforts, even in a late medieval castle like Hailes, another habitual resting-place of

Queen Mary. The castle is ruinous; all that remain are the lower rooms, cellars, two pits for prisoners, the bakehouse, chapel and solar above, but the plan makes it clear that comfort was getting the upper hand over security, since there was only one line of defence. All the same the outer walls were eight feet thick. This was the pattern: later Scots tower-houses had very substantial walls, but the actual defences were confined to battlements, bartizans, strong grilles on windows, and gun-loops in the wall bases. There is a good example at Elcho Castle, once the home of the Wemyss, elegantly sited on the River Tay below Perth, and excellently restored. The domestic arrangements of a sixteenth-century stronghold designed primarily as a dwelling-house emerge here very clearly; there are, for instance, three separate stair-systems, which added greatly to the family's convenience as well as making a small garrison go further. This was a reasonably comfortable house to live in, and could be defended against anything short of an actual army.

At Crathes, in Kincardine, there is another good example, built 1553–96, with a noble great hall on the first floor, a vaulted tower-room adorned by a curved Elizabethan fireplace. There are well-preserved painted ceilings, and a long gallery (for exercise on wet days) which runs across the whole building. The turrets were probably designed more for domestic convenience than military strength; but it is to be noted that the outer corners were still rounded, to prevent enemies from prising out the stones. Domestication of the castle went a stage further at Kirkcudbright, where McLennan's Castle, though it dominates the harbour very successfully, follows essentially the plan of a house. Kirkcudbright was an active port right up to the eighteenth century, but troubled by pirates on the coast, notably Leonard Robertson, of whom Queen Elizabeth's government complained repeatedly. The Scots privy council ordered him and his men to cease their 'tuelyeing and harlotrie' and to leave the kingdom; the castle was built to enforce the decision, but its function is clearly post-medieval; it was not built to stand an army siege.

All the same, Scots lairds not only continued to call their new houses castles but insisted on making them genuinely defensible until well into the seventeenth century. For a perfect example of a well-preserved seventeeth-century tower-house one must go to Amisfield, five miles from Dumfries, and not easy to find (Elshieshiels Tower, near Lochmaben, a few miles away, is by the same architect). It is tall, narrow, thirty feet square and nearly eighty high, with four main rooms one above the other, the stairs being neatly enclosed in a circular turret. As often in Scotland, a more modern house was built by its side, but the tower was lived in, absolutely unaltered, until quite

recently. A bigger and more famous example is Craigievar in Aberdeenshire, an architectural masterpiece in pink harled granite. It can be argued that the tower-house, in its mature seventeenth-century form, is Scotland's greatest contribution to European architecture, for though its Gallic affiliations are plain enough, the style is unique. At Craigievar, over six storeys high, the skill of the designer in crowding such functional convenience and security into a comparatively narrow compass is plain to even the uninstructed. The castle was finished in 1626 by a prosperous laird, William Forbes, known as William the Merchant, who took over the estate and half-finished building from the impoverished Mortimers. It is, perhaps, the work of a famous Aberdeenshire stonemason, John Bell, and there is a much fine decorative work inside. Though most of the curtain-wall and corner-towers have gone, virtually nothing else has changed. Craigievar has the distinction of being the last of the true tower-houses, since after the Civil War styles and tastes changed and Scotland was about to embrace classicism.

Only in the far north did castles linger on as military instruments. They played a perceptible role in the rising of the Old Pretender in 1715, and if any one action signalled the end of the castle in Britain it came one day in 1719, in the aftermath of the rising, when a Royal Naval ship-of-the-line, HMS *Worcester*, was sent up to Loch Duich, on the north-west highland coast, to reduce the great stronghold of the Macraes, Eilean Donan. It was defended by a gallant company of Spanish soldiers but the ship's cannon reduced it to rubble in a matter of hours. And rubble it remained until the twentieth century, when a Macrae who had married a maltster heiress spent a million pounds on restoring it and making it habitable. Eilean Donan is actually on an island (as its name implies) linked to the land by a stone bridge; and its magnificent setting on the sea-loch has made it perhaps Scotland's most photographed castle. But it was the last of the line; the new forts and fortified barracks which the Hanoverian crown built to hold down the highlands were very different conceptions. And in 1774, when Boswell and Johnson toured Skye and stayed at Dunvegan Castle, another very ancient fortress, their hostess Lady Macleod complained bitterly about its inconveniences and said she longed to live in a more domesticated home. So by then the castle, as a prolongation of a medieval form of building, was effectively extinct even in wildest Scotland.

Opposite: Eilean Donan is on a sea-island linked to the coast by a stone bridge. A stronghold of the Macraes, it was levelled by the guns of *HMS Worcester* in 1719, then restored in the 1920s at a cost of £1 million.

CHAPTER SEVEN

STONE WALLS
AND
GUNPOWDER

Previous page
right: Ludlow Castle.

left: Bolton Castle.

The medieval castle made a rapid disappearance from the English architectural scene with the advent of the Tudors. In Scotland and in France the rich and well born continued to call the new houses they built 'castles', but in England sixteenth-century men already regarded the term as archaic. Probably the last of the old-style castles to be built was Thornbury in Gloucestershire, put up by the Duke of Buckingham in 1511. But this was no rugged castle; rather, a development of the highly decorative defensible palace, of the type Lord Cromwell built at Tattershall. The duke was a very grand personage, with more titles to hereditary distinction than the Tudors themselves; and the gateway swarms with the carved shields of his family, the Stafford knot and the Bohun Swan, his garter insignia, and an inscription:

> Thys gate was begon in the yere of owre Lorde Gode MCCCCXI. The ii yere of the reyne of Kynge Henri the VIII by me Edw Duc of Bukkyngha. Erll of Herforde Stafforde and Northampto.

But the castle was an anachronism, and so was its builder, the last of the medieval superlords, whose claims and possessions were incompatible with the schemes of the New Monarchy. In due course Henry VIII removed Buckingham's head, and confiscated his castle.

We find a more characteristic sixteenth-century development (one among many) with the delightful ruins of Moreton Corbet Castle in Shropshire. Here the ancestral stronghold of the Corbet family, not far from the Welsh border, with a keep built about the year 1200, was brought up to date not in a military sense but in a strictly domestic one by the addition of a magnificent Elizabethan range. This fascinating essay in the Elizabethan renaissance, dating from 1579, with its five-light windows, Tuscan and Ionic columns, and ornamental metope frieze, has more in common with the totally undefended palace of the Thynnes at Longleat than Thornbury, and is light-years away from the Middle Ages. Indeed, the great new men of the Tudor age, the Wolseys, the Bacons, the Cecils, the Hattons,

built not castles but tremendous houses, like Hampton Court, Burghley, Gorhambury, Theobalds and Holdenby, with only the merest decorative genuflections to the military style.

Yet castles continued to serve a variety of important purposes in the sixteenth century, and were therefore maintained and even added to in a number of cases. The strength of the Tudor monarchy, and the efficiency of its central administrative machine, made the fortified castle unnecessary and almost obsolete in normal times – inventories of royal castles made at the beginning, and shortly after the end, of Elizabeth's reign tell a sad tale of neglect, decay and ruin. But the moment the succession was in doubt or, still more, actively challenged, castles sprang into military life again. Thus, in 1553, when Queen Mary's title was impugned by the upstart Duke of Northumberland on behalf of his daughter-in-law, Lady Jane Grey, the queen instantly retired to her great castle at Framlingham in Suffolk. This was, and is, a building of exceptional interest. It was a creation of the Bigods, Earls of Norfolk, although the original twelfth-century castle was smashed to bits by Henry II. About 1190–1210, Roger, the 2nd earl, built a revolutionary new castle, with a vast curtain-wall laced with thirteen strong towers. The new concept, which enabled a large force including cavalry to be kept in the area of maximum defensibility, replaced the Conisbrough type with its dominant keep. It reflected crusader experience, which itself echoed Byzantine walls and towers, notably at Constantinople: Framlingham was, in a sense, an adumbration of Caernarvon. The castle passed from the Bigods, through crown possession, to the Mowbrays, Dukes of Norfolk, who made it their chief residence throughout the fifteenth century, and embellished and enlarged it, transforming the castle and the streets and buildings which surrounded it into a fortified town. In 1476 the castle went through the female line to the first Howard Duke of Norfolk, killed at Bosworth in 1485. His son, the 2nd duke, pardoned by Henry VII and later the victor of Flodden, modernized the castle, making copious use of brick. He added the splendid bridge and gatehouse which now form the main

Framlingham's sheer size enabled it to serve as a concentration point for an entire army. Queen Mary Tudor used it as such to gather the forces needed to put down the Duke of Northumberland's coup d'état.

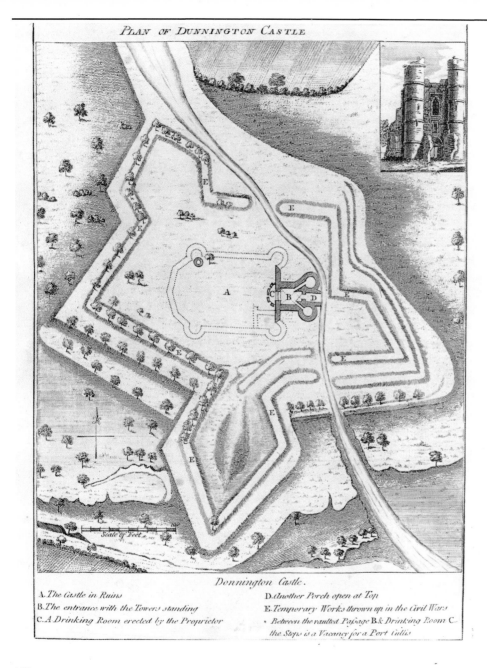

PLAN OF DUNNINGTON CASTLE

Donnington Castle.

A. The Castle in Ruins
B. The entrance with the Towers standing
C. A Drinking Room erected by the Proprietor
D. Another Porch open at Top
E. Temporary Works thrown up in the Civil Wars
* Between the vaulted Passage B & Drinking Room C. the Steps is a Vacancy for a Port Cullis

entrance, and he perched on top of the towers a series of magnificent Tudor chimneys, all, save one, purely decorative. Henry VIII in his old age imprisoned the 3rd duke and confiscated Framlingham; and Edward VI gave it to his elder half-sister, Mary. As Mary's chief support came from East Anglia, and as Framlingham's outer bailey encompassed most of the town, thus providing defensible accommodation for an entire army, it was a natural rallying point for her forces. They flocked to join her there, and within a week the measure of her support was so formidable that Northumberland abandoned his venture.

Mary doubtless had her own action in retiring to Framlingham in mind when she later, during the Wyatt rebellion, accused her half-sister Elizabeth of doing the same thing at her castle of Donnington, near Newbury. In fact Elizabeth was inevitably the cynosure of all Protestant plots under Mary, and in times of trouble it was natural for her servants to put Donnington, the only defensible home she had, in a state of readiness; though Elizabeth, under interrogation, at first denied she even owned the place. Donnington, not yet 'slighted', was then a formidable castle. As queen herself, Elizabeth rarely deigned to lock herself up in a castle even when her life was under threat; during the Armada scare, for instance, she continued to live at her houses near or in London. The only exception was in 1569, when she briefly allowed herself to be persuaded to occupy Windsor (one of her principal homes anyway), which the military experts regarded as the strongest place in the kingdom.

Outside the south and midlands, and especially in the north and on the Welsh Marches, castles continued to serve important administrative and defence purposes. The Council of the North, which was a major prerogative system of justice, as well as a military and financial machine, operated from Clifford's Tower, within the vast circumference of York Castle. Ludlow Castle, in Shropshire, was the seat of the Council of the Marches of Wales, over which, in Elizabeth's time, Sir Henry Sidney (Sir Philip's father) presided for so many distinguished

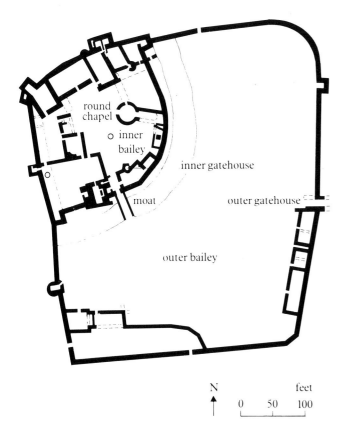

round chapel

o inner bailey

inner gatehouse

moat

outer gatehouse

outer bailey

N feet

0 50 100

Milton's masque, *Comus*, was first staged. The castle, on high ground overlooking the left bank of the Teme, was for centuries regarded as the chief key to the Welsh Marches, and has been fairly termed one of the most powerful and complete examples of medieval military architecture in the country. But it is also a complete administrative centre, a sort of miniature Whitehall in the dress of the English renaissance – indeed, in Sir Henry's time it was a centre of English culture too.

Until the mid-seventeenth century such governmental castles were operated on the assumption that they might have to withstand a siege; though, as it happened, sixteenth-century sieges in England and Wales were few and brief. When the Earls of Northumberland and Westmorland rose on behalf of Catholicism and Mary Queen of Scots in 1569, they took Durham Castle without a shot (it was virtually undefended) but they failed completely to take Henry II's grim fortress-keep at Newcastle, and their own still-powerful castles were not even defended when the rebellion collapsed in ignominy and cowardice. The two earls, together with the Countess of Northumberland, the 'Grey Mare', who was the Duke of Norfolk's sister and the real agitator behind the revolt, fled to the Dacre Castle at Naworth, but Leonard Dacre refused to harbour them. Then they rode to the notorious Liddesdale, and the protection of the Armstrongs. Northumberland was betrayed to the Scots regent, Moray, and eventually beheaded, while Westmorland found refuge and safety in the tower-house of Ferniehurst Castle.

Of course, the earls' castles were forfeit; and thereafter the great strongholds on the fringes of the English heartlands, which were still kept up under Elizabeth, served chiefly as prisons, for prisoners of state and recusants. This was the fate, for instance, of Framlingham, of Wisbech in Cambridgeshire (an early Norman motte-and-bailey, now a species of Regency villa), and of magnificent Beaumaris, which housed Fr William Dai, regarded by many Welsh Catholics as a saint. Mary Queen of Scots, during her nineteen years as a state guest under house-arrest, sampled a number of castles, including several

Far Left: Donnington's ground plan shows its Civil War defences, so successful that it four times beat off parliamentary seiges. When it finally surrendered in 1645, its garrison received 'as honourable Conditions as Could be given'.

Left: Ludlow's ground plan shows that outer protection was necessary only on the east and south, where concentric walls were built. The cliffs on which the inner castle is built fall steeply to the Teme on the west and to the Corve on the north.

years. It still is one of the biggest and most impressive of British castles. The main gateway leads to an enormous courtyard or outer bailey; in one corner there is a deep dry ditch, from which most of the stone to build the castle was produced, guarding the inner bailey. Sir Henry's splendid coat-of-arms is over the inner gateway, and within, on its right, the Elizabethan chamber where the judges of the court resided. The inner castle contains the Pendower Tower, where Edward IV's two luckless boys were held before being brought to London; a Norman keep and towers; the magnificent fourteenth-century state apartments, modernized in Elizabethan times; and, not least, the vast council hall, where the Court of the Marches sat, and where

Carlisle was the capital of the West March and remained a fortified town until the late 18th century. Henry VIII transformed its medieval castle into a powerful gun-fort garrisoned with 800 German mercenaries.

belonging to the ultra-warlike Talbots, Earls of Shrewsbury. Her first proper English residence, in fact, after she was moved from Carlisle Castle, was Bolton, which looks down over Wensleydale, and was built, as we have noted, by Richard de Scrope at roughly the same time as Bodiam. Even today the towers stand almost to their full height, though gutted inside; and in Elizabeth's time, Sir Francis Knollys, her vice-chamberlain, sent to inspect it in 1568, reported that it 'appeareth to be very strong, very fair and very stately after the old manner of building. . . . It is the highest walled house that I have seen'.

Another of Mary's prisons was the Earl of Shrewsbury's Tutbury, in north Staffordshire, overlooking the River Dove. This huge castle occupied a hill on the extreme verge of Staffordshire and Derbyshire, and was originally built for John of Gaunt, though by Mary's time it was in bad repair, very damp, and with rooms of wood and plaster which failed to keep out the wind. Mary thought nothing of its magnificent views; she said it sat squarely on the top of a mountain in the middle of a plain, and was 'exposed to all the malice of the heavens'. But in some ways it was a more attractive place than Fotheringhay, twenty miles south-west of Peterborough, in Northampton-shire. This was originally a motte-and-bailey on the River Nene, and later became a prime Yorkist castle after being completely rebuilt under Edward III. Richard Crouchback was born there in 1452. Henry VII turned it into a state prison. Catherine of Aragon, in her long rearguard action against her ferocious husband, successfully pleaded not to be sent there; she thought it might be fatal. So Mary must have realized it was the end of the line for her. The castle had a fine, north-facing gateway, a strong keep, a double moat along three sides and the river on the fourth. Mary's trial was held in the Great Chamber, seventy feet long and twenty-one feet wide, which was directly over the Great Hall. For her execution, which had to be a semi-public act, the hall itself was used, and crammed with 300 people. A twelve-foot square stage, hung with black, was erected, and the two Royal Commissioners, the Earls of Shrewsbury and Kent,

sat on it. Mary's eyes were bound with a white cloth embroidered in gold. The first blow of the axe struck the back of her neck; the second severed the head, all but a sinew. Mary was forty-four, but prematurely aged; when the executioner lifted up her head by the hair, he found himself clutching an auburn wig, while the head, short-cropped and grey, rolled on the floor. At this point Mary's Skye terrier, which had been hiding under her skirts, crept out and tried to cling to the head.

Elizabeth herself was no castle-fancier. All her life she hated cold houses, and preferred modern homes, with wooden boards, low ceilings and vast fireplaces, to the stone discomforts, however distinguished and romantic, of castles. In her time, of course, much of the architectural idiom of the medieval world, as well as its customs, were being relegated to deliberate antiquarianism, or play-acting. The famous tilts, held on the anniversary of her accession, in the tilt-yard at Whitehall Palace, were elaborately and self-consciously staged by Sir Henry Lee, her Master of Ceremonies, to conjure up a vanished world of chivalry. Elizabeth was not averse to a castle forming the background to such mumming, provided it contained a modernized suite of apartments for herself. At Kenilworth, the vast De Montfort water-castle, Robert Dudley, Earl of Leicester, transformed the castle buildings to suit her taste, and to serve as a staging post on her royal progresses. Dudley was accomplished in all the arts, military as well as civil, and the manner in which he transformed the fortress into a Renaissance palace, without essentially damaging its martial properties, was a triumph of architectural skills. Kenilworth was a working castle: Dudley kept an artillery train there, as well as powder and a great stock of firearms and armour. But in its state rooms and outbuildings it could also accommodate the court for lengthy stays. Elizabeth resided there for nearly three weeks in 1575, and was sumptuously entertained, perhaps in a last bid by Dudley to win her hand. The chief feature of the visit was, of course, the water-pageants. But there was also bear-baiting with dogs, fireworks, discharge of cannon, mystery plays by the Coventry Men, and masques. Elizabeth herself dubbed five

knights and touched nine persons for the 'Queen's Evil'. Sir Henry Lee was in charge of a romantic entertainment about knights and ladies, with poems probably by Sir Edward Dyer; and the events were described in prose by Robert Laneham, the gifted Keeper of the Privy Council Door, and in verse by Thomas Gascoigne. But already we are closer in spirit to Sir Walter Scott, and the Eglington Tournament of 1838, than to the world of Edward III's Round Table.

Nevertheless stone and brick still had a major part to play in warfare in the sixteenth century, and castles continued to be built, even under the Tudors, though they were of a radically different sort. As in the fourteenth and fifteenth centuries, the motive was coastal defence, and the circular forts set up by the Tudors had, as their distant ancestor, Edward III's Queenborough, then of course still intact and garrisoned. But they were built primarily for heavy artillery, and marked an enormous technical leap forward from the crude designs of the mid-fifteenth century. As a matter of fact, the first in the series, Dartmouth Castle in Devon, is pre-Tudor, since it dates from 1481; it was built by the townsmen to head off a French invasion in support of Henry Tudor, the Lancastrian claimant, and it was paid for by money supplied by Edward IV and Richard III. It consists of two artillery towers, on either side of the haven, linked by a heavy chain barrier. These towers had the first proper big-gun ports, two and a half feet high and two feet wide, giving the gunners a decent field of fire. (It is notable that only the year before Canterbury was still putting in primitive gunports in the style of the 1380s.)

Henry VIII took up the new type of fort with his customary enthusiasm. Among his many accomplishments was a profound knowledge of artillery. Like Henry IV, he knew how guns were cast, and it is certain that he was personally responsible for the design of at least one of his sea-castles. In the 1520s he built St Catherine's Castle at Fowey. It is still medieval in appearance, but it has the wide gunports of Dartmouth (six at floor level), and incorporates another innovation – a much lower profile. The king built castles on similar lines at Bayard's

Cove, Dartmouth, and the Little Dennis Fort, below Pendennis Castle in Falmouth. It is not quite clear whence he derived his ideas. In 1520–1 Albrecht Dürer had been called in to advise on the defences of Antwerp, and in 1527 he published in Nuremberg the first known work on the subject of artillery fortifications. This included detailed instructions on how to add artillery bastions to existing walls, and contained plans for an ideal fortress and town. But his gunports were not so advanced as in Henry VIII's later castles. Indeed, in 1532, a Calais document referred to 'splaies' instead of 'lowpes' for big guns, 'which the King's Grace hath devised', and it may be that on this point at least Henry was the real innovator, though in the light of his activity in other spheres it is more likely that he beefed-up the ideas of others. Certainly he was keen to employ Continental experts, especially Italians. At the time several Italian cities were rebuilding their defences for artillery; and the Italians were, almost certainly, the first to develop the new science of angled bastioning. But the Scandinavians were also building gun-forts in Henry's day.

The big scare came at the end of 1538, when the Pope succeeded in reconciling Henry's two Catholic enemies, Charles V and Francis I; there was then a prospect of a joint Imperial-French invasion, to enforce the Pope's excommunication of Henry in December. Whatever his faults Henry was a man of immense vigour and dispatch, and he acted promptly to meet what the documents call 'the pretended invasion'. As Lambarde, the Elizabethan historian of Kent, put it, the king 'determined (by the aid of God) to stand upon his own guard and defence; and without sparing any cost he builded castles, platforms and blockhouses in all needful places of the Realm'. This is no exaggeration; in the short space of two years, Henry carried through the most comprehensive defence scheme in Britain since Roman times.

On the Thames itself he had five forts or bulwarks. There was the Hermitage, alias 'Johnes Bulwark' on the Essex side near Gravesend, later known as 'Tilbury Fort'; the 'Bulwark at Tylbery', otherwise East Tilbury; a fort at Gravesend itself,

Opposite: Dartmouth Castle in Devon, dating from 1481, was the precursor of the coastal artillery forts built by Henry VIII. It has the first of the proper gun-ports (two feet wide), giving the gunners a wide field of fire.

known as Crane's Bulwark; Milton Bulwark, or 'Mr Cobham's Bulwark', which was a blockhouse at Milton; and finally the 'Bulwerk at Heigham'. These defences cost £5,000 in all. By March 1540 guns were already installed in three of them, and their captains and garrisons were named in the 'book' kept by the overall commander, Sir Christopher Morris. Next came the three castles guarding the anchorage in the Downs – Sandown, Deal and Walmer. Work on them proceeded throughout 1539, and by early 1540 they were in a state of readiness; Deal, referred to as 'the great castle', being already garrisoned by a captain and thirty-four others of all ranks. At Dover, three new bulwarks – Moates, under the cliff, Archcliff Bulwark and another which soon went out of use – were added, all recorded as 'furnished' in Sir Christopher's book by March 1540.

Next came the 'castle at Floston', otherwise Sandgate Castle, near Folkstone. This cost £5,000 and was begun in March 1539; it was still incomplete eighteen months later, but armed and garrisoned. On the other, or western, side of Dungeness was the 'castle at Rye', or 'Chambre', now known as Camber Castle. Then came the main defences of the Solent, both on the Isle of Wight and the mainland. These consisted of castles at Calshot and Hurst, in Hampshire, and East and West Cowes on the island. In 1539, a report by the Earl of Southampton and Lord St John emphasized that these four forts commanded all the normal approaches to Southampton Water, certainly all those with an easterly wind. But other defences were put up: another fort called Sandown (not to be confused with the Kentish castle) and a fort called Worsley's Tower or Carey's Sconce, opposite Hurst Castle, which was modernized at the same time. Of course the largest and strongest fortress on the Isle of Wight was Carisbrooke, with its mighty fourteenth-century gate-house. This was put under the charge of a vigorous artillery expert, Richard Worsley, whose family had long been associated with the castle; he rebuilt the fortifications, clearing space for the big guns, issued firearms to the island's militia, and defeated two French invasion bids. (But it should be noted that the principal Tudor additions at Carisbrooke were carried out

by the Italian military architect Federigo Gianibelli, under Queen Elizabeth.) Finally, the defences west of the Solent were strengthened by a new artillery bulwark at Portland Castle, completed in 1540.

These forts stretching from the Thames to Dorset were all in working order, if not complete, within eighteen months of Henry setting the programme in hand. Obviously, Henry wanted to cover as quickly as possible the stretch of coastline where a landing was most likely to be made. By the middle of 1540 Charles and Francis had quarrelled again, and the worst pressure was off. But work on south-coast defences continued, at a more leisurely pace, for many decades to come. By 1544, for instance, Southsea Castle, guarding Portsmouth Harbour, was nearly finished; it was 'His Majesty's own device', and is the only castle we can be sure was Henry's own work. At St Mawes an artillery fort was put up to a single clover-leaf plan; but it was sited on the slope of a hill, and so was utterly indefensible from the land side. In the Civil War it was taken by parliament without a shot. By contrast, Pendennis was a formidable piece of work, on a headland, with a flat top and steep sides. It was also provided with a four-acre enclosure or *enceinte*, straight-sided and with corner bastions; the gunports were arranged to rake all the walls, and so to make a direct assault with ladders as suicidal as could be. But this belonged to the Elizabethan age, when siege-warfare was developing rapidly.

Contemporaries complained that these gun-forts 'stank of gunpowder and dogs'. All the same, there was nothing quite like them on the continent of Europe. The biggest and most impressive were the three castles of the Downs, known as 'the device of the king for three new Blockhouses or Bulwarks to be made in the Downs'. This appears to suggest that Henry designed them himself, but we have no proof of this. As a matter of fact their circular shape was not entirely satisfactory. Pointed and angled bastions, giving a complete field of fire to the defenders, were first set up in the Portsmouth area, and 'eared' bastions of the true Italian form appeared at Yarmouth Castle, in the Isle of Wight, around 1547, right at the end of

Right: Carisbrooke was the centre from which the Governor of the Isle of Wight administered the island, living in some splendour. However, the 16th-century fortifications were highly professional, designed by Elizabeth I's favourite military architect, Gianibelli.

Far right: Walmer, Sandgate and Camber castles show variations on the concentric designs of the Tudor gunforts. Contemporaries complained that these forts 'stank of gunpowder and dogs', and the circular shapes proved unsatisfactory. By the end of Henry VIII's reign they were being superseded by pointed and angled bastions, giving a complete field of fire to the defenders.

Henry's reign. The designer may have been Sir Edward Ryngley (he was certainly the overseer), former Comptroller of Fortifications at Calais. At Calais his assistant was Stephen von Hashenperg, and this Moravian military engineer was brought over to help on the Downs castles; we know, for instance, that he designed the earthwork bulwarks which linked the three castles into one defensive system, and he was also described as the 'deviser' as well as the supervisor of Sandgate. He later worked on the defences of Carlisle, but was sacked in 1543 because he 'appeared to have behaved lewdly and spent great treasure to no purpose'. Certainly the gunports he put in at Sandgate are inferior to those at Deal and Walmer, and he may therefore have been a fraud.

The royal accounts for these operations are not complete, but they provide much illuminating information. At Sandgate the number of men rose in 1539 until the daily average was about 500; less than half labourers, the rest bricklayers and stonemasons, and over fifty carpenters and 'sawyers'. Altogether, in May 1539, there were 1,400 men at work on the Downs castles. The total rose further during the summer, fell in the winter of 1539–40, then rose again the following spring. The splendid Caen stone used in the Downs castles came from the suppressed Carmelite Friary at Sandwich, and other ecclesiastical sources were St Radegund's Abbey, Horton Priory and Christchurch, Canterbury. As in Edward III's time, pressing was used to grab skilled labour – some of the Sandgate stonemasons came from Somerset and Gloucester. There was trouble with the labourers at Deal in June 1539, for the king was paying 5d a day, below the national average. Sir Edward Ryngley reported: 'This week we had business with the King's labourers here, saying they would have 6d a day; but after I had spoken with them I caused them to return to work. . . . I have sent the nine first beginners, five to Canterbury Castle and four to Sandwich gaol.'

Deal is the most impressive of the forts and by far the best preserved in its original shape, though the present battlements date from 1732. It had a clover-leaf design, like St Mawes, only

doubled. The linked defence system of the castles allowed them to reinforce and reprovision each other, and thus saved manpower and money; and, in addition, they were brilliantly designed to emphasize mobility within each unit, for reinforcing and re-ammunitioning the defences on each sector. Thus at Deal great ingenuity went into the construction of a central tower, or hollow pillar, with a water-well below, and a double set of staircases above. The garrison was a mere captain and twenty-four other ranks; but the firepower the castle could provide was formidable. The main armament was mounted on the outer ring, but guns were also fired from the top of the keep, and the inner bastions or lunettes attached to it. Altogether, there were five tiers of gunports or embrasures, and there can have been few more strongly defended citadels in any period. There were no less than 145 openings for firearms; combinations of cannon and handgun ports ensured that every part of the wall of the keep was covered by fire, and that the whole of the space between the keep and the outer curtain could be swept by the guns. There was, too, a furnace for heating round-shot, particularly useful against wooden ships; and elaborate provision was made to keep the powder secure.

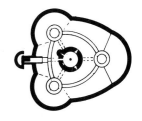

Walmer was similar in plan to Deal, but smaller; and Sandown, which has now almost totally disintegrated into the sea, had a Walmer-type plan. We do not know what guns they had in Henry's day; but in 1597, at Walmer, there were one cannon, one culverin, five demi-culverins, a saker, a minion and a falcon. Since we know from contemporary evidence that the saker had a range of a mile, and a cannon of a mile-and-a-half, the guns effectively covered the Downs anchorage. At the end of the Elizabethan period, there were ten trained gunners at Sandown, eleven at Walmer and sixteen at Deal; but they could be supplemented by locals in case of emergency; in the reign of Charles II, the numbers were much the same. Deal was, and is, preserved almost as Henry built it and the sheer beauty of its functionalism makes it one of the most fascinating castles in Europe. Walmer, by contrast, became the official residence of the Warden of the Cinque Ports, and so was domesticated and

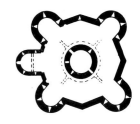

made into what one warden, the Duke of Wellington, who died there, called 'the most charming marine residence he had ever seen. The queen herself has nothing to compare with it.'

The Tudors were also active farther north in England, for fear of the Scots was acute until the 1580s, and there was always a chance of their descending on Carlisle, or on the north-east coast in conjunction with the French (and later the Spanish). Henry VIII was at Hull in October 1540, inspected the defences, and ordered a castle and two blockhouses to be erected at once. A few years before, in Verona, the engineer Michele Sanmichele had built a new kind of bastion, with curtain projections which were no longer circular or curved towers, but solid, angular structures, of earth revetted with a battered wall of stone, brick or timber. The structures which went up at Hull in 1541 in pursuance of Henry's orders were of this type, and can thus be considered the first modern forts in England. The king also built forts at Langer Point (now Landguard Fort), opposite Harwich, and in 1542 on Beblowe Crag, on the Holy Island in Northumbria. This last was a perfect natural site for a fortification, overlooking the harbour, and it is curious that through its long history the island had never been fortified before, being given over completely to the ecclesiastic activities of Lindisfarne Priory. But Henry was just the man to change the situation. Stone from the priory was used to build the fort, and the church became the garrison's main storehouse. The fort was complete by 1550, three years after Henry's death. It was never attacked, though briefly occupied by the Jacobites for one night, and remained in a state of defence until after the Napoleonic Wars, when the guns were removed. At the end of the century it was bought by Edward Hudson, editor of *Country Life*, who employed the architect Sir Edwin Lutyens to reconstruct it with great skill and fidelity.

Although Tudor defensive operations were dominated by the prodigious activities of Henry VIII, they should be seen as a whole, since separate monarchs tended to carry through programmes initiated by their predecessors. On the north-west coast, Henry had, as we have noted, Hashenperg, known as

Far left: Deal is the most perfectly preserved of the massive series of coastal forts built – and in some cases designed – by Henry VIII during the French invasion scare of the 1530s and 1540s.

Left: Lindisfarne, on Holy Island off the Northumberland coast, was built as a gun-fort by Henry VIII and finished in 1550. Around 1900 it was bought by the editor of *Country Life*, who employed Lutyens to restore it.

Tilbury Fort on the Thames was the centre of the great armed camp set up during the Armada scare in 1588, and Queen Elizabeth made her famous address to her troops there. However, the works which survive date from 1670.

'the Almain', as his engineer. He, and his successor William Garforth, helped the Earls of Derby, Lords of the Isle of Man, to reconstruct for big guns Castle Rushen and Peel Castle, as well as to build several new gun-forts. But their main work was at Carlisle, which Henry transformed from a powerful and well-preserved medieval castle into a formidable gun-fort, garrisoned with 800 German mercenaries. Work seems to have been suspended under Edward VI and Mary, for in 1558 Lord Scrope, Warden of the West March, reported to Queen Elizabeth that both the castle and the town walls were partly ruinous. The walled city in those days was a lozenge-shaped enclosure of forty-five acres, strongly protected in front by the River Eden, and on the flanks by the Petterill and the Caldew. Intensive repairs to the whole *enceinte* were carried out under Elizabeth, and Carlisle continued to be an important fortified town until after the 'Forty-five'.

Elizabeth's greatest military work, however, was the refortification of Berwick. This was the first English town to be equipped with the new bastions built according to Italian principles. In 1554 Zanchi published the standard treatise on the subject, and the new works were set in train by Queen Mary in the following year. In 1562 Peter Whitehorne produced a treatise in English, and this may well have influenced the works at Berwick. The Elizabethan defences are still in a remarkable state of preservation, and repay careful study and investigation on the spot (their lines are not always obvious). By the standards of the day they were very formidable, better even than the famous walls of Valetta, built after the Great Siege of Malta in 1567. They have a very thick curtain and huge angular bastions, spaced at intervals; all the bastions have flankers, that is two-storey chambers in the flank, in which guns were mounted to rake the ditch. Guns were also, of course, mounted on the tops of the bastions. Building these defences involved shifting enormous quantities of earth, and diggers and other workmen were pressed and dispatched from as far away as Suffolk, Gloucestershire and Kent. Although the works were pushed ahead vigorously they were still incomplete in 1568, when Elizabeth's cousin, Lord Hunsdon, the warden, urged her to provide another £5,000, 'when no sudden approach of the French need be feared'. The designer and engineer was Sir Richard Lee, Elizabeth's Surveyor of Fortifications. But another engineer active in the north was Rowland Johnson. Plans preserved at Hatfield, carrying his signature, show proposals to transform Wark and Norham in the same style, though the work at Norham was never in fact carried out.

Despite her long reign, and the threat to her coast-line in its closing decades, Elizabeth carried out no schemes on the scale of her father's. But she did not neglect the nation's defences, preferring to make do and mend rather than embark on fresh and impoverishing projects. At Upnor Castle in Kent, opposite the naval base at Chatham, she built a new bulwark in 1561–2, using stone from the outer curtain-wall of old Rochester Castle. This lacks the strict functionalism of Henry VIII's work, and indeed has too high a profile, being thus in strict contrast to Berwick; in fact it is adorned with antiquarian Gothic details, which indicates that even as early as Elizabeth's reign amateur architects felt that a medieval touch was necessary for any 'castle'. As a rule, though, Elizabethan work was strictly professional. In 1598–9 the engineer Paul Ivry rebuilt Pendennis, turning it into one of the strongest fortresses in western Europe; and, two years later, Gianibelli, Elizabeth's favourite military architect, completed the refortification of Carisbrooke, under the direction of one of the greatest of the Isle of Wight's Governors, the 2nd Lord Hunsdon.

It was Gianibelli, too, who reconstructed the fort most closely associated with Elizabeth herself, at Tilbury. Here Henry VIII had built a D-shaped blockhouse at the crucial point where the Thames narrows to a mere 800 yards. Gianibelli hastily reconstructed and enlarged it early in 1588, and it became the focus of the great armed camp which the Earl of Leicester, appointed head of the army, assembled in the summer and which Elizabeth addressed in her most famous speech. But it should be noted that the fortifications at Tilbury which still exist are not Gianibelli's but more modern works built in 1670, after the naval defences of London were exposed as inadequate in the Dutch wars. Other Elizabethan forts fared better in the seventeenth century. Pendennis, in fact, proved virtually impregnable during the Civil War, only literal starvation compelling surrender. The gallant commander of the garrison, Colonel John Arundell, was known to his men as 'Old Tilbury' because, as a boy, he had been present in the fort to hear Elizabeth speak.

The crown continued to build fortifications of a sort to defend Britain's sea-coasts until the Second World War. But they gradually ceased to be classifiable, even under the loosest definition, as castles. Perhaps the last great working castle to be built was Fort George (about 1770), guarding the approach to the Murray Firth, in Inverness-shire. The first proper barracks,

as such, had been built half a century before (perhaps from a design by Vanbrugh) inside the perimeter at Berwick; it is still functioning and worth a visit. But Fort George was not only a full-scale barracks, planned to hold two battalions, or 1,600 men, with its own bakehouse, brewery, chapel and so forth, and an immense and scientifically designed magazine; it was also a huge, and up-to-date artillery fortress, mounting guns which commanded the approaches to Inverness harbour. It was planned by William Skinner, Chief Engineer of Great Britain, and its first governor. The motive behind its construction was yet another French invasion scare, that of 1759, and the fort was hastily armed while still unfinished – work going on for the whole of the next decade. The buildings of the interior, in which the Adam brothers had a part, were (like Henry VIII's big forts) constructed to astonishingly high standards, down to such details as elegant regimental cyphers on the leaden drainpipes, and Adam fireplaces in the governor's house. One is not surprised to hear it cost £210,000. When it was finished one clan leader, Sir Aeneas MacKintosh, commented: 'Houses and rooms fit for a royal palace, and superior to Sir James's'. Not long afterwards, in August 1773, Boswell and Johnson were hospitably entertained there by the governor, Sir Eyre Coote. Johnson said at the time: 'I shall always remember this fort with gratitude.' And in his subsequent book he minuted: 'Fort George, the most regular fortification in the island, well deserves the notice of a traveller.' A hundred years after it was built it was still regarded as an artillery station, though re-equipped with 68-pounders and 10-inch shell guns. And, even today, the buildings are fully in use by the army, and continue to deserve the traveller's notice.

But we are running ahead of our story: we have yet to consider the last period in which British castles and fortresses were to see action on a considerable scale – the Civil War.

CHAPTER EIGHT

CASTLES AND SIEGES OF THE CIVIL WAR

Previous page

left: Corfe is a splendid
natural site for a castle, a
steep-sided hill on a spur
of the Purbeck range. The
shattered silhouette
reflects the parliamentary
mines and gunpowder
used to 'slight' it during
the Civil War.

right: Sherborne Castle.

The great English Civil War in the 1640s was the last age of the military castle in Britain. Medieval castles, ancient town walls and even strongly built mansions proved surprisingly defensible. What was new were the complicated 'lines of circumvallation' and earth-work bulwarks and bastions which were more or less scientifically thrown up around these strongpoints. If the sixteenth century had been the age of the Italian military engineers, during the seventeenth century it was the Dutch (and later the French) who took the lead. From their experiences during the long war of sieges against the Spanish army in the Netherlands, Dutch experts had effectively tilted the balance in favour of the defender, and during the Civil War they were in considerable demand on both sides.

In some ways siege techniques had not changed all that substantially since the Middle Ages. The big works created by the besiegers were, in purpose and design, not unlike the *malvoisins* of Philip Augustus and Richard Coeur de Lion; and medieval-style siege-towers, known as sows, were actually used on several occasions. Guns were less effective than was generally expected. They failed to dominate field actions because of their slow rate of fire and poor traction. In sieges, of course, they could be deadly in the hands of a real expert. They could make a breach even in very stout defences. At Leicester, in May 1645, the royalists breached the city walls with six 'great cannon', which included (to use their technical names), two demi-cannon, each firing a twenty-seven-pound shot, two culverins, with fifteen-pound shot, and two twelve-pounders. The cannon proper, with a crew of five, fired a forty-seven-pound shot. But such guns were rare, and difficult to shift. The largest cannon-balls found at Newark, where there were extensive artillery duels over a long period, weigh about thirty-one pounds, and appear to have been fired from a demi-culverin. These guns had a range of 400 yards fired point-blank, and up to 2,400 yards at ten degrees elevation; the culverin could stretch to 2,650 yards.

Guns, however, were not much use against fixed defences at extreme range. Mortars, which fired crude shells or grenades, were on the whole more feared by defenders than cannon; they caused more casualties. But guns of any size were not common. When Newark finally surrendered, the parliamentary commander, General Poyntz, had twenty-three big guns, regarded as an unusually powerful siege-train. Sir George Belasyse, the royalist Governor, had a parliamentary monster he had captured, known as 'Sweet Lips', eleven other big guns, two mortars, and a number of small pieces called draks. Ammunition was less of a problem. In August 1641 parliament had abolished the royal monopoly in the manufacture of gunpowder, which until then had been leased to the Evelyn family at Long Ditton, and at Chilworth in Surrey, within easy reach of the Tower. When the war began powder mills were set up wherever necessary. All they involved was extracting and refining the saltpetre from 'earth' found in decomposing organic matter, in cattle sheds, sheep pens, dovecotes and so forth; blending it with charcoal and brimstone, and milling the mixture finely. The process was a dangerous one, but not exactly difficult.

Earlier in the war, the royalists had a distinct advantage in siege-work, both offensive and defensive, for they had many more English and foreign veterans and, in particular, hired the services of the Dutchman Bernard de Gomme, the greatest military engineer of the age, who built many of their best systems. Ideally, according to the best Dutch thinking, a defended town or castle ought to have a complete circumvallation, with bastions at regular intervals, plus detached works, or satellite forts, in advance of the main line. Towns with continuous bastion-systems included the naval bases of Portsmouth and Hull. Gomme set up a new, and very strong, Dutch system at Oxford, as outlined on the map he drew in 1644; parliamentary leaders thought it the strongest fortified town in the kingdom, though there are virtually no traces of it today. Gomme planned a similar system at Liverpool, but shortage of cash prevented it from being completed. Reading had a continuous *enceinte* (punctuated by the river), though with only a few bastions. But it had a fine advance fort, Harrison's Barn.

Probably the best 'detached work' was the Queen's Sconce at Newark, with its elborate bastions, a castle in itself. Other towns with continuous *enceintes* were Carmarthen and Bridgwater. There was another at Bristol, built by parliament, with artillery bastions, Colonel Fiennes being the engineer. But this was successfully stormed by Prince Rupert in July 1643. Gomme was then called in and immensely strengthened the defences, turning one of Fienne's forts, Windmill Hill, into a massive pentagonal castle. The king thought the city impregnable, and it was Rupert's surrender of it to Cromwell and Fairfax in 1645, with the loss of his 140 guns, which led to Charles's bitter quarrel with his most dashing commander.

There were alternatives to the complete *enceinte* on 'scientific' lines. At King's Lynn bastions were simply added to the medieval walls (as had been done at Carlisle in the previous century). The same procedure was followed at Yarmouth. At London, Plymouth and Chester, forts were made out of medieval portions of the defences, then linked with a bank and ditch. At other towns, such as Colchester and Worcester, bastions and ravelins were added on to earlier defences – in the case of the latter, six bastions placed in front of its medieval wall on the north and east sides. At Dorchester in Dorset a prehistoric fort, Mumbury Rings, was transformed into an isolated bastion, just beyond the edge of the town. At Barnstaple, refortified by the parliamentarians, the accounts tell a typical tale: 'In disbursements for Materials and Wages to build the Fort in which were mounted 28 pieces of ordnance, £1,120. For entrenching the town, £450. In Fortifying the castle, building three defensible gates and making 16 platforms, £660.' Here we have an 'unscientific' combination of updated medieval defences, an unrelated but newfangled gun-fort, and firing platforms – and not a very effective one either, since in 1643 Prince Maurice took the town without great difficulty.

There were also a number of forts or castles built at isolated strategic points, to guard road junctions, river crossings and so on. At Earith in Huntingdon, for instance, the parliamentarians built The Bulwark, to guard one of the approaches to Ely. In 1645 the royalists built two forts at Dartmouth, Gallant's Bower, and Mount Ridley on the Kingswear side. And forts were built by both sides in the Isles of Scilly (for example, at the south end of Tresco, and the batteries at St Mary's).

Much cogitation and argument went into the best types of defence (as no doubt they did in Angevin times, when the Framlingham system was challenging Conisbrough and Dover). One point of contention was the relative merit of wet and dry moats. At Newark much use of water was made by both sides; towards the end, the royalist general, Belasyse, 'fell into a ditch on the Towne Gradd, where his Lordship slipped in mud, so dirty he was scarce known'. But the Earl of Rutland noted in his diary that Sir Jacob Astley, a veteran of the Netherlands and one of the most experienced royalist commanders, 'was of opinion that a dry ditch and a good rampyer is stronger and better to be defended, with men enough in the town, than a ditch moted, by reason they can in a dry ditch change and turne to worke at pleasure'. Ditches of either kind were reinforced by palisades, which served as a kind of barbed wire, especially against cavalry. A royalist observer, Richard Symonds, inspected Boarstall Castle, on the Oxfordshire and Buckinghamshire border, a fourteenth-century structure of which only the gatehouse now remains, and found: 'A palizardo or rather a stockade without the graffe; a deepe graffe and wide, full of water; a palizardo above the false bray, and another six or seven above that, neare the top of the curten.' At Woodstock he noted that at the old defensible palace, later demolished by the 1st Duchess of Marlborough, 'the palizardoes stand on the top of the curten . . . and the like at the foot of the false bray.' (A false bray was a defence on the berm itself.) Symonds found at Worcester that 'Prince Maurice has made without the ditch (that is dry on that side that goes to Droitwiche) a low breast work, and stockade without that: the top of the breast worke is not a foot above the ground on the outside. Very necessary to safeguard a dry ditch and wall.'

Generally speaking the royalists had the best of it, at any rate for the first two years. The defences the parliamentarians set up

Chirk Castle, Clwyd is a unique, unaltered example of a border castle of Edward I's time. It is the only one of all the castles in North Wales to be continuously inhabited.

at London and Bristol were much inferior to the ones built or planned at Newark, Reading, Carmarthen, Oxford and Liverpool, or the later royalist defences at Bristol, parts of which can still be distinguished from the more amateurish parliamentary efforts. In addition to Gomme, the king had on his payroll the French 'fireworker', Bartholomew La Roche, and such experts as Sir John Henderson, the first commander at Newark, who had been governor of the great fortress at Ulm. Most of the parliamentary commanders and advisers were ordinary country gentlemen, who had never poked their noses beyond the Channel. Later parliament, too, found veterans: Poyntz, for instance, who had fought under the great Wallenstein, and the two leading Scots commanders, Lord Leven and David Leslie, both also veterans of the Thirty Years War. Poyntz's final siege-works outside Newark were laid with as much skill as anyone on the royalist side possessed.

There is little doubt that the best-defended city in the whole theatre of war was Oxford, for much of the time Charles's headquarters. Of course Oxford had had a strong castle since early Norman times – in 1071 Robert Doyly built a tower on a mound 250 feet in diameter, and sixty-four feet high. Later the castle was extended, though only the chapel crypt and one tower remain (now forming part of Oxford prison). Under Henry III the city was given a strong wall, enclosing 120 acres, with six gates, though the only substantial part remaining now is in New College garden. When the king decided to circumvallate Oxford, the royalist experts, led by Gomme, virtually ignored the old walls, except as inner defences, and pushed out the lines to keep cannon shot as far from the town centre as possible. These works cost £30,000 and involved forced labour by all the city's male inhabitants, from sixteen to sixty, on pain of a shilling fine for every day's non-appearance. The Oxford defences may be said to have served their purpose completely, in that they successfully deterred a mass-attack; the city remained inviolate until the king's cause was lost.

It was at Newark, the strongest royal city after Oxford, that the defences were really tested. This city on the Trent had been regarded as a strategic one since very early times; it marked the point where two great prehistoric routes intersected at a Trent crossing. There were Roman defence works at two places, later superseded around 900 by the 'New Work', from which the town got its name, set up against the Danes. Early in the twelfth century, the town and manor went to the bishops of Lincoln, who built a fine stone castle, described by Henry of Huntingdon in 1138 as magnificent, and of very ornate construction. Occupying a commanding position overlooking the river, bridge and road, its fortifications were added to and strengthened throughout the Middle Ages and beyond, and in the seventeenth century it was still one of the largest and most powerful river-castles in the kingdom.

At the end of 1642 the king's generals decided to garrison and fortify Newark in the greatest possible strength, to make it, in fact, the centre of a large fortified area, used as a rallying point for armies and a supply centre. They needed to hold Newark, where the Great North Road bridged the Trent and bisected the main road linking Lincoln to Nottingham and Leicester, in order to maintain communications between the king's headquarters in Oxford and his strongholds in Yorkshire and Newcastle, where his arms-convoys from the Netherlands usually landed. Holding Newark also made it possible for the king's army of the north, under the Earl of Newcastle, to mount a thrust into the territory of the Eastern Association, which was the main source of parliamentary military power. Newark Castle, and its defensive system, was linked to other royalist castles in the area, such as Belvoir, all of them garrisoned. The defensive zone was used to milk a huge area of supplies and manpower, and to mount cavalry raids into neighbouring parliamentary territory.

Parliament made three major attempts to take the city. In February 1643 Major General Thomas Ballard attacked with 6,000 men and ten guns, mostly small six-pounders. He fired eighty shots into the town. But a fierce counter-attack cost him three of his guns and sixty prisoners, and the siege was broken off. The second parliamentary attack, in February 1644, was even less successful. Sir John Meldrum surrounded the defensive zone with 2,000 horse, 5,000 foot, eleven cannon and two mortars. The cannon included the famous 'Sweet Lips', a 'great basilisk' from Hull, four yards long and probably installed in the sixteenth century – it was called after a notorious Hull whore of that time. It was 'Sweet Lips' which deposited the thirty-pound balls unearthed at Newark in modern times. Meldrum built a bridge of boats over the Trent to help an intensive investment of the royalist lines, but he was surprised and surrounded by Prince Rupert and compelled to surrender, in perhaps the worst single parliamentary disaster of the war. He was allowed to march away but lost all his guns, his small-arms, and his ammunition-train.

The third siege began in November 1645, when the main Scots army joined General Poyntz and his English force. For the first time the Newark defenders under Lord John Belasyse, were up against real professionals. The Scots built a great battering-fort, Edinburgh, the seventeenth-century equivalent of a *malvoisin*; while Poyntz had his own giant bastion, called Colonel Grey's Sconce. They not only set up two bridges of boats, but brought up an armed pinnace, mounting two guns and manned by forty musketeers, which penetrated the Trent defences to within half a mile of the castle itself. Then Poyntz dammed the River Smite and the arm of the Trent running immediately under the castle, putting the town mills out of action. By the end of March, 7,000 Scots and 9,000 English had the town 'closely invested', to within a range of 'about a cannon shot'. By April Poyntz had diverted both rivers away from Newark, had sapped right up to the Queen's Sconce, its main outwork, and had built a battery 'within musket shot' of one of the town gates; meanwhile the Scots had the castle itself within range of their guns. The surrender came in May. Belasyse had done his best to provision the town the previous winter; he had even issued his own diamond-shaped Newark coinage. But soon the garrison was down to horseflesh. Plague broke out. By May Newark, deprived of water for cleansing and washing, had become 'a miserable, stinking, infected town'. Even so,

when ordered to surrender, Belasyse burst into tears, for his men were still in good heart; he marched out with about 1,500. Poyntz was voted by the Commons a £200 sword and lands worth £300 a year. Newark was the last major action of the First Civil War; Oxford itself surrendered the following month.

One other respect in which the royalists, initially at least, enjoyed a huge advantage over their opponents was in their possession of a large number of fortified dwellings and castles. Properly garrisoned and provisioned they could cause a surprising amount of trouble, especially if they were provided with even quite primitive earthworks, to keep the besiegers' cannon from firing point-blank at the walls and towers. Thus at Lathom House, near Ormskirk, the Countess of Derby put up a desperate and protracted resistance against heavy odds. At Corfe, in Dorset, a new artillery bastion was built up against the curtain of the inner ward. At Sherborne Castle, a ravelin outwork, set up thirty-five yards in front of the south-west gatehouse, helped the defender to hold out for thirty-five days against the triumphant Sir Thomas Fairfax in 1645.

Two castles which gave parliament enormous trouble were Donnington, Elizabeth's old fourteenth-century stronghold, and Basing House, near Basingstoke, the ancestral home of the Marquess of Winchester. Both survived for most of the war on the borders of an area otherwise dominated by parliament, and impeded the advance and communications of its armies. Donnington was not, as it happened, even owned by the king: he had sequestered it from John Packer, Private Secretary to the Duke of Buckingham, for refusing a forced loan in 1640. As it commanded the Bath–London road, Charles decided to fortify it in September 1643 and sent Colonel John Boys with 200 foot, twenty-five horse and four cannon. Boys built a complete set of 'star' earthworks round it, at a cost of £1,000 – money well invested. In July 1644 the Earl of Essex sent General Middleton to take it with 3,000 dragoons and light cavalry. Middleton had no big guns, and lost 300 men in a hopeless attempt to attack with scaling ladders. In September Colonel Horton took over, with a siege-train. He shot at it for twelve days and 'beat down three towers and a part of the wall', but could not compel surrender. In October the Earl of Manchester wanted to try another storm, but, according to Clarendon, his men 'being well informed of the resolution of those within, declined that hot service'. They had expended over 1,000 great shot in nineteen days 'upon the walls without any further damage to the garrison than the beating down some old parts thereof'. Donnington was invested again towards the end of 1645, Cromwell detailing Colonel Dalbier to take it. Boys delayed the end by building a big satellite bastion on the castle hill, from which he launched sorties. But he could not match a giant mortar which Dalbier had acquired, and which he mounted near the present lodge. A large hole in the staircase tower of the gatehouse, though repaired in brick, testifies to its force; and it was reported to have fired seventeen rounds in one day, presumably a high rate. After parley, in March 1646, Boys surrendered with 200 men, twenty barrels of gunpowder and six pieces. His men marched out in some style, 'with bagge and baggage, musckets charged and primed, mache in Coke, bullate in mouthe, drumes beatinge and Collurers fleyinge. Every man tane with hime as much amunishion as hee could carye. As honourable Conditions as Could be given'.

The end of Basing House was less satisfactory. This enormous place, reckoned in Tudor times to be the largest private house in England, was originally a motte-and-bailey built by one of the Conqueror's companions, Hugh de Port. This survives in the shape of two baileys and a shell-keep, with a few ancient stones and sixteenth-century brick. The castle went to the Paulets in 1428, and a century later Sir William Paulet, Lord Treasurer for many years and later Marquess of Winchester, got a licence to crenellate a new house. The enormous early Tudor palace he built has gone, except for a gatehouse, but it seems to have had four or five broad towers, all with angle turrets. John Paulet, the 5th Marquess, was a very pious Roman Catholic, and a fanatical supporter of King Charles. He was said to have scratched *Aimez loyauté* on every window in the house with a diamond. He made Basing, on the main West Road, 'the onlie

rendezvous for the Cavaliers and Papists thereabouts'. Paulet put Humphrey Vanderblin, described as 'the ingenious and valient German', in charge of refashioning the defences, and he built a complete set of earthworks, some traces of which remain, outside and to the south of the ditches surrounding the medieval curtain.

Basing was an object of peculiar detestation to the Puritans. It was said to be stuffed with treasure and Papist priests. Actually, among those sheltering there were Inigo Jones and the engraver Wenceslaus Hollar. Cromwell finally determined to put an end to the nuisance in October 1645. He had five 'great guns', two of them demi-cannons, one a whole cannon, and two culverins; these guns could breach holes in any building. At Sherborne a similar siege-train under Fairfax had breached the castle in two days; at Winchester, they had made, in a single day, a breach in the wall wide enough for thirty men to enter. Cromwell spent the night before the assault in prayer, pondering a text from the 115th Psalm: 'They that make them are like unto them, so is every one that trusteth them' – an ominous thought. He attacked from both sides and carried the castle at the point of the sword. In such circumstances quarter was rarely given. Indeed, one of his officers, later the regicide General Thomas Harrison (hanged, drawn and quartered at the Restoration), killed a royalist major in cold blood, saying: 'Cursed be he, that doth the Lord's work negligently.' The Marquess himself was found in a bread-oven, saying his rosary. Inigo Jones was carried out stark naked, wrapped in a blanket. A quarter of the garrison, including six priests and a woman, were slaughtered; one was a giant, said to be nine feet high. Cromwell's chaplain called the interior 'fit to make an emperor's court'. The cellars were broached, and drunken soldiers accidentally set fire to the house. The Marquess, watching the flames, insisted that 'if the king had no more ground in England but Basing House, he would adventure as he did, and so maintain it to the uttermost'. Coldly, Cromwell had the structure 'knocked down and utterly slighted'.

There was a somewhat similar tale, though happily no

Far left: Sherborne Castle, updated during the Civil War by a ravelin outwork set up in front of the gatehouse, held out for thirty-five days against Sir Thomas Fairfax in 1645.

Left: Window of the Great Hall, Raglan Castle, seen from the Pitched Stone Court.

indiscriminate slaughter, at Raglan, the last of the great aristocratic homes to fall. This castle-palace of the Somersets, Earls of Worcester (and later Dukes of Beaufort) was the centre of a vast estate, with an annual rental of £24,000. The earl, a fanatical royalist, was reputed to be the richest man in England, and his family later claimed he had given over £1,000,000 to the king's cause. It was also said that the 'keeping of the garrison of Raglan, towards which till the very last there was never a penny contribution raysed or exacted, amounted to at the very least £40,000'. Certainly, the castle was a curious piece of the old society which the Civil War destroyed. It was run on patriarchal lines. The earl would permit neither swearing nor drinking. He was a learned man of great taste, who had built up a magnificent collection of works of art, and he had inherited an immense library, which included the finest collection of Welsh bardic manuscripts in existence, as well as thousands of other treasures. Raglan had other marvels, including much hydraulic machinery, installed by Lord Herbert, the earl's heir; it made roaring noises and terrified the rustics. But Herbert was not at Raglan; he was the king's general in South Wales, and the defence of the castle was entrusted to his younger brother, Lord Charles Somerset.

The earl took a number of precautions before the castle was invested. He had the trees in the home park cut down. He burnt down cottages in the line of fire. The fireplace and panelling in the best oak parlour were taken down and sent to one of his lesser houses (they are now at Badminton). Unfortunately he did not remove the library. As to siege-works, Lord Charles built a battery 500 yards north-east of the castle gatehouse, in the style recommended in official artillery handbooks; and he created an entirely new bastioned *enceinte*, covering the south, east and north sides, where attack was most expected. As a matter of fact, the siege itself was unnecessary, since by 1646, when Fairfax demanded the castle's surrender, it was clear the king's cause was lost. Other garrisons were freely submitting. But the earl (now promoted to marquess) was a proud man. It was boasted that 'Raglan and Pendennis, like winter fruit, hung long on.' The kind had issued general orders about yielding, but the earl was upset that Raglan was not referred to in them by name. So after exchanges of many messages, his obstinacy triumphed and he defied the parliament men: 'So I submit myself and yourself to do what you think fitting.'

The castle had a daily bombardment of sixty shot, each of eighteen to twenty pounds. They made little impression on the Great Tower, beyond destroying its battlements, but they did immense damage to other parts of the castle. In addition, the parliamentary chief engineer, Captain Hooper, planted 'four mortar pieces in one place and two mortar pieces at another, each mortar piece carrying a grenado shell twelve inches diameter'. These killed and wounded many. Worcester had 800 horse and foot in his castle and they made 'diverse desperate sallies'; but after the fall of Oxford the besieging force rose from 1,500 to 3,500, and the garrison was 'reduced to more caution and taught to lie closer'. In August, Worcester was induced to surrender to Fairfax. He and his household waited in the hall and 'could see through the window the general with all his officers entering the Outward Court, as if a floodgate had been let open'. Inside the castle were found twenty cannon, a huge powder magazine, and a powder mill capable of making three barrels a day; 'great store of corn and malt, wine of all sorts and beer'; the horses were 'almost starved for want of hay . . . and therefore were tied with chains'; there was also 'great store of goods and rich furniture'.

Raglan was 'the first fortified and the last rendered', for Pendennis had fallen two days before. The garrison were treated with great leniency, considering the eleven-week siege, and allowed to leave with colours flying and drums beating; the hundred officers, gentlemen and squires were even permitted to retain their arms, bag and baggage. But Worcester himself was detained in parliamentary custody, under the Black Rod, and died a few months later. His library, and much else of value, was deliberately burned, under the supervision, ironically, of Henry Herbert of Coldbrook, a direct descendant of the William ap Thomas, who had collected the rare manuscripts

Opposite: Raglan, one of the grandest of all medieval castles, was beseiged and heavily bombarded during the Civil War of the 1640s, and was afterwards 'slighted'. It still looks formidable.

Opposite: Montgomery, once a strong castle occupying a superb site on the Welsh borders, was demolished by the parliamentarians at the end of the Civil War and is now a romantic ruin.

and built the Great Tower. This last caused some trouble to the 'slighters': 'The Great Tower, after tedious battering the top thereof with pickaxes, was undermined, the weight of it propped with the timber, whilst the two sides of the six were cut through: the timber being burned it fell down in a lump, and so still firmly remains to this day.' It is interesting that the parliamentarians, in dealing with a superb piece of masonry like this tower, could think of nothing better than the old mining technique used by medieval siege-engineers – and fortunate, too, for enough was left, and still remains, of Raglan to give the visitor a strong idea of its former strength and magnificence.

The victorious parliamentary armies slighted the castles they stormed or which surrendered to them partly because the very existence of such strong points on balance favoured the royal interest; but partly also because the general public mood was hostile to castles, symbols of 'the Norman yoke' and of feudal services – now at last abolished in law by the Long Parliament – and of the expensive and cruel habits of an over-privileged aristocracy. Hence castles were demolished or rendered uninhabitable or indefensible even when there was no warrant from military necessity. Monmouth, the superb marcher castle in whose Great Tower Harry of Monmouth, the future Henry v, had been born, was another property of the Somersets. It surrendered peacefully to Sir Trevor Williams and Colonel Morgan in 1646, but was nevertheless largely destroyed the following year, the townspeople joining enthusiastically in pulling down the Great Tower and other strongpoints. At Montgomery, once the key to the central sector of the Welsh Marches, there seems to have been no fighting. Indeed, its owner, Lord Herbert of Cherbury, brother of the poet George Herbert, had built a new house within the walls of the old castle, already crumbling, in what had been the middle ward. The castle was neither defensible nor garrisoned. Nevertheless, in 1649 parliamentary commissioners ordered its destruction. As Izaak Walton wrote in his *Life of George Herbert* (1670): 'The Heirs of the Castle saw it level with that earth, that was too good

to bury those wretches that were the cause of it.'

But Walton's was the minority voice of the antiquarian and the connoisseur. Most people were glad to see the castles go. Even in 1660, when the whole ghastly business of the Civil War and its aftermath was over, opinion was still in favour of pulling down castles. At Caernarvon a demolition order was made, the local authorities agreeing, 'conceiving it to be for the great advantage of ourselves and posterity to have the Castle of Caernarvon and the strengths thereof demolished'. A hundred years later, when the first 'romantic' tourists began to arrive, the city fathers were mightily glad that, for some reason unknown to us, the order was never carried out!

Where the parliamentary generals were undoubtedly justified in tearing down walls and towers was during what Cromwell called the wholly 'mischievous' and unnecessary Second Civil War. For in these cases the castles which defied parliament were commanded by officers who had broken their oaths, and turned their coats in order to put up a futile fight for royalty. Cromwell, who was heavily involved in this business, was particularly angry that men who had taken parliament's shilling should now provoke the terrible hardship and bloodshed involved in storming heavily defended fortresses. This was the case, for instance, at a number of strong Welsh castles, such as Tenby, Chirk, Chepstow and Pembroke. At Chirk, held for the king by the former parliamentary commander Sir Thomas Myddleton, General Lambert was obliged to bring up a heavy siege-train and blast down the walls and towers. Afterwards one complete curtain, complete with towers, was demolished. At Chepstow, yet another castle of the Somersets, Sir Nicholas Kemeys, commanding a garrison of 120, was the turncoat. There, Cromwell's men built a four-gun heavy battery, deprived the garrison of its artillery by knocking down the battlements, and then breached the curtain-wall. The garrison then deserted, and Sir Nicholas was put to the sword during the assault.

At Pembroke, with its gigantic round keep, one of the strongest castles in the Commonwealth, Cromwell had a great

Right: Chepstow, an important medieval castle on the South Wales border, was besieged and taken by Cromwell during the Second Civil War. He put its commander to the sword. Later it served as a prison for the regicide Henry Marten.

Far right: Pontefract, where Richard II was put to death, was perhaps the strongest castle in England in the 1640s, but succumbed to Cromwell's artillery and was then levelled. Virtually nothing now remains.

deal of trouble during a siege that lasted seven weeks. Its mayor, John Poyer, had originally garrisoned it for parliament, but sided with the king in 1648, and was joined by Colonel Laugharne and other renegades; Cromwell described them as 'a very desperate enemy, very many of them gentlemen of quality and thoroughly resolved, and one of the strongest places in the country'. He was handicapped by the fact that he himself had an acute attack of gout, and no siege-train, since the ships carrying it foundered in a storm in the Bristol Channel, and ended up on the beach at Berkeley. For a time he made do with no guns at all, then borrowed some from the warship *Lion*, commanded by Captain Crowther – a reminder of how important it was that the navy sided with parliament. Even so, Pembroke was not battered into surrender. It gave in because the food was down to 'a little bisquit' and because, by means of treachery within the garrison, Cromwell was able to block the route to Wogan's Cavern, which contained the castle's water supply. Cromwell was very bitter against Poyer and Laugharne; he said he judged 'their iniquity double, because they have sinned against so much light, and against so many

evidences of Divine Presence'. Poyer was eventually shot in the piazza of Covent Garden. At Pembroke Cromwell did not trouble himself with trying to knock down the Great Tower, which might well have proved an even tougher nut than Raglan; but he brought down the outer walls and towers. Chepstow was made over to him by parliament, so he left it intact and garrisoned it; one of its towers survived to become the comfortable life-prison of Cromwell's fellow regicide, Henry Marten, before the castle was eventually dismantled as a military base in 1690.

Cromwell was even more enraged by the stout resistance put up by Pontefract, the great thirteenth-century Yorkshire stronghold, with its quatrefoil keep, rather like Clifford's Tower at York. He wrote to the Speaker: 'The place is very well known to be one of the strongest inland Garrisons of the Kingdom. Well watered; situated upon a rock in every part of it, and therefore difficult to mine. The walls very thick and high, with strong towers; and, if battered, very difficult to access, by reason of the depth and steepness of the graft.' Cannon proved useless; so did proffered bribes; and after a continuous siege of twelve

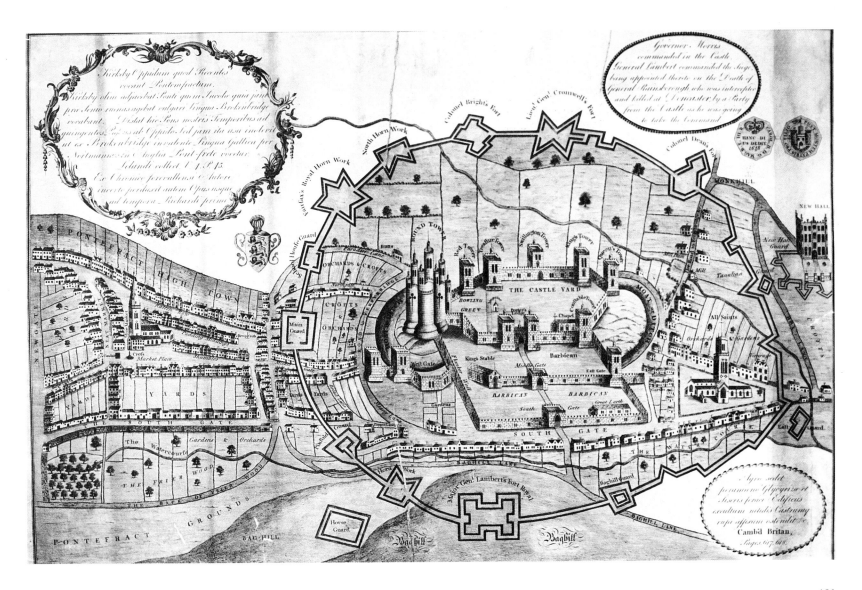

Monmouth was once an important Marcher castle. Henry V was born in its great tower. It surrendered peacefully during the Civil War but was nonetheless largely demolished by parliament and local people.

months the castle only surrendered because its supplies were gone and the execution of the king had made resistance pointless. In this case the slighting was carried out regardless of cost and with a thoroughness which left only a chunk of walling at the base of the tower, and fragments of the curtain. So once-impregnable Pontefract now only serves as a children's recreation ground.

The most important siege of the Second Civil War, and the only one comparable in scale to Newark, was at Colchester. There, over ten weeks, a major battle raged, for the three royalist commanders, Sir Charles Lucas, Sir George Lisle and Sir Bernard Gascoigne, had managed to concentrate in the town a force of 4,000 men, of whom 2,500 were well-armed, and 600 cavalry. Colchester, of course, was the oldest defended town in Britain, and it was perhaps appropriate that it should be the scene of the last great British siege. Ditches were dug, defending forts built, and the Balkerne Gate, originally a Roman triumphal arch, later a Roman defended gatepost, was turned into an artillery bastion. Colonel Ransborough, a parliamentary siege-expert, was put in charge of the investment, and later Fairfax brought a siege-train of forty guns from London. There were several desperate sorties, and much slaughter. Some 186 houses were destroyed and hundreds more damaged by the artillery bombardment. The Colchester people were anti-royalists, but helpless before such a large garrison. By mid-August 1648 food had run out, and the townsfolk begged the royalist commanders to surrender. The terms, negotiated at the end of the month, were harsh. Even the town was fined £14,000 and its walls torn down. Many of the garrison were transported as slaves to the West Indies. Lucas and Lisle were immediately secured in the castle, and told they would be shot forthwith. Both had been captured before, and had broken parole; they argued that their parole had been extracted under duress, and that in any case this was a new war; but in the bitter mood the casualties of the siege had brought about such excuses were brushed aside, and they were promptly dispatched by firing-party in the castle ditch.

Geoffrey's Window, Monmouth Castle.

How many castles in all were slighted by the parliamentary forces is hard now to discover exactly: probably about fifty or sixty. Few complained. When the monarchy was restored, it proved scarcely less ruthless. Many other royal castles simply went out of service and were allowed to decay. And, everywhere, the stone and lead thieves moved over the ruins, an ant-like army, working away industriously for decades, to remove the traces of the Middle Ages. But, such being the perversities and contradictions of human nature, while this work of erosion was still proceeding a few men of means were beginning a movement to reinvigorate the medieval castle in a new and less objectionable form.

CHAPTER NINE

'THE MONSTROUS PRACTICE OF CASTLE BUILDING'

St James's Palace, with its Tudor battlements designed for artistic rather than military purposes, is an early example of the practice of putting fake defensive features on palaces. Henry III invented the idea in the 13th century.

Previous page
left: Cardiff Castle.

right: Castle Drogo in Devon is a brilliantly designed but entirely fanciful exercise in castle architecture by Sir Edwin Lutyens. It is stunningly sited, with panoramic views.

It is not entirely surprising that the castle should have been resurrected as an architectural style, as opposed to a military instrument. Indeed in some respects the idiom of castellation had never been abandoned, having been adopted as a mainly or even purely decorative feature quite early in the history of the medieval stone castle. Henry III put 'fake' battlements on some of his country houses and hunting-boxes. He thus inaugurated a habit of conscious antiquarianism, or pseudo-chivalry, which became a feature of genuine castles in the fifteenth century, of Tudor town and country palaces (such as St James's) and which, in the case of some Oxbridge colleges, persisted into the second half of the seventeenth century.

The Tudors, although anxious to dissociate themselves from so many social and political aspects of the Middles Ages, were devoted to the (to them) romantic embellishments – pedigrees, coats-of-arms, joustings and mock-combats. It was inevitable that the kind of revivalism illustrated by Leicester's entertainments for Queen Elizabeth at Kenilworth should also express itself in architecture. And so it did. Sir Francis Willoughby came from an ancient family; but, like many other Elizabethan gentlemen, he was a *nouveau riche*. His estate at Wollaton, near Nottingham, was one of the richest coal-mining sites in the country (it also produced iron ore), and he profited hugely from the vast expansion of the coal trade which was so marked a feature of Elizabeth's day. Some £80,000 of his income he devoted to building a sumptuous castle-palace at Wollaton, in the years just before the Armada. While other rich men, like the Thynnes at Longleat, were embracing Renaissance classicism, the scheme at Wollaton exhibits a deliberate harking-back to medieval ideas. It consists of a central square 'keep', surrounded by four *corps de logis*, with square angle-towers. It differs from a castle in that there is no internal courtyard, for the building is solid; the keep occupies a dominant place, as in a castle, because it towers above the large central hall around which the living-rooms lie. The hall is fifty-three feet high, and its windows are thirty-five feet above the floor. Its roof, with its hammer-beam construction, is also a medieval hark-back, and the castle-gothic idiom appears likewise in the keep's windows.

Wollaton may have been a rarity; but it was not unique. It was the work of Robert Smythson, a master-mason active also at Longleat and Wardour, and who is described on a tomb in Wollaton Church as the 'architect and surveyor' of Wollaton Hall. Not so far away, at Bolsover Castle in Derbyshire, his son John Smythson built for Sir Charles Cavendish, son of the famous Bess of Hardwick, a keep-like structure. This seventeenth-century exercise in medievalism is of four storeys, the lower two vaulted, built square with three small angle-turrets, and with 'antique' hooded fireplaces.

The true medieval–romantic revival, however, did not take place until nearly a hundred years later, when leading aesthetes and craftsmen began to react forcefully against the rigidity and symmetry of classicism. Culzean, as remodelled by Robert Adam, Vanbrugh Castle and Walpole's Strawberry Hill were signs of the times. The first real centre of the cult was Herefordshire, already rich in ruinous castles of the Welsh Marches. One of them, Croft Castle, was owned by Richard Knight, the son of a wealthy iron-master from Shropshire, then in the first stages of the Industrial Revolution. The castle dated from the late fourteenth and early fifteenth centuries, and was large, quadrangular, with four round corner-towers. In the decade 1750–60, Knight 'gothicized' it, inside and out. His nephew, Richard Payne Knight, carried the process a stage further. In 1772–8 he built Downton Castle in the Herefordshire forest of Bringewood, originally bought by the Knights to supply fuel to their furnaces. Building the castle was an exercise in landscaping. The theory ultimately derived from the paintings of Claude, Poussin and Salvator Rosa: a truly perfect landscape was incomplete without a building, preferably ruinous, and woods and gorges, in particular, demanding buildings that were castellated. In Bringewood forest, on a magnificent site overlooking the River Teme with woody crags below, Knight found the ideal setting for his house, one of the earliest contrived mansions in the castle style. He was thinking entirely in terms of landscape and externals: the interiors are

classical. But he argued that regularity was more appropriate to ecclesiastical buildings; irregularity made a new type of gentleman's house possible, since the comfort of the internal arrangements did not have to be sacrificed to a tyrannical symmetry. Moreover, as he pointed out, once an irregular outline became acceptable, sons and grandsons would be able to add to the house at will, as their distant ancestors had done, without fear of spoiling the 'shape'. (An appropriate thought in the case of Downton, which was greatly altered in the nineteenth century.)

In 1794, Payne Knight elaborated the new aesthetic of irregularity in his poem *The Landscape*; and the same year saw the publication of two complimentary works – *Essay on the Picturesque*, by a neighbouring Herefordshire squire, Uvedale Price; and *Sketches and Hints on Landscape Gardening* by the great

Bolsover, in Derbyshire, is a 17th-century exercise in medievalism, with a 'keep' of four storeys, the lower two vaulted, and three small angle-turrets. There are antique hooded fireplaces and other conscious anachronisms.

Humphry Repton. It was Repton's collaboration with the architect John Nash, who was taken up by the Prince Regent and many other wealthy amateurs, which really began the vogue of castle-building. At Luscombe, in Devon, the banker Charles Hoare commissioned the pair to create for him a gothic castle and its setting, and the opportunity was taken to translate theory into perfect practice. Price had pointed out, in his *Essay*, that the building of a house should not only reflect the irregularity of nature, but should emulate its light and shade, and its varieties of texture. Repton rejected the idea of building Hoare a villa because 'if the Grecian or modern style were adopted here, the roof would be unsightly from every part of the grounds'. On the other hand, by giving the house 'the Character of a Castle', he could blend 'a chaste correctness of proportion with bold integrity of outline, its deep recesses and projections producing broad masses of light and shadow, while its roof, enriched by turrets, battlements, corbells and lofty chimneys, has infinitely more picturesque effect'. He also argued, putting a more commercial point, that irregularity added to 'the Consequence' of a house, since 'the offices and mere Walls', which in an ordinary house 'it would be essential to conceal', could be made much of by castellation, and so would 'extend the Site and make it an apparently considerable pile of building'.

In fact at Luscombe the effect is not of weightiness, but of a delightful airiness and lightness, emphasized by the large, low, delicate gothic windows, and the seemingly fragile Chippendale furniture installed within. But perhaps inevitably, and certainly in lesser hands, gothicization tended to produce the ponderous. At Eastmore, again in Herefordshire, Sir Robert Smirke (architect of Covent Garden) built for the 2nd Lord Somers, from 1812, a gigantic replica of what he imagined a medieval castle should be. Stones were dragged by mules from the Forest of Dean at a reputed cost of £12,000; but a shortage of timber led to the use of cast-iron stanchions in the roof. Inside a vast hall was constructed, fifty-five feet long, which was speedily festooned with suits of armour; a library, by G. E. Fox, was designed and decorated in the Italian style, apparently based on the sacristy of Santa Maria delle Grazie in Milan; and finally a gothic drawing-room, swarming with heraldic devices and hung with gigantic brass chandeliers modelled on those in Nuremberg Cathedral, was supplied by Augustus Pugin, almost the last thing he did before his death in 1852.

Still farther away from the Nash–Repton mode was Penrhyn Castle in Gwynedd, built for the Welsh slate-millionaire George Hay Dawkins-Pennant, from 1827 onwards. Penrhyn was the original home of the Tudor dynasty in the fourteenth century, and had already been reconstructed as a 'medieval' house by Samuel Wyatt in 1782. But then, with the publication of Scott's *Ivanhoe* in 1820, came the 'Norman Revival', and Thomas Hopper was brought in to 'Normanize' the castle. Hopper could design in any mode and based his enormous practice on the principle: 'It is an architect's business to understand all styles and to be prejudiced in favour of none.' For Penrhyn he shipped over hard grey 'Mona Marble' from Anglesey, and followed a Norman decorative mode throughout. The keep, 115 feet high and 62 feet broad, was square, sombre, and modelled on Rochester and Hedingham. There was a circular 'Ice Tower', a barbican, and defensible walls; even the drawing-room and the library were 'Norman', and remarkably well done too. Hopper used the material on which the fortune of the family was built, slate, for his interiors. Thus for the state bedroom he had carved a 'Jacobeathan' four-poster bed, with 'Norman' mouldings, out of a slate-block weighing four tons. This was set aside for the use of Queen Victoria, when she stayed in the castle in 1851; she declined, on the ground that 'It is interesting but uninviting.'

With Penrhyn, and other vast gothic piles put up at the same period, such as Toddington Manor in Gloucestershire, the impulse changed from the purely aesthetic, of Nash and Repton, to the historical and the quest for reproductive accuracy. Rich men began to want to relive medieval scenes against an appropriate architectural background. There was a good deal of snobbery in this, a hankering for a hierarchical system in an age when the middle class was fighting hard to grab power. There was also a partly sublimated religious impulse, expressed in the cult of chivalry. Its notions were described in great detail by Kenelm Digby's *Broadstone of Honour*, published in 1822, and a steady seller for many years (it was Burne-Jones's favourite bedside book). There was, finally, the sheer love of pageantry, inflamed by the enormously successful Scott novels, which poured from the presses, sometimes two a year. George IV had set the tone publicly with the elaborate antiquarian arrangements he made for his coronation in 1820. But when Victoria was crowned, in 1838, Lord Melbourne insisted on dropping much of the medieval pageantry, on the grounds of expense. This annoyed the more romantic members of the aristocracy, and especially the young Lord Eglington, whose stepfather had a hereditary right to a part in the ceremony. Hence he decided, the following year, to stage a compensatory tournament at Eglington Castle, his neo-baronial home on the west coast of Scotland. It was held on 28 August 1839, and attracted enormous publicity and a crowd of 100,000 people. Samuel Pratt of Bond Street supplied the armour; Lady Seymour, granddaughter of the playwright Sheridan, was the Queen of Beauty, and the bill came to £40,000. The affair was a fiasco, since it poured with rain, and meretricious to a degree. But it symbolized an age when the new parliament buildings were being gothicized inside and out, and architects and decorators were searching industriously for the concrete reality of medievalism.

But was 'the real thing' desirable? Nash, for instance, had used a gothic vernacular, but he had not aimed to create authentic castles; quite the contrary. But by the 1840s and 1850s that was precisely what architects and their patrons were doing. Sir George Gilbert Scott, the leading theorist, did not approve of the trend. Architecture, he felt, should indeed reflect the nature of society:

> Providence has ordained the different orders and gradations into which the human family is divided, and it

Opposite: Eastnor, in Herefordshire, is a gigantic mock castle, built from 1812 onwards by the architect Sir Robert Smirke for the 2nd Lord Somers. It has a baronial hall fifty-five feet long.

Penrhyn, a massive Welsh mock castle, was built for a slate-millionaire from 1827 onwards. Inspired by Sir Walter Scott's *Ivanhoe*, it was designed in Norman style with a keep modelled on Rochester.

is right and necessary that it should be maintained. . . .
The position of a landed proprietor, be he squire or
nobleman, is one of dignity. . . . He is the natural head of
his parish or district . . . in which he should be looked
up to as a bond of union between the classes. . . . He has
been placed by providence in a position of authority and
dignity, and no false modesty should deter him from
expressing this, quietly and gravely, in the character of his
house. (*Remarks on Secular and Domestic Architecture*, 1857.)

But Sir George thought that this argument, though sound, was
a delicate one, easily brought into contempt and ridicule, and
he feared that that was precisely what the cult of imitation
castles was liable to do – especially, though he did not say this,
since so many of them were built by men who had made their
money in trade:

The monstrous practice of castle-building is, unh-
appily, not yet extinct. . . . The largest and most carefully
and learnedly executed Gothic mansion of the present
day is not only a castle in name – it is not a sham fortress,
such as those of twenty years back, whose frowning
gateway is perhaps flanked on either side by a three-foot
clipped hedge – but it is a real and carefully constructed
medieval fortress, capable of standing a siege from an
Edwardian army. . . . Now this is the very height of
masquerading. The learning and skill with which the
pageant has been carried out reflect the highest credit
upon the architect; yet I cannot but feel it to have been a
serious injury to our case, that so unreal a task should
have been imposed on him.

Scott obviously had in mind the architect Anthony Salvin,
and his extraordinary creation, Peckforton Castle in Cheshire.
Salvin was perhaps the best, and purest, of the imitation-castle
designers. He was himself a pupil of Nash, and as a young man
he had restored the Great Hall at Brancepeth Castle, in his

native Durham. He actually understood what medieval military
engineering was about; but he was no head-in-the-air romantic.
When Lionel, 1st Lord Tollemache, decided to build at
Peckforton in 1844, Salvin was recommended to him (by his
colleague Alfred Waterhouse) as 'celebrated for the way in
which he can combine the exterior and plan of an Edwardian
castle with nineteeth-century elegance and comfort'. This was
just what Tollemache wanted. As a landowner with a 26,000-
acre estate, he was an enlightened despot, a believer in feudal
hierarchy and *noblesse oblige*. He seems to have invented the
policy of 'three acres and a cow' for all, and wrote: 'The only real
and lasting pleasure to be derived from the possession of a
landed estate is to witness the improvement in the social
conditions of those residing on it.' Thus he spent £280,000 on
building new farmhouses and cottages, but he also set aside
£68,000 for a castle to emphasize his own position at the head
of the pyramid.

Inverary, home of the
Dukes of Argyll, is a
16th-century castle,
completely reconstructed
as an eclectic 18th-century
château in blue-green
granite, and topped by
green Victorian
cone-towers.

For his purposes (whatever may be thought of them) Salvin's creation was exactly right. He had the gift for grouping, essential for creating the feeling of medieval authenticity. Peckforton is minatory, but its towers are not too high for use, and it gives the impression – as Scott feared – of actually being defensible. From Salvin's beautiful watercolours and drawings, it is evident that he composed it pictorially, paying great attention to colour, light, shade, silhouette and texture. This is a real castle, if not a functional one, not a stone veneer for a palace. In fact Salvin put the kitchen sixty yards from the dining-room, something no medieval baron would willingly have permitted, unless he entertained a morbid dread of fire. On the other hand, the stonework and attention to detail is superlative, in the best tradition of James of St George and Henry VIII himself.

There were other rich men, like Tollemache, who built castles to reinforce social theory. Salvin advised on the construction of Bayon's Manor, Lincolnshire, for Charles Tennyson d'Eyncourt, though the actual architect was a local man. Here, largely by accident, the life-rhythm of a true medieval castle was followed. First came a gothic manor-house, with a tower; then, from 1839, it was surrounded with a huge series of fortifications, outer curtain and wall, with towers and bastions, and a second wall, surrounding the whole house. The inner wall had two gateways, but the outer one, defended by barbican, moat and drawbridge, had only one, so that visitors had to make a series of detours and circumnavigations to get to the house, and in the course of their wanderings saw all the delights of the castle, including a huge keep, built as a ruin, on a mound inside the inner wall. Like all imitation castles of the period, Bayon's had a great hall, its owner believing, with Pugin, that 'under the oaken rafters of their capacious halls, the lords of the manor used to assemble all their friends and tenants at those successive periods when the church bids all her children rejoice, while humbler guests partook of their share of the bounty dealt to them by the almoner beneath the ground entrance of the gatehouse'. It is not known whether Bayon's had an almoner

Far left: Cardiff Castle was transformed by the Victorian architect William Burges from a ruined Anglo-Norman fortress into a sumptuously decorated Gothic palace with medieval military decor.

Left: Powis Castle is an old Welsh stronghold, held by both the Herbert and the Clive families. Intelligently restored by the architect G. F. Bodley in the 1900s, it is notable for its gardens and art collection.

but in 1842 a banquet on the lines indicated by Pugin was held there to celebrate the birth of the Prince of Wales and the departure of the eldest son of the manor to join his regiment abroad. Alas, like many true castles, Bayon's Manor became derelict and ruinous with the passage of time, and in 1965 was brutally 'slighted'.

But other Victorian exercises in the castle-style survive, notably the two masterly reconstructions which William Burges created for the 3rd Marquess of Bute at Cardiff and Castell Coch. The Butes were an old and wealthy Scottish family, with extensive estates in Wales, who made themselves multi-millionaires in the mid-nineteenth century by developing the docks and city of Cardiff. The young 3rd marquess, who became a catholic, was fascinated, almost mesmerized, by the medieval past, and by the desire to re-create it; and he had an income of £151,000 a year. In 1865, he joined forces with Burges,

who had already noted the possibilities offered by the ruined Norman castle of Cardiff (a prison of the wretched Robert, Duke of Normandy, the Conqueror's eldest son), which had been given a veneer of Georgian gothic by Capability Brown in about 1776. Burges, like Bute, was a passionate medievalist, who hated industrialization, wore antique clothes in the privacy of his rooms, and numbered Pre-Raphaelites like Rossetti and Simeon Solomon among his friends. He was a skilled decorator as well as an architect, and his plans for Cardiff were both monumental and riotously elaborate. He worked there from 1868 until his death in 1881, and the building and decorating continued long after.

Burges first altered and enlarged a suite of lodgings, on medieval foundations. Then he added a 150-foot clock tower, at one angle of the castle enclosure. This was essentially a bachelor tower-suite, with winter and summer smoking-

rooms, a bedroom and offices, and servants' rooms. (Bute did not marry until 1872.) Off the bedroom was a magnificent Roman bath, a genuine article, converted to Victorian plumbing, and the summer smoking-room, which led to a magnificent viewpoint on the top of the tower. This room was a fantasy of rich Victorian decoration, complete with a vast gilt chandelier, in the shape of the rays of the sun, with a gold Apollo standing triumphantly at the centre. Then, over the years, Burges added a sixteenth-century style tower, with a high-pitched roof, an octagonal fifteenth-century tower, finished off with a timber flèche, a new domestic wing and tower, and the main Bute Tower – all five towers designed to be seen clustered together, producing a skyline of enormous complexity and busyness. The Bute Tower had bedrooms, bathrooms and other facilities for the Marquess, now married. But Burges's favourite building was, perhaps, the flèche tower, which had an octagonal staircase, decorated with a carved crocodile at the top of the balustrade, feasting its eyes on a plump carved baby on the rail beneath – a brilliant touch showing how well Burges knew how to recapture medieval sculptural fancies.

Of course Cardiff does not look like any medieval castle that ever existed; in this respect it has more in common with the creations of mad King Ludwig of Bavaria than anything Salvin designed. But at Castell Coch, also in Glamorgan, on the site of an old motte-and-bailey castle which had been destroyed in the fifteenth century, Burges came much closer to the Salvin manner in the use of massive stonework. He followed the original ground plan, but he used grey limestone instead of the red sandstone with which the original castle was built; and, above the bases, his concept of the shape and height of the towers and curtain was purely conjectural. Thus he made the towers much higher than they probably were in reality, and of unequal height, with high pitched roofs in the continental style. The courtyard, too, though immensely impressive in its massive strength, is unlike any medieval model anywhere. Bute's bedroom was immediately over the drawbridge, which was a

Far left: Castell Coch, in South Wales, is on the site of an old motte-and-bailey castle, but is actually a fanciful exercise in romantic imagination by William Burges. He built it for the multi-millionaire 3rd Marquess of Bute.

Left: Castell Coch has some spectacular internal decorations by William Burges, including this drawing-room fireplace surmounted by the Three Fates. He died before the castle was finished, however, and his successors toned down his exuberance.

working one, but Burges was obliged to cheat with the machinery so as not to interfere with his patron's comfort. On the other hand, the well is genuine, there are proper 'murder holes' above the gateway, and the cellar-dungeon has an authentic look.

Burges died before work on the interior decorations at Castell Coch really began in earnest, and left only outline plans, the exuberance of which his successors toned down. So there is none of the spectacular magnificence of Cardiff. But some curious details, in the Burges style, were inserted. Lady Bute's round bedroom, at the top of the main tower, with a curved and domed roof, contains not only a great bed of state, adorned with glittering crystal balls, and worthy of Henry III himself, but an ingenious dressing-table and washstand, with porcelain towers containing water – a device for which there is at least one medieval precedent, at Battle Hall, Kent, as we have noted.

Opposite: Belvoir, in Leicestershire, is the dramatic hill-fortress of the Dukes of Rutland. Lived in for almost a millenium, it has been rebuilt three times and what we now see is mostly 19th-century work.

Bute could never have enough of such details. At Castell Coch, in 1875, he insisted on planting his own vineyard, to supply wine for his table (as he believed had been done there in the Middle Ages). He liked to ask his guests what they thought of the results, 'Well now, Lord Bute,' said Sir Herbert Maxwell, 'it is what I should call an interesting wine.' Perhaps the comment could serve for both the Bute–Burges ventures.

Meanwhile many of the stately castles of England were undergoing less imaginative but equally thoroughgoing restorations and transformations. There was plenty of money to do it, for many ancient families found their incomes multiplied in the nineteenth century, as a result of coalmining, the rise in the value of agricultural land (at least until the 1880s) and, above all, by the boom in house property in London and other cities. Thus the Grosvenors were able to spend £600,000 on the new palace at Eaton Hall, the Howards of Arundel must have laid down over £1 million on a series of restorations, and it cost the 4th Duke of Northumberland £250,000 to 'restore' Alnwick. These expensive undertakings produced very mixed results. At Dunster Castle, in Somerset, once a Mohun stronghold, Anthony Salvin did some splendid work in the years following 1867, and the result is one of the most attractive architectural medleys in Britain, though this castle, apart from its foundations, is essentially a Victorianized Elizabethan–Jacobean–Restoration manor-house, rather than a medieval stronghold. Salvin's work at Alnwick, especially his massive vaulted entrance-way and the inner court to which it leads, is also of a very high standard. At Powis Castle, an old Welsh stronghold later held by the Herberts and the Clives – it thus unites two magnificent artistic collections, and is rich in artistic objects of all kinds – the architect G. F. Bodley carried out a very well-judged restoration in the 1900s.

Sometimes, however, there were several layers of refurbishing. At Arundel, in some ways the most magnificent of all English medieval castles, the 10th Duke of Norfolk spent £600,000 embellishing the walls and towers in 1780s gothic – only to have the 15th duke sweep all away at the end of the nineteenth century in a vast programme of 'Normanization'. The visitor will find great quantities of the original medieval masonry and detail of all periods, from the twelfth century onwards, but he must look for it. At Belvoir, the superb hill-fortress of the Manners, Dukes of Rutland, the castle was completely rebuilt in 1654–68 (after a Commonwealth demolition), by a pupil of Inigo Jones. But Restoration Belvoir was swept away by James Wyatt, who rebuilt it in the gothic style in the early nineteenth century; and this, in turn, was damaged by a fire in 1816, which destroyed the whole of the north-east and the north-west fronts, the grand staircase crumbling into powder from the heat. The rebuilding which followed was an amateur affair by the Reverend Sir John Thoroton, the 5th duke's chaplain, with the help of the duchess, though Wyatt's sons acted as advisers. In 1846, *White's Directory* called it 'by far the most superb architectural ornament of which Leicestershire can boast'. Modern opinion is more critical; but it is, perhaps, desirable to bring a very open mind and catholic tastes to the contemplation of any historic castle which has been lived in for nearly a millennium.

North of the Border the castle had never been abandoned as the customary habitation of the upper classes, but there too it enjoyed an architectural revival in the closing decades of the eighteenth century, just as the clan system was dissolving as a military force. At Inveraray the Dukes of Argyll completely reconstructed their early sixteenth-century castle, according to an eclectic château-plan devised in 1743 by Roger Morris. The result, completed in 1770, with its blue-green granite and Victorian green cone-towers, is a magnificent essay in castellated *pastiche*, and the source of much later architectural idiom in the highlands. A decade later, Robert Adam turned Culzean Castle, Ayrshire, on its wild, cliff-top site, into a stately Georgian mansion with Gothic embellishments, adding another brilliant set of much-imitated conventions to the northern architectural vocabulary.

With the nineteenth century, and the commercial boom in the highland way of life, many great tower-house castles of the

Dunrobin, on the Sutherland coast, was transformed in 1844–50 from a mixture of medieval castle and Renaissance house into a vast Victorian château with a silhouette of breathtaking extravagance.

fifteenth, sixteenth and seventeenth centuries were expanded and modernized. Glamis was more than doubled in size, not really to the advantage of its appearance. At Dunrobin, on the coast of Sutherland, a modest medieval castle was transformed, in 1844–50, into a vast and highly decorative château, with a silhouette of breathtaking extravagance, thanks to the immense fortune of the 2nd Duke of Sutherland. These are all matters of taste. So, too, are the brand new exercises in Scottish baronial which date from the middle years of the nineteenth century and later. At Balmoral, in 1848, Queen Victoria and Prince Albert, having bought a highland property they had never seen, arrived to find 'a pretty little castle in the old Scotch style'. In fact, it had been built less than twenty years before by John Smith, an Aberdeen architect. (Before that it had been a fifteenth-century tower-house.) Albert described this house as 'of granite, with numerous small turrets, and whitewashed, and situated on rising ground . . . the air is glorious and clear, but cold'. Victoria, who had been recommended to the pure, dry air of Deeside by her physician, also liked the place: 'All seemed to breathe freedom and peace, and to make one forget the world.' But in 1852 she was left a large fortune by John Camden Nield, a learned barrister and miser, who denied himself the barest necessities to accumulate cash for the monarch. With this the royal couple bought the fee-simple of the estate, demolished the 'pretty little castle', and built Balmoral, believed to be the largest castle in Scotland. The architect was William Smith (son of John Smith of Aberdeen), but he merely looked after the details: the castle was, as the queen said: 'My dearest Albert's own creation, own work, own building, own laying out.' The great square tower is eighty feet high, and to some may seem top-heavy. The ballroom is sixty-eight feet long, and the dining- and drawing-room correspondingly ample; and, even today, the castle is capable of sleeping 130 people.

Balmoral has had its critics. Its decorations were described as 'tartanities'. Lord Clarendon thought the plaids there 'would rejoice the heart of a donkey'; the whole place he summed up as 'the scramble of rural royalty'. Disraeli hated it (it rained for the entire five days he was there). He found the library a mess: it contained twenty-six identical guide-books, thirty-two *Ladies of the Lake* and a round dozen of Sir William Vernon's *Rob Roy*. Harcourt called it 'a hole'; Lady Dalhousie said: 'I never saw anything more uncomfortable and that I coveted less.' In 1878 Prince Leopold expressed such 'intense aversion' to the castle that he refused to go there at all, an act of rebellion which his mother, the queen, declared had 'placed the whole authority of the Sovereign and the Throne in jeopardy'.

But others, beside the queen, liked Balmoral, and still do. For it, and its many imitations, seemed to sum up the spirit and aspirations of those who refuse, even today, to believe that the age of the castle is entirely dead, and who still try to prolong it into an alien and mundane epoch.

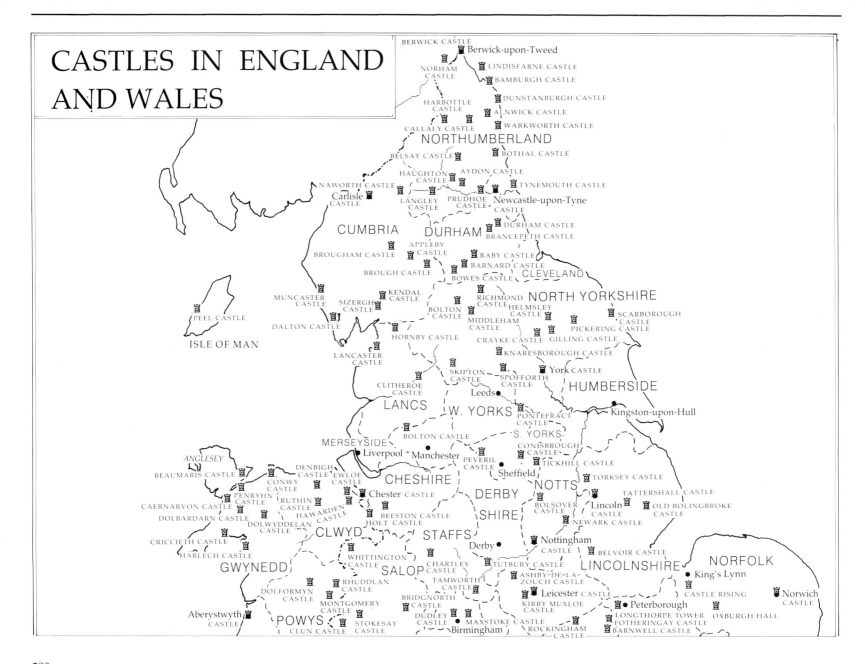

CASTLES IN ENGLAND AND WALES

BERWICK CASTLE
Berwick-upon-Tweed
NORHAM CASTLE
LINDISFARNE CASTLE
BAMBURGH CASTLE
HARBOTTLE CASTLE
DUNSTANBURGH CASTLE
ALNWICK CASTLE
CALLALY CASTLE
WARKWORTH CASTLE
NORTHUMBERLAND
BELSAY CASTLE
BOTHAL CASTLE
HAUGHTON CASTLE
AYDON CASTLE
NAWORTH CASTLE
TYNEMOUTH CASTLE
Carlisle CASTLE
LANGLEY CASTLE
PRUDHOE CASTLE
Newcastle-upon-Tyne
CUMBRIA
DURHAM
DURHAM CASTLE
BRANCEPETH CASTLE
APPLEBY CASTLE
RABY CASTLE
BROUGHAM CASTLE
BARNARD CASTLE
BROUGH CASTLE
CLEVELAND
BOWES CASTLE
MUNCASTER CASTLE
KENDAL CASTLE
RICHMOND CASTLE
NORTH YORKSHIRE
SIZERGH CASTLE
HELMSLEY CASTLE
SCARBOROUGH CASTLE
PEEL CASTLE
BOLTON CASTLE
DALTON CASTLE
MIDDLEHAM CASTLE
PICKERING CASTLE
ISLE OF MAN
HORNBY CASTLE
CRAYKE CASTLE
GILLING CASTLE
LANCASTER CASTLE
KNARESBOROUGH CASTLE
SKIPTON CASTLE
York CASTLE
SPOFFORTH CASTLE
CLITHEROE CASTLE
Leeds
HUMBERSIDE
LANCS
W. YORKS
Kingston-upon-Hull
PONTEFRACT CASTLE
BOLTON CASTLE
S. YORKS.
MERSEYSIDE
CONISBROUGH CASTLE
Liverpool Manchester
PEVERIL CASTLE
TICKHILL CASTLE
ANGLESEY
Sheffield
TORKSEY CASTLE
BEAUMARIS CASTLE
DENBIGH CASTLE
EWLOE CASTLE
CHESHIRE
NOTTS
TATTERSHALL CASTLE
CONWY CASTLE
DERBY
PENRHYN CASTLE
RUTHIN CASTLE
Chester CASTLE
BOLSOVER CASTLE
Lincoln
OLD BOLINGBROKE CASTLE
CAERNARVON CASTLE
HAWARDEN CASTLE
SHIRE
CASTLE
DOLBARDARN CASTLE
BEESTON CASTLE
NEWARK CASTLE
DOLWYDDELAN CASTLE
HOLT CASTLE
CLWYD
STAFFS
Derby
Nottingham
CRICCIETH CASTLE
BELVOIR CASTLE
CASTLE
WHITTINGTON CASTLE
CHARTLEY CASTLE
TUTBURY CASTLE
LINCOLNSHIRE
NORFOLK
HARLECH CASTLE
GWYNEDD
SALOP
TAMWORTH CASTLE
ASHBY-DE-LA-ZOUCH CASTLE
King's Lynn
RHUDDLAN CASTLE
Leicester CASTLE
DOLFORMYN CASTLE
BRIDGNORTH CASTLE
KIRBY MUXLOE CASTLE
CASTLE RISING
Norwich CASTLE
MONTGOMERY CASTLE
Peterborough
LONGTHORPE TOWER
OXBURGH HALL
Aberystwyth CASTLE
DUDLEY CASTLE
MAXSTOKE CASTLE
FOTHERINGAY CASTLE
POWYS
STOKESAY CASTLE
ROCKINGHAM CASTLE
BARNWELL CASTLE
CLUN CASTLE
Birmingham

200

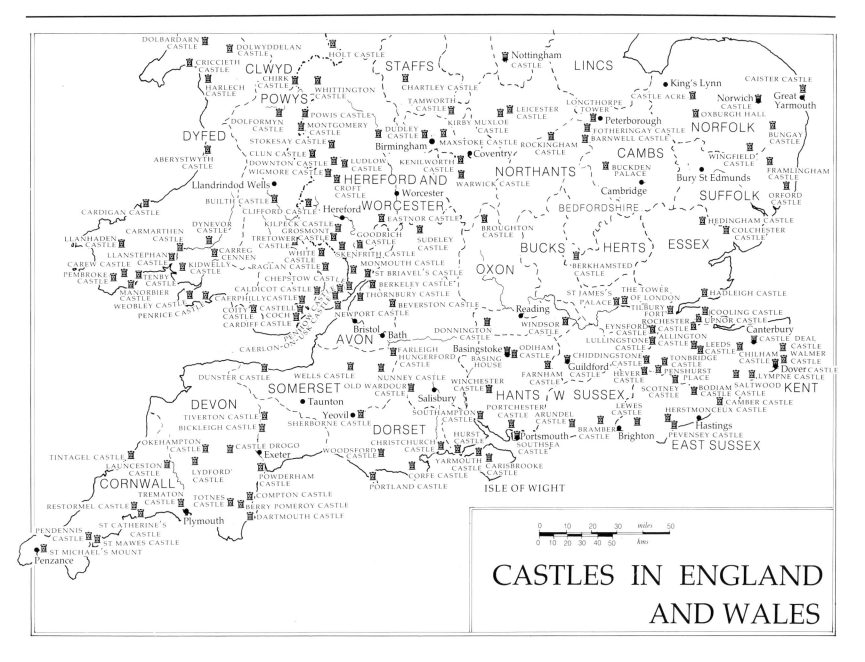

CASTLES IN ENGLAND
AND WALES

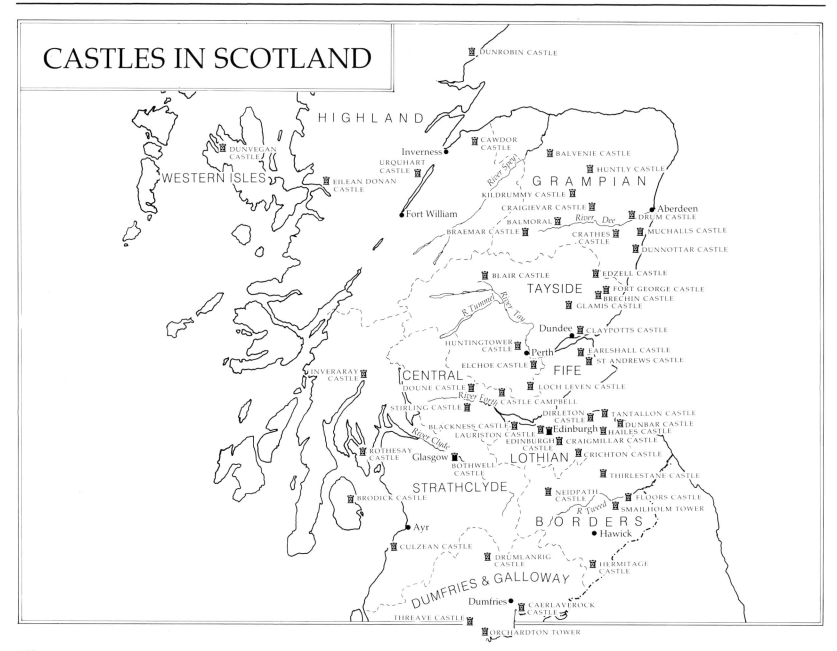

CASTLES IN SCOTLAND

DUNROBIN CASTLE

HIGHLAND

DUNVEGAN CASTLE

WESTERN ISLES

Inverness

CAWDOR CASTLE

BALVENIE CASTLE

URQUHART CASTLE

HUNTLY CASTLE

GRAMPIAN

EILEAN DONAN CASTLE

River Spey

KILDRUMMY CASTLE

CRAIGIEVAR CASTLE

Aberdeen

Fort William

BALMORAL

River Dee

DRUM CASTLE

BRAEMAR CASTLE

CRATHES CASTLE

MUCHALLS CASTLE

DUNNOTTAR CASTLE

BLAIR CASTLE

EDZELL CASTLE

TAYSIDE

FORT GEORGE CASTLE

R Tummel

River Tay

BRECHIN CASTLE

GLAMIS CASTLE

Dundee

CLAYPOTTS CASTLE

INVERARAY CASTLE

HUNTINGTOWER CASTLE

EARLSHALL CASTLE

Perth

ST ANDREWS CASTLE

ELCHOE CASTLE

FIFE

CENTRAL

DOUNE CASTLE

LOCH LEVEN CASTLE

River Forth

CASTLE CAMPBELL

STIRLING CASTLE

DIRLETON CASTLE

TANTALLON CASTLE

BLACKNESS CASTLE

DUNBAR CASTLE

LAURISTON CASTLE

Edinburgh

HAILES CASTLE

River Clyde

EDINBURGH CASTLE

CRAIGMILLAR CASTLE

ROTHESAY CASTLE

Glasgow

LOTHIAN

CRICHTON CASTLE

BOTHWELL CASTLE

STRATHCLYDE

THIRLESTANE CASTLE

BRODICK CASTLE

NEIDPATH CASTLE

FLOORS CASTLE

R Tweed

SMAILHOLM TOWER

Ayr

B O R D E R S

Hawick

CULZEAN CASTLE

DRUMLANRIG CASTLE

HERMITAGE CASTLE

DUMFRIES & GALLOWAY

Dumfries

CAERLAVEROCK CASTLE

THREAVE CASTLE

ORCHARDTON TOWER

GAZETTEER
Selected castles open to the public

Every effort has been made to provide accurate information regarding opening times but they do change from year to year and it would be advisable to check with the castle concerned before a visit, especially during Public and Bank Holidays.

Last admission times, unless stated otherwise, are half an hour before closing.

NT   – National Trust
NTS – National Trust for Scotland
AME – Ancient Monument, England (English Heritage)

AMS – Ancient Monument, Scotland (Scottish Development Department)
AMW – Ancient Monument, Wales (Cadw)

ENGLAND

Alnwick Castle
Alnwick, Northumberland   Tel. (0665) 602207
May–Sept: Sun–Fri & Bank Hol. Sat 1–5

Arundel Castle
Arundel, West Sussex   Tel. (0903) 883136
Apr–last Fri in Oct: Sun–Fri 1–5 (opens 12 June–Aug)

Bamburgh Castle
Bamburgh, Northumberland   Tel. (066 84) 208
Apr–last Sun in Oct: daily 1–5 (4.30 in Oct)

Berkeley Castle
Berkeley, Gloucestershire   Tel. (0453) 810332
Apr & Sept: daily except Mon 2–5; May–Aug: daily except Mon 11–5, Sun 2–5; Oct: Sun 2–4.30

Bodiam Castle
Bodiam, near Robertsbridge, East Sussex
Tel. (058 083) 436
Apr–Oct: daily 10–6 (sunset if earlier); Nov–Mar: Mon–Sat 10–sunset
(NT)

Bolsover Castle
Bolsover, Derbyshire   Tel. (0246) 823349
15 Mar–15 Oct: Mon–Sat 9.30–6.30, Sun 2–6.30; 16 Oct–14 Mar: Mon–Sat 9.30–4; Sun 2–4
(AME)

Bolton Castle
Castle Bolton, North Yorkshire   Tel. (0969) 22300
Easter–Oct: daily 10–5

Carisbrooke Castle
Carisbrooke, Isle of Wight   Tel. (0983) 522107
15 Mar–15 Oct: Mon–Sat 9.30–6.30, Sun 2–6.30; 16 Oct–14 Mar: Mon–Sat 9.30–4, Sun 2–4
(AME)

Carlisle Castle
Carlisle, Cumbria   Tel. (0228) 31777
15 Mar–15 Oct: daily 9.30–6.30; 16 Oct–14 Mar: Mon–Sat 9.30–4, Sun 2–4
(AME)

Castle Drogo
Drewsteignton, Devon   Tel. (064 73) 3306
Apr–Oct: daily 11–6
(NT)

Colchester Castle
Colchester Essex   Tel. (0206) 712222
Apr–Sept: Mon–Sat 10–5, Sun 2.30–5; Oct–Mar: Mon–Fri 10–5, Sat 10–4

Conisbrough Castle
Conisbrough, South Yorkshire   Tel. (0709) 863329
15 Mar–15 Oct: Mon–Sat 9.30–6.30, Sun 2–6.30; 16 Oct–14 Mar: Mon–Sat 9.30–4, Sun 2–4
(AME)

Corfe Castle
Corfe, near Wareham, Dorset   Tel. (0929) 480921
Mar–Oct: daily 10–6 (sunset if earlier); Nov–26 Feb: Sat & Sun 12–4 (weather permitting)
(NT)

Deal Castle
Deal, Kent   Tel. (0304) 372762
15 Mar–15 Oct: Mon–Sat 9.30–6.30, Sun 2–6.30; 16 Oct–14 Mar: Mon–Sat 9.30–4, Sun 2–4
(AME)

Donnington Castle
Donnington, near Newbury, Berkshire
Tel. (0635) 40615
All year, at reasonable times
(AME)

Dover Castle
Dover, Kent   Tel. (0304) 201628
15 Mar–15 Oct: daily 9.30–6.30; 16 Oct–14 Mar: 9.30–4, Sun 2–4
(AME)

Dunstanburgh Castle
Embleton, near Craster, Northumberland
Tel. (066 576) 631
15 Mar–15 Oct: daily 9.30–6.30; 16 Oct–14 Mar: 9.30–4, Sun 2–4
(AME)

Durham Castle
Durham, Co. Durham   Tel. (0385) 65481
Apr, July–Sept: Mon–Sat 10–12 & 2–4.30; rest of year:
Mon, Wed & Sat 2–4.30
Subject to closure for university functions

Framlingham Castle
Framlingham, Suffolk   Tel. (0728) 723330
15 Mar–15 Oct: daily 9.30–6.30; 16 Oct–14 Mar: Mon–Sat
9.30–4, Sun 2–4
(AME)

Goodrich Castle
Goodrich, Ross-on-Wye, Hereford and Worcester
Tel. (0600) 890538
15 Mar–15 Oct: daily 9.30–6.30; 16 Oct–14 Mar: Mon–Sat
9.30–4, Sun 2–4
(AME)

Hedingham Castle
Castle Hedingham, near Halstead, Essex
Tel. (0787) 60261/60804
Easter weekend & May–Oct: daily 10–5

Hever Castle
Hever, Edenbridge, Kent   Tel. (0732) 865224
Apr–Oct: daily 11–6, Castle opens 12 (last admission 5)

Kenilworth Castle
Kenilworth, Warwickshire   Tel. (0926) 52078
15 Mar–15 Oct: daily 9.30–6.30; 16 Oct–14 Mar: Mon–Sat
9.30–4, Sun 2–4
(AME)

Kirby Muxloe Castle
Kirby Muxloe, Leicestershire   Tel. (0533) 386886
15 Mar–15 Oct: Mon–Sat 9.30–6.30, Sun 2–6.30;
16 Oct–14 Mar: Mon–Sat (except Wed pm & Thurs)
9.30–4, Sun 2–4
(AME)

Leeds Castle
Maidstone, Kent   Tel. (0622) 65400
Apr–Oct: daily 11–5; Nov–Mar: Sat & Sun 12–4

Lincoln Castle
Castle Hill, Lincoln, Lincolnshire   Tel. (0522) 511068
Summer: Mon–Sat 9.30–5.30, Sun 11–5.30;
Winter: Mon–Sat 9.30–4

Lindisfarne Castle
Holy Island, Berwick-upon-Tweed, Northumberland
Tel. (0289) 89244
Apr–Sept: daily except Fri (open Good Fri) 11–5;
Oct: Sat & Sun 11–5
(NT)

Ludlow Castle
Ludlow, Shropshire   Tel. (0584) 3947
May–Sept: daily 10–6.30; Oct–Nov & Feb–Apr: 10.30–4
(closed Dec & Jan)

Norham Castle
near Berwick-upon-Tweed, Northumberland
Tel. (028 982) 329
15 Mar–15 Oct: Mon–Sat 9.30–6.30, Sun 2–6.30; 16
Oct–14 Mar: Mon–Sat (except Tues & alternate Mons)
9.30–4, Sun 2–4
(AME)

Orford Castle
Orford, Suffolk   Tel. (03945) 4727
15 Mar–15 Oct: Mon–Sat 9.30–6.30, Sun 2–6.30;
16 Oct–14 Mar: Mon–Sat (except Thurs and Fri am)
9.30–4, Sun 2–4
(AME)

Pevensey Castle
Pevensey, East Sussex   Tel. (0323) 762604
15 Mar–15 Oct: Mon–Sat 9.30–6.30, Sun 2–6.30;
16 Oct–14 Mar: Mon–Sat 9.30–4, Sun 2–4
(AME)

Portchester Castle
Portchester, Hampshire   Tel. (0705) 378291
15 Mar–15 Oct: Mon–Sat 9.30–6.30, Sun 2–6.30;
16 Oct–14 Mar: Mon–Sat 9.30–4, Sun 2–4
(AME)

Restormel Castle
Lostwithiel, Cornwall   Tel. (0208) 872687
15 Mar–15 Oct: daily (except Tues & Wed am) 9.30–6.30;
16 Oct–14 Mar: Mon, Wed pm, Thurs–Sat 9.30–4,
Sun 2–4
(AME)

Richmond Castle
Richmond, North Yorkshire   Tel. (0748) 2493
15 Mar–15 Oct: daily 9.30–6.30; 16 Oct–14 Mar: Mon–Sat
9.30–4, Sun 2–4
(AME)

Rochester Castle
Rochester, Kent   Tel. (0634) 402276
15 Mar–15 Oct: Mon–Sat 9.30–6.30, Sun 2–6.30;
16 Oct–14 Mar: Mon–Sat 9.30–4.30, Sun 2–4
(AME)

Sizergh Castle
near Kendal, Cumbria   Tel. (053 95) 60070
Apr–Oct: Sun, Mon, Wed & Thurs 2–5.45
(NT)

Tilbury Fort
Tilbury, Essex   Tel. (037 52) 78489
15 Mar–15 Oct: Mon–Sat 10–6, Sun 2.30–6; 16 Oct–14
Mar: Mon–Sat 10–4, Sun 2.30–3.30
(AME)

Tower of London
Tower Hill, London EC3   Tel. (01) 709 0765
Mar–Oct: Mon–Sat 9.30–5, Sun 2–5;
Nov–Feb: Mon–Sat 9.30–4
(AME)

Warkworth Castle
Warkworth, Northumberland   Tel. (0665) 711423
15 Mar–15 Oct: daily 9.30–6.30; 16 Oct–14 Mar: Mon–Sat
9.30–4, Sun 2–4
(AME)

Warwick Castle
Warwick, Warwickshire   Tel. (0926) 495421
Mar–Oct: daily 10–5.30; Nov–Feb: daily 10–4.30

Wells
Bishop's Palace, Wells, Somerset   Tel. (0749) 78691
Easter–Oct: Thurs, Sun & Bank Hol. Mon, and daily in
Aug 2–6; May–July & Sept: also Wed, 11–6

Windsor Castle
Windsor, Berkshire   Tel. (0753) 868286
Precinct: daily, Jan–29 Mar & 26 Oct–Dec: 10–4.15; 30
Mar–30 Apr (closed am 21 Apr) & Sept–25 Oct: 10–5.15;
May–Aug (closed 16 June): 10–7.15
State Apartments: 3 Jan–9 Mar & 26 Oct–7 Dec: Mon–Sat
10.30–3; 10 May–1 June & 28 June–23 Oct: Mon–Sat
10.30–5, Sun 1.30–5
Subject to closure at short notice.
Check opening times for other areas of the Castle.

SCOTLAND

Caerlaverock Castle
Caerlaverock, near Dumfries, Dumfries and Galloway
Apr–Sept: Mon–Sat 9.30–7, Sun 4–7; Oct–Mar: Mon–Sat
9.30–4, Sun 2–4
(AMS)

Castle Campbell
Dollar, Central   Tel. (02594) 2408
Apr–Sept: Mon–Sat 9.30–7, Sun 2–7; Oct–Mar: Mon–Sat
9.30–4, Sun 2–4
(AMS)

Craigievar Castle
Lumphanan, Grampian   Tel. (033 983) 635
Castle: May–Sept: daily 2–6 (last admission 5.15)
Grounds: all year 9.30 – sunset
(NTS)

Crathes Castle
Banchory, Grampian   Tel. (033 044) 525
Easter, May–Sept: daily 11–6; Apr & Oct: Sat & Sun 11–6
(NTS)

Culzean Castle
Maybole, Strathclyde   Tel. (065 56) 274
1–10 Apr, May–Aug: daily 10–6; 11–30 Apr, Sept–Oct:
daily 12–5
(NTS)

Doune Castle
Doune, Central   Tel. (0786) 841203
Apr–Sept: Mon–Sat 9.30–7, Sun 2–7; Oct–Mar:
Mon–Wed & Sat 9.30–4, Sun 2–4
(AMS)

Edinburgh Castle
Edinburgh, Lothian   Tel. (031) 225 9846
Apr–Sept: Mon–Sat 9.30–5.50, Sun 11–5.50; Oct–Mar:
Mon–Sat 9.30–5.05, Sun 12.30–4.20 (last admission 45
mins before closing)
(AMS)

Eilean Donan Castle
Dornie, Wester Ross, Highland   Tel. (059 985) 202
Apr–Sept: daily 10–12.30 and 2–6

Fort George
Ardersier, Inverness-shire, Highland
Apr–Sept: Mon–Sat 9.30–7, Sun 2–7; Oct–Mar: Mon–Sat
9.30–4, Sun 2–4
(AMS)

Glamis Castle
Glamis, Tayside   Tel. (030 784) 242
Easter & May–Sept: daily except Sat 1–5;
Oct–Apr: by appointment only

Hermitage Castle
Liddlesdale, Borders
Apr–Sept: Mon–Sat 9.30–7, Sun 2–7; Oct–Mar: Mon–Sat
9.30–4, Sun 2–4
(AMS)

Huntingtower Castle
near Perth, Tayside   Tel. (0738) 27231
Apr–Sept: Mon–Sat 9.30–7, Sun 2–7; Oct–Mar: Mon–Sat
9.30–4, Sun 2–4
(AMS)

Inveraray Castle
Inveraray, Strathclyde   Tel. (0499) 2203
1 Apr–9 Oct: Mon–Sat 10–1 & 2–6, Sun 1–6 (April–June,
Sept, closed on Fri); July–Aug: Mon–Sat 10–6, Sun 1–6

Loch Leven Castle
Kinross, Tayside
Apr–Sept: Mon–Sat 9.30–7, Sun 2–7
(AMS)

Neidpath Castle
near Peebles, Borders   Tel. (087 57) 201
Easter & May–Sept: Mon–Sat 10–1 & 2–5, Sun 1–5
(subject to availability of staff)

Orchardton Tower
Palnackie, Dumfries and Galloway
Apr–Sept: Mon–Sat 9.30–7, Sun 2–7; Oct–Mar: Mon–Sat
9.30–4, Sun 2–4
(AMS)

Stirling Castle
Upper Castle Hill, Stirling, Central   Tel. (0786) 62517
Apr–Sept: Mon–Sat 9.30–6, Sun 10.30–5.30; Oct–Mar:
Mon–Sat 9.30–5, Sun 12.30–4.20
(AMS)

Tantallon Castle
North Berwick, Lothian   Tel. (031) 556 8400
Apr–Sept: Mon–Sat 9.30–7, Sun 2–7; Oct–Mar: Mon–Sat
(except Wed & Thurs am) 9.30–4, Sun 2–4
(AMS)

WALES

Beaumaris Castle
Beaumaris, Anglesey, Gwynedd   Tel. (0248) 810361
15 Mar–15 Oct: Mon–Sat 9.30–6.30, Sun 2–6.30;
16 Oct–14 Mar: Mon–Sat 9.30–4, Sun 2–4
(AMW)

Caernarvon Castle
Caernarvon, Gwynedd   Tel. (0286) 673094
15 Mar–15 Oct: daily 9.30–6.30; 16 Oct–14 Mar: Mon–Sat
9.30–4, Sun 2–4
(AMW)

Caerphilly Castle
Caerphilly, Mid Glamorgan   Tel. (0222) 883143
15 Mar–15 Oct: daily 9.30–6.30; 16 Oct–14 Mar: Mon–Sat
9.30–4, Sun 2–4
(AMW)

Cardiff Castle
Cardiff, South Glamorgan   Tel. (0222) 822000/822083
Mar, Apr & Oct: 10–5; May–Sept: 10–6;
Nov–Feb: 10–4.30

Castell Coch
Tongwynlais, South Glamorgan   Tel. (0222) 810101
15 Mar–15 Oct: daily 9.30–6.30; 16 Oct–14 Mar: Mon–Sat
9.30–4, Sun 2–4
(AMW)

Chepstow Castle
Chepstow, Gwent   Tel. (029 12) 4065
15 Mar–15 Oct: daily 9.30–6.30; 16 Oct–14 Mar: Mon–Sat
9.30–4, Sun 2–4
(AMW)

Chirk Castle
Chirk, Clwyd   Tel. (0691) 777701
Apr–Sept: daily (except Mon & Sat, but open Bank Hol.
Mon) 12–5; Oct: Sat & Sun 12–5
(NT)

Conwy Castle
Conwy, Gwynedd   Tel. (049 263) 2358
15 Mar–15 Oct: daily 9.30–6.30; 16 Oct–14 Mar: Mon–Sat
9.30–4, Sun 2–4
(AMW)

Harlech Castle
Harlech, Gwynedd   Tel. (0766) 780552
15 Mar–15 Oct: daily 9.30–6.30; 16 Oct–14 Mar: Mon–Sat
9.30–4, Sun 2–4
(AMW)

Kidwelly Castle
Kidwelly, Dyfed   Tel. (0554) 890104
15 Mar–15 Oct: daily 9.30–6.30; 16 Oct–14 Mar: Mon–Sat
9.30–4, Sun 2–4
(AMW)

Pembroke Castle
Pembroke, Dyfed   Tel. (0646) 6815 0
Easter–Sept: daily 9.30–6; Oct–Easter: Mon–Sat 9.30–4

Penrhyn Castle
Bangor, Gwynedd   Tel. (0248) 353084
Apr–Oct: daily (except Tues) 12–5 (opens 11, July &
Aug)
(NT)

Powis Castle
Welshpool, Powys   Tel. (0938) 4336
2 Apr–June, Sept & Oct: daily (except Mon & Tues, but
open Bank Hol. Mon) 12–5; July–Aug: daily (except
Mon, but open Bank Hol. Mon) 11–6
(NT)

Raglan Castle
Raglan, Gwent   Tel. (0291) 690228
15 Mar–15 Oct: daily 9.30–6.30; 16 Oct–14 Mar: Mon–Sat
9.30–4, Sun 2–4
(AMW)

Rhuddlan Castle
Rhuddlan, Clwyd   Tel. (0745) 590777
15 Mar–15 Oct: 9.30–6.30, Sun 2–6.30; 16 Oct–14 Mar:
Mon–Sat 9.30–4, Sun 2–4
(AMW)

Skenfrith Castle
Skenfrith, Gwent
All year, at reasonable times
(NT, AMW)

GLOSSARY OF TECHNICAL TERMS

Abacus: flat portion on top of a capital.

Aisle: space between arcade and outer wall.

Ambulatory: aisle round an apse.

Apse: rounded end (usually of chancel or chapel).

Arcade: row of arches, free-standing and supported on piers or columns; a blind arcade is a *dummy*.

Arch: can be round-headed, pointed, two-centred or drop, that is arch struck from centre on the springing-line; *ogee*: pointed arch with double curved sides, upper arcs convex, lower concave; *lancet*: pointed arch formed on an acute-angle triangle; and *depressed*: flattened or elliptical.

Ashlar: worked stone with flat surface, usually of regular shape and square edges.

Aumbry: recess to hold sacred vessels, often found in castle chapels.

Bailey: castle courtyard and surrounding buildings.

Barbican: outwork defending the entrance to castle.

Barrel roof: like a covered wagon, or inverted ship; *barrel vault* is a plain vault of uniform cross-section.

Bartizan: overhanging battlemented corner turret, corbelled out; common in Scotland (and France).

Bastion: solid masonry projection.

Batter: inclined face of wall; hence *battered*.

Battlements: parapet with indentations or embrasures, with raised portions (merlons) between; also called crenellations.

Bays: internal divisions of building, marked by roof principals or vaulting piers.

Berm: level area separating ditch from bank.

Bivalate: a hillfort defended by two concentric ditches.

Bond: arrangement of bricks in courses.

Bratice: timber tower, or projecting wooden gallery.

Bronze Age: in Britain, *c*. 1800 to 600 BC.

Buttress: projection from wall for additional support.

Castellan: officer in charge of a castle.

Chamfer: surface made by smoothing off the angle between two stone faces.

Chevron: zig-zag moulding (twelfth century).

Clunch: hard chalk material.

Cob: unburnt clay mixed with straw.

Constable: official in charge of castle in owner's absence.

Cornice: decorative projection along top of wall.

Counterfort: defence work of besieging force.

Counterscarp: outer slope of ditch.

Course: level layer of stones or bricks.

Crenel: gap in battlemented parapet; *crenellate*: to fortify.

Crosswall: interior dividing wall of castle.

Curtain: connecting wall 'hung' between towers of a castle.

Diaper work: decoration of squares or lozenges.

Dogtooth: diagonal indented pyramid.

Donjon: principal tower of castle; keep.

Dormer: window placed vertically in sloping roof.

Drawbridge: movable bridge; originally moved horizontally like a gangway.

Dressing: carved stonework around openings.

Drum-tower: large, circular tower, usually low and squat.

Drystone: unmortared masonry.

Embattled: battlemented.

Embrasure: small opening in fortified parapet, usually splayed on inside.

Fillet: narrow flat band.

Fluting: concave mouldings in parallel.

Foliated: carved with leaves.

Footings: bottom part of wall.

Forebuilding: block in front of keep, to form lobby or landing.

Fosse: ditch.

Freestone: high-quality sandstone or limestone.

Fresco: painting on wet plaster wall.

Gable: wall covering end of roof-ridge.

Gallery: long passage or room.

Garderobe: latrine; privy.

Great chamber: lord's solar, or bed-sitting room.

Groined: roof with sharp edges at intersection of cross-vaults.

Half-shaft: roll-moulding on either side of opening.

Hall: principal room or building in complex.

Herringbone: brick or stone laid diagonally.

Hillfort: Bronze or Iron Age earthwork of ditches and banks.

Hood: arched covering; when used to throw off rainwater, called hood-mould.

Impost: wall bracket to support arch.

Iron Age: in Britain from *c.* 600 BC to Roman period.

Jamb: side of arch, door or window.

Joist: timber stretched from wall-to-wall to support floorboards.

Keep: main tower.

Lancet: long, narrow window with pointed head.

Light: component part of window, divided by mullions and transoms.

Lintel: horizontal stone or beam bridging opening.

Loop: narrow opening.

Louvre: opening in roof (often with lantern over) to allow smoke to escape from central hearth.

Machicolation: projecting gallery on brackets, on outside of castle towers or walls, with holes in floor for dropping missiles, etc.

Mangonel: siege-engine whose projectile arms turn against fixed stop.

Merlon: solid part of embattled parapet.

Meutrières: murder holes.

Mine gallery: siegework to cause wall-collapse.

Motte: artificial earth-mound for keeps of eleventh- and twelfth-century castles.

Motte-and-Bailey: earth-mound with wood or stone keep, surrounded by ditched and palisade enclosure (or courtyard).

Moulding: masonry decoration.

Mullion: vertical division of window.

Multivallate: hillfort with three or more concentric lines of defence.

Mural: wall (adjectival).

Nailhead: pyramid moulding.

Newel: centre-post of circular staircase.

Nookshaft: shaft set in angle of jamb or pier.

Oolite: granular limestone.

Open joint: wide space between faces of stones.

Oratory: private chapel in house.

Oriel: projecting window in wall; originally a form of porch, often of wood.

Palisade: timber defensive screen or fence.

Parados: low wall on inner side of main wall.

Parapet: low wall on outer side of main wall.

Pediment: low-pitched gable over porticos, doors, windows, etc.

Perpendicular: English architectural style, *c.* 1330–1540.

Pier: support for arch, usually square as opposed to pillar (round).

Pilaster: shallow pier used to buttress wall.

Pinnacle: ornament crowning spire, tower etc.

Piscina: handbasin, usually set in or against wall, with drain.

Pipe-roll: Exchequer accounts, rolled on narrow wooden cylinders.

Pitch: roof slope.

Pitching: rough cobbling.

Plinth: projecting base of wall.

Portcullis: grating dropped vertically from grooves to block passage or gate in castle; of wood, metal or a combination of the two.

Postern: back door of castle.

Quadrangle: inner courtyard.

Quoin: dressed stone at angle of building.

Rampart: defensive stone or earth wall surrounding castle or town.

Rath: low, circular ringwork.

Ravelin: outwork with two faces forming a salient angle.

Re-entrant: recessed.

Refectory: communal dining-hall.

Revetment: retaining wall.

Rib: raised moulding dividing vault.

Ring-work: circular earthwork of bank and ditch.

Romanesque: prevailing architectural style, eighth to twelfth century, with rounded arches.

Roofridge: summit line of roof.

Rubble: unsquared stone not laid in courses.

Rustication: worked ashlar stone, with faces left rough.

Saltire: diagonal, equal-limbed cross.

Scarp: slope on inner side of ditch.

Shaft: narrow column.

Shell-keep: circular or oval wall surrounding inner portion of castle.

Soffit: underside of arch or opening.

Solar: upper living room of medieval house or castle; often over the hall.

Splay: chamfer, or sloping face.

Squint: observation hole in wall or room.

Stringcourse: continuous horizontal mouldings on wallface.

Tracery: intersecting ribwork in upper part of window.

Transom: horizontal division of window.

Trebuchet: siege-engine with unequal counterpoise arm.

Trefoil: three-lobed.

Turret: small tower, round or polygonal.

Vault: stone roofing.

Vitrified: material reduced to glass by combustion.

Voussoir: wedged-shaped stone in arch.

Wall-stair: staircase built into thickness of wall.

Wall-walk: passage along castle wall.

Weathering: sloping surface to throw off rainwater.

Wing-wall: wall down slope of motte to protect stairway.

Yett: iron gate.

SELECT BIBLIOGRAPHY

The History of the King's Works vols I–III, general editor H. M. Colvin (HMSO 1963–70), has been the basis for the sections on royal castles and the author and publishers are particularly grateful for the use of this documentary material. Other important works of reference which have been extensively consulted are: Sir Nikolas Pevsner (editor), *The Buildings of England*, 44 volumes (London 1951–76) and *The Victorian County Histories*; Sydney Toy, *The Castles of Great Britain* (London 1954); W. Douglas Simpson, *Castles in England and Wales* (London 1969); G. T. Clark, *Medieval Military Architecture*, 3 vols (London 1884); L. F. Salzman, *Building in England down to 1540* (Oxford 1952); and the various individual guides to castles and fortifications in the care of the Department of the Environment, published by the HMSO.

For the earliest period, the most useful general survey is A. H. A. Hogg, *Hillforts of Britain* (London 1975); but see also D. Hill and M. Jesson (eds), *The Iron Age and its Hillforts* (Southampton 1971) and J. Forde-Johnston, *Hillforts of the Iron Age in England and Wales* (Liverpool). For the Roman period, see especially the HMSO publications on *Caerlon-on-Usk*, *Housesteads Roman Fort*, *Chester* and *The Forts of the Saxon Shore*. For the Anglo-Saxon period, see H. M. and J. Taylor, *Anglo-Saxon Architecture* (Cambridge 1965) and Sir Frank Stenton, *Anglo-Saxon England* (Oxford 1955).

For the medieval period, see Warren Hollister, *Military Organisation in Norman England* (London 1940); R. Allen Brown, 'A list of Castles 1154–1216', *English Historical Review*, lxxiv and *English Medieval Castles* (London 1954); D. F. Renn, *Norman Castles in Britain* (2nd edn ed. John Baker, London 1973); A. Hamilton Thompson, *Military Architecture in England during the Middle Ages* (Oxford 1912); Margaret Wood, *The English Medieval House* (London 1965) and E. S. Armitage, *The Early Norman Castles of the British Isles* (London 1912). On the political side, see Sir Frank Stenton, *The First Century of English Feudalism* (Oxford 1955); H. A. Cronne, *The Reign of Stephen, 1135–54* (London 1970); and W. L. Warren, *Henry II* (London 1973). Lord Curzon, *Bodiam Castle, Sussex* (London 1926) is an interesting curiosity.

For Wales, see especially J. E. Morris, *The Welsh Wars of Edward I* (Oxford 1950); J. G. Edwards: 'Edward I's castle-building in Wales', *Proceedings of the British Academy*, 1946; and A. J. Taylor, *The King's Works in Wales, 1277–1330* (HMSO 1974), reprinted from the main *History of the King's Works*.

For the Borders, see Geoffrey Watson, *The Border Reivers* (London 1974); D. L. W. Tough, *The Last Years of a Frontier* (London 1928); T. R. Rae, *The Administration of the Scottish Frontier, 1513–1603* (London 1966) and R. Hughill, *Border Castles and Peels* (London 1970). For Scotland, see T. C. Smout, *A History of the Scottish People* (London 1969); David MacGibbon and Thomas Ross, *Castellated and Domestic Architecture of Scotland*, 5 vols (Edinburgh 1887–92); and a more modern survey, Hubert Fenwick, *Scotland's Castles* (London 1976).

The best survey of the impact of cannon on castles and early gun-forts is B. H. St. J. O'Neil, *Castles and Cannon* (Oxford 1960). The best introduction to the sieges of the Civil War is the Royal Commission on Historical Monuments Survey, *Newark-on-Trent: the Civil War Siegeworks* (HMSO 1964). Other sieges of interest are described in Walter Money, *The First and Second Battles of Newbury and the Siege of Donnington Castle, 1643–46* (London 1881) and G. N. Godwin, *The Civil War in Hampshire and the Story of Basing House* (London 1904).

For the revival of castellated architecture, see Christopher Hussey's two volumes, *English Country Houses: Mid-Georgian, 1761–1800* (London 1956) and *English Country Houses: late Georgian, 1799–1841* (London 1958); and Mark Girouard, *The Victorian Country House* (Oxford 1974). Girouard also deals with the early modern period, including Wollaton and Bolsover, in *Robert Smythson and the Elizabethan Country House* (London 1983). For the Eglington Tournament, see Ian Anstruther, *The Knight and the Umbrella* (London 1963).

INDEX

page numbers in *italics* refer to illustrations

ACKNOWLEDGEMENTS

The author and publishers would like to thank the following institutions and photographers for permission to reproduce illustrations and for supplying photographs:

Aerofilms Ltd   *13*, 90, *176*; James Austin   54; John Bethell   35, 38, 64–7, 94, 97, 100, 116, 131, 164, 180, 187, 195; British Museum   152, 175; The British Tourist Authority   109, 136; Cambridge University Collection   123, 162; Department of the Environment, Crown Copyright Reserved   53, 151; Department of the Environment, Edinburgh   127, 139; Castle plans by Line and Line, from Richard Humble, *English Castles*   39, 46, 68, 82, 88, 153; Michael Holford   173; A. F. Kersting   11, 14, 19, 29, 41, 61, 89, 95, 106, 142, 146, 156, 163, 182, 183, 193, 186; National Army Museum   181; National Trust for Scotland (Woodmansterne Publications Ltd)   144, 145; Hugh Palmer   198; Royal Commission on Historical Monuments   18; Walter Scott   47; Edwin Smith   188, 191; Patrick Sutherland   84 (© 1987 Weidenfeld and Nicolson Ltd); from Sidney Toy, *Castles: A Short History of Fortifications*   21, 40, 75, 76, 138, 161; The Welsh Office   194; Tim Woodcock   *167*, *174*, *179*; Weidenfeld & Nicolson Archives   16, 48, 113, 144.

Numerals in italics indicate colour illustrations

Jacket photograph of Bodiam Castle kindly supplied by S. & O. Mathews Photography

The publishers have taken all possible care to trace and acknowledge the source of illustrations. If any errors have accidentally occurred, the publishers will be happy to correct them in future editions, provided they receive notification.

215